Flying out of this World

Peter Greenaway

Flying out of this World

The University of Chicago Press
Chicago and London

Before beginning his career as a director, Peter Greenaway trained as a painter. His films include the *The Draughtsman's Contract; The Cook, the Thief, His Wife and Her Lover;* and *Prospero's Books.*

The University of Chicago Press, Chicago 60637
The University of Chicago Press, Ltd., London
© 1994 by The University of Chicago
All rights reserved. Published 1994
Printed in the United States of America
03 02 01 00 99 98 97 96 95 94   1 2 3 4 5
ISBN: 0-226-30636-4 (cloth)
        0-226-30637-2 (paper)

Originally published in a bilingual format as *Le bruit des nuages,* © Éditions de la Réunion des musées nationaux, 1992; © SPADEM, ADAGP, Paris, 1992

Library of Congress Cataloging-in-Publication Data

Greenaway, Peter.
    [Bruit des nuages. English]
    Flying out of this world / Peter Greenaway.
        p.   cm. — (The Parti-Pris series)
    Includes index.
    ISBN 0-226-30636-4. — ISBN 0-226-30637-2 (pbk.)
    1. Flight in art.   2. Art, Modern.   3. Art—Philosophy.
  I. Title.   II. Series: Parti pris (Paris, France)
N8217.F6G7413   1994
704.9′4—dc20   93-32976
                                                   CIP

♾ The paper used in this publication meets the minimum requirements of the American National Standard for Information Sciences—Permanence of Paper for Printed Library Materials, ANSI Z39.48-1984.

Contents

Contents

Flying out of this World

The impossibility of personalised flight has naturally made it a prime subject matter for depiction as a frozen moment in two dimensions. A mocking perversity. Flight violently contradicts those two states of being. However, I, for one, am always eager to respect the intention of all those optimistic pictorial intimations that say, "This is how you could fly if you could fly." They are evidence.

In the English language, flight also means escape. In French, to fly is to steal. Flyers are thieves escaping. Alas, despite wing implants, feathers and wax, and carnal associations with swans, we will never grow wings. Alas, any true flight we make will always be externally assisted. Alas, the best we can do is fall and believe ourselves flying. Alas, not until air grows as heavy as water could we push ourselves up and off. Alas, not until gravity exerts considerably less than it presently does on the human body, will we be able to flap our arms and drift away from the earth.

In Europe we do not believe in levitation—or only in spirit. We say we are floating on air, when we are really only feeling light-headed.

Desire for personal flight is universal and without time barriers. If Heaven of any description is undoubtedly above us, then it is reachable by flight alone. No tower of Babel will suffice. Mechanical contrivances fall far too short of our desire. No amount of mechanical noise about us is going to satisfy, and the awesome fear of imminent fall if the engine stops or the wind drops is going to unquestionably disqualify a machine. We want wings on our feet or on our shoulders, or an unrestricted permission to directly thwart gravity by some other means.

The thesaurus of flight images in three thousand years of Western culture is most persistent and nearly unlimited. Such a large heritage can only be tackled a little at a time. This exhibition of drawings is a small contribution to the History of Imagined Flight and to all its concomitant mocking frustrations. Each image has been chosen as though it was a clue, an instruction, a pointer, a directive, an aide-memoire into the mysteries and the hubris of flying, sacred and profane. Each image is an example of the ecstatic delights of flying success or the consequences of flying failure. Who knows, when put together, positive and negative, they might form a template of how we too can take to the air, certainly metaphorically. Literally? Perhaps.

As to the order in which we can approach these pictorial instructions, I have been interested in a certain melodramatic curve of flight through the air for a long time. It is the trajectory of a thrown stone. It follows the hump of a humped-back whale from nose to tail. It's bounded like a smooth, sheep-cropped, grassy hill. It is a graph-line through a grey, blue, and then a grey again, sky. A thrown-stone-trajectory is a good metaphor for so many phenomena: the curve of an event, any event; the curve of life, any life; the curve of a hypothesis; the curve experienced in the manufacture of a work of art; the curve of interest experienced in the manufacture of a catalogue. We should not be so superior in our imaginative geometry, for blood, vomit, and urine can exit the human frame in a similar trajectory.

In the past, I have considered this curve of flight in so many contradictory ways, that, like Hogarth's serpentine line, whilst its hold on the imagination is strong, its grasp on science is tenuous.

The history of flying is like being hungry and unsuccessful with omelettes after breaking too many eggs. And eggs are a bird's way of passing on flying delights. You can see that too many qualifications are disastrous. Trying to fly without being prepared to say it's impossible is like trying to learn to swim without water, though we must admit that swimming can be like flying in water. All qualifications make any flight wavering and bumpy, and besides, they demean the very straightforward demands of gravity. So, concentrating the credulity of a, by now, understandably suspicious audience, I am going to cut this flight trajectory into nine sections, like cutting a frozen, curved-back eel into nine parts for the frying-pan, and, with this nine-part template, I am going to arrange the flying images. I am going to write of them as though they might be an argumentative, discursive excuse for a film, and prepare the exhibition as though I am going to the theatre, and accompany flying in general with a sound-track, if only to justify the French title, *Le bruit des nuages,* which is what I eventually wish to hear when I am truly airborne. With this multifarious approach, we can hope to service the idea a little more expansively, hoping that if our feet will not leave the ground, our minds might.

There is, however, one great contradiction in all this. The act of flying itself. I have never yet read or heard an apt description of unassisted flying that describes the phenomenon with any real adequacy. But then how would I know? How would you know? I feel it is possible to purposefully convey enthusiasm and information about standing and running, sitting and lying down. Falling and jumping? Certainly not. The act of falling is quickly terminated, and all thoughts are on the crash-landing. Jumping is too quick. There is no time for contemplation in a jump. The vocabulary of flying peculiarly contradicts itself. It is a vocabulary of approximation that cannot use its tools to introduce or explain its purposes with any great efficacy. It must also be remembered that take away the "f" from flying and we have lying. "F" is such a little used consonant. "Lying" in the English language is often confused with "lying" as in lying down, which is contrary to all principles of flight. Believing that a satisfactory model will not be found, I will therefore largely pursue the particular obligation of acknowledging flying as though no-one has flown, and in that I can not be contradicted, for I do not count being transported in any mechanical dirigible as flying. A flying exhibition without flying? Is it like an opera without music? A sea without water? An absurdity? I am not so sure.

Earth-bound with Gravity

We start with a grounded section, replete with heavy examples. They are reminders that our feet are only permitted short steps and small leaps before they must be stuck down again on the earth. But there are mocking intimations of a lift-off set about with allegorical presumption and evil mischief. From these examples, flight may just be a proposition.

1
REDON
The Ball (The Prisoner)

As a bold and unequivocal instructive, we start with a simple volume that will never fly. It is the first imperative. Gravity as a ball underground. At the bottom of the hill. A heavy full stop realised as a volume. The end of a sentence that we have not yet written. A re-imploded black hole made whole. And it is as shiny as a cannon-ball . . . which, of course, under suitable conditions, will fly, though the bore in the barrel of the gun to take this missile would suggest a barrel of inordinate length and a massive power of propulsion. A cannon devised by Boullée, Etienne-Louis Boullée, master of the heavy mass, guardian of gravitational spirit. There are cannon-balls like this one in Crevalcore, as unexpected a metaphysical toy for John the Baptist as it might be here for this philosopher. In Crevalcore they may be perfunctory, whilst being enigmatic. Here, with Redon, the enigma is complete. Science-fiction is familiar with the story of the metal cone as big as a cherry, but one thousand times as heavy as its expected size would suggest. All who possessed it had holes in their pockets, in their floorboards, in their lives. This ball is made of the same material.

For particulars, in those trying to squeeze meaning for the beginning of a flight journey, this huge ball is perhaps a meter in diameter and it could squeeze its companion philosopher out of his pictorial space. This drawing is three quarters ball, one quarter philosopher, which might be about the right space to keep a philosopher in his place. This ball, so like a dark planet or a black world, could roll and crush the philosopher. The slightest pressure and it would slowly roll off its table, its catafalque, its keeping place. And who is the philosopher? He has a chunky face like a Disney dwarf and is as ball-headed as the ball itself. Is he Daedalus contemplating difficulties with gravity?

The ball is set against a column in a dark space. Is the dark space night or is it a secret and an underground cell? If it's underground, then flight is even farther away. The drawing is called *The Prisoner.* Is this philosopher chained to this ball? Is this ball the familiar ball of the ball-and-chain that tells in shorthand that a man is a prisoner in so many caricatures and cartoons? If this potential flying philosopher is chained to this ball, then there is no chance he can fly. No. The philosopher is free to come and go. The ball is the prisoner.

More important particulars, for seldom does an artist waste time with what he considers as unimportant. The ceiling is low, thus increasing the indoor pressure and accentuating the claustrophobia. The philosopher is tonsored, so is this a monkish circumstance, or is it a nod to a mode of worship, secular or religious, that is far older than Christianity? Has he some ear-ornament? We must not give up looking for clues that might help. Has this philosopher an earring that looks heavy enough to have extended his ear unnaturally? And is this philosopher blind? Or is it that his eyes are so heavily lidded, they look to the ground in embarrassment or modesty or respect? And if he is blind, then here is a philosopher whose right hand may tell him more than his eyes ever can. He wears an ancient dress, and he carries his hand on his hip in a philosopher's stance.

A symbol of heaviness contemplated by a bearded philosopher of se-mitic pedigree, in an underground cell, in a dark dungeon where this heavy ball has gravitated. It will take a great deal of energy to lift it upstairs. Perhaps it is Redon's Philosopher's stone, the Philosopher's Ball, the perfectly spherical loadstone, the lead into gold catalyst. A sphere is curiously faceless. It might be a mirror but it's not going to show you your face as you know it.

If we feel so much negativity in this black sphere, consider its opposite. Its opposite is a balloon, an air-filled balloon, that will float easily on any draught in the dark dungeon. Is there any way we can see this ball as a hollow sphere with a thin crust? And when the philosopher-prisoner taps it—as he is about to do—will it ring like a bell? Or will it crack under the tap like the spherical black egg of the Roc?

By contemplating this epitome of gravity, this dense dark mass, with its own gravity-field, that at the very least attracts dust like the planet Jupiter attracts meteorites, we and the philosopher can understand what makes gravity jealous.

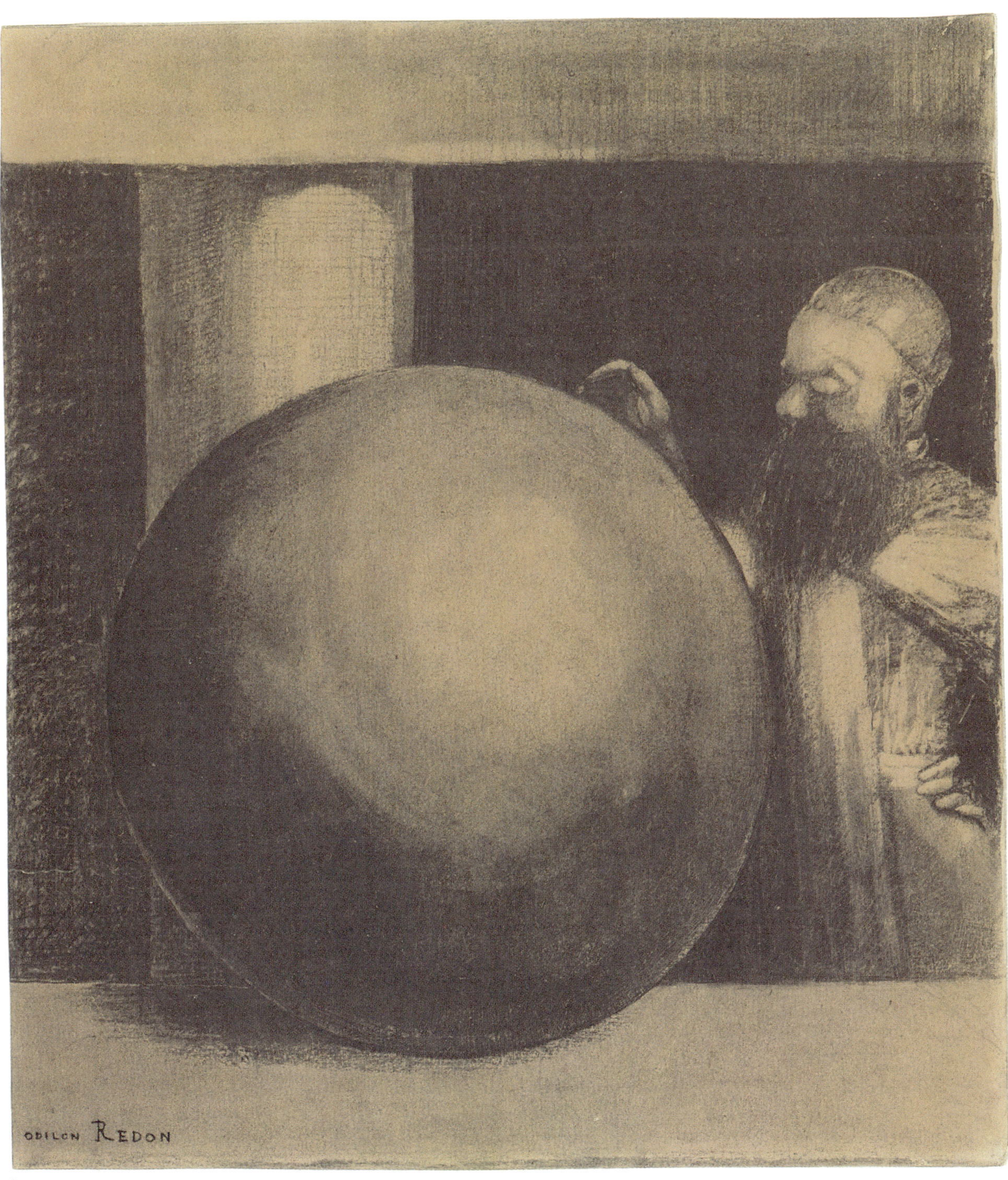

odilon REDON

2
GOYA
The Porter

This drawing is at the opposite end of the scale of engimas to Redon. Goya's little sweating carrier of bundles, of bigger-than-man-sized packages, fully comprehends the weight of his load. But he is grinning beneath the weight of his bundle. How do we know he is grinning, we cannot see his face? He's grinning all right. In bitter agony at carrying so much weight and being drawn by Goya at the same time. Goya has asked him to stand still. What's in his package? Are there further bundles inside, working down to a thing so small he could have carried it in his pocket? Has he the world in his bundle, expertly disguised by packaging specialists? Is it full of perishable goods, or eider feathers for filling mattresses for the likes of him to lie down on when he's finished work? Or bird feathers for making wings? Or is there a body amongst those wrappings? His grandmother? His mother? His wife? One visitor says he's grinning because he is carrying a dead relative in his bundle. Another visitor, determined to find continuity among these pictorial instructions, thinks he is carrying Redon's philosopher.

This little man's own shadow is entirely obscured by the shadow of his package, his great burden. And, if we are looking closely for clues, some solid impediment has fastened itself to the brown ink of the shadow. Perhaps this impediment is made up of the self-same substance that the porter has in his bundle. Perhaps this impediment is the substance of shadow itself. It's a pity we cannot see his face. After he's finished grinning, it will be all straining and stressing. And it is certain that he blames the circumstances of life for his burden, not Mr. Newton. This is a true warning that we are trapped on the earth.

This man's flesh is completely covered in clothing. He is a rarity in this exhibition, for most of our protagonists are naked. With this porter, there is no parting between his shoes and his trousers, between his trousers and

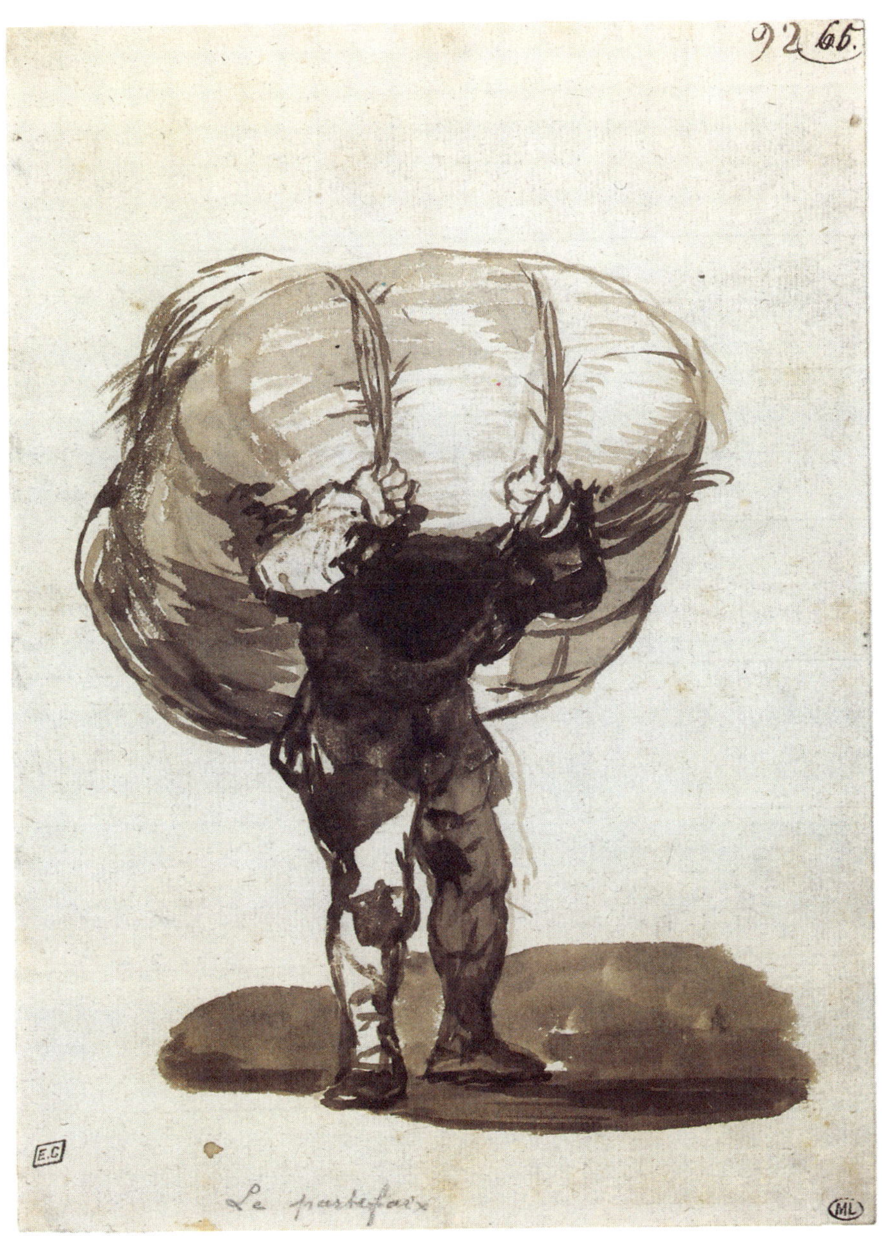

his shirt, even between his jacket-collar and his hat. For he is hatted. And he might very well be wearing knee-pads. These could be clues. For this man could well be prepared to face the cold rarified air of the upper reaches, and his knees are well prepared for a heavy landing. His fingers are curled around the ropes that bind his parcel together like the fingers of a man used to holding the strings of a parachute.

One curiosity, this drawing has, in brown ink, the same colour ink as the drawing, a number ninety-two written in its top right corner. Ninety-two is the atomic number of uranium. Perhaps this man is carrying a bomb. We could be blown into the sky.

3
Annibale CARRACCI
Hercules bearing the celestial globe

4
Giulio PIPPI (Giulio Romano)
Atlas

Atlas, the man who carries the world, becomes the book of the maps of the world. An example of man, or God, into book. Few have that honour.

Redon's blank enigmatic sphere and Goya's ambiguous bundle have not been graced with a specific identity. We have no doubt of what is carried by Atlas (or Hercules) in the Carracci and Romano drawings, though the sphere be empty and featureless. However, without the identity of the drawings being made known, by title or by our recognition of the classical archetype, the weight they carry is just as enigmatic. Bearing the weight of the world for Atlas is a punishment. He is a Titan, an old God, disinherited by the new regime and exiled to the Atlas Mountains of North Africa where he is to everlastingly support the heavens, or, more pertinently for us, the skies. It's a short step from the circular Heavens to the circular Earth.

Carracci gives Hercules a muscular body and a set of facial features that barely make an individual identity. He is a body, a presence, holding up the world with muscle. Romano gives Atlas a crown, a beard, a blowing cloak and a footrest. Romano makes him an older man and permits him a gesture like a scene-shifter manoeuvring a difficult part of the universal scenery. Perhaps he's in the act of passing the burden over to Hercules. Or just leaving to plant his orchard of golden apples, or just excusing himself to father numerous rain-bringing daughters. These distractions apart, he is supposed to be rooted to his responsibilities. However, according to Romano, he could not hold the pose for long. Gravitational

heaviness would tip him into the void on his left handside. How convenient is the footrest? Is it a draughtsman's device, or is it the start of a
staircase going up to Heaven, or going down to Hell? The drawn geomet-
ric arc that circumscribes the world, touches the tip of his nose, and slices
behind his upper right arm, is in opposition to the cube of the stair, and

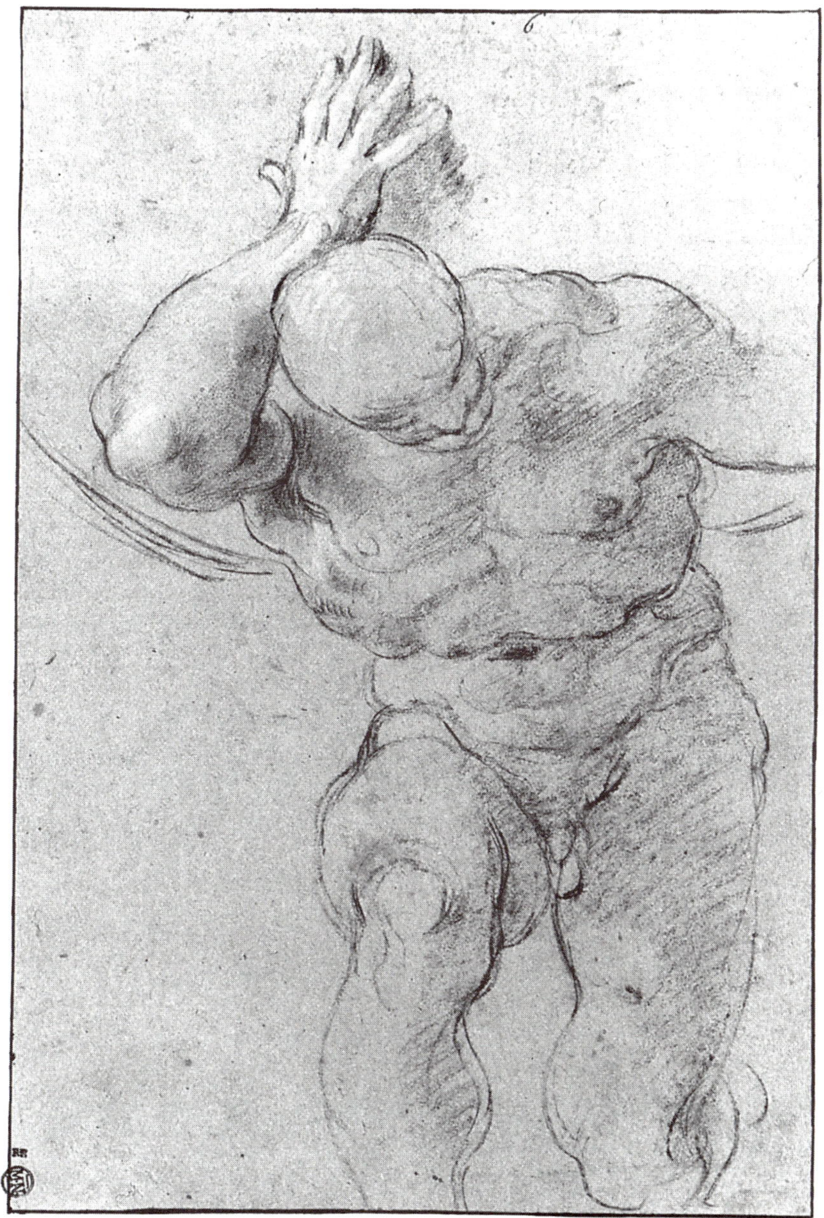

3

between these two Platonic solids is the most serpentine of hem-folds wriggling eight times like a serpent in water.

What makes Atlas a king? Crown or no crown, either way, Gravity is king, and flight for both of these immortals is an impossibility. These gentlemen cannot even take a break to blow their noses. Unlike Goya's porter, they cannot move a step from their responsibilities. The iconography says they must stand and grow like trees. No possibility of flight for them.

If the world rests on the shoulders of Atlas, what does Atlas stand upon? Tortoises, turtles, the bottom of the sea? All talk of there being no spherical world unless Copernicus and Galileo say so, is bogus. Carracci here is the more advanced theoretical practitioner, his globe is certainly circular, his body tells us so. Giulio Romano is an opportunist, he's keeping his options open. For him, the world could just be a large disk in the sky. In fact his thumb-finger relationship anatomically spread around so brief a curvature on the drawing's right, almost confirms he is a flat-earther. Yet even Romano thinks, if the world is a disk, it's a thick disk. Like a biscuit. In fact the closer you look, you can see Giulio Romano has truly hedged his bets, for no head could be that close to those hands if the world was truly a sphere.

As it is, both worlds are featureless. Carracci and Romano could be agreeing with Redon. The world is a blank, ripe for planting, ripe for colonisation, ripe for exploitation, ripe for flying around. Material, and perhaps Time, have tried a little to rectify the sphere's emptiness. The paper of the Carracci drawing is stained and flecked with impurities, even with hints of rogue colour, just like the world, and Time and wear have made Hercules more mortal, less God, more man. There is a paper crease across his belly where all men bend—just like a book.

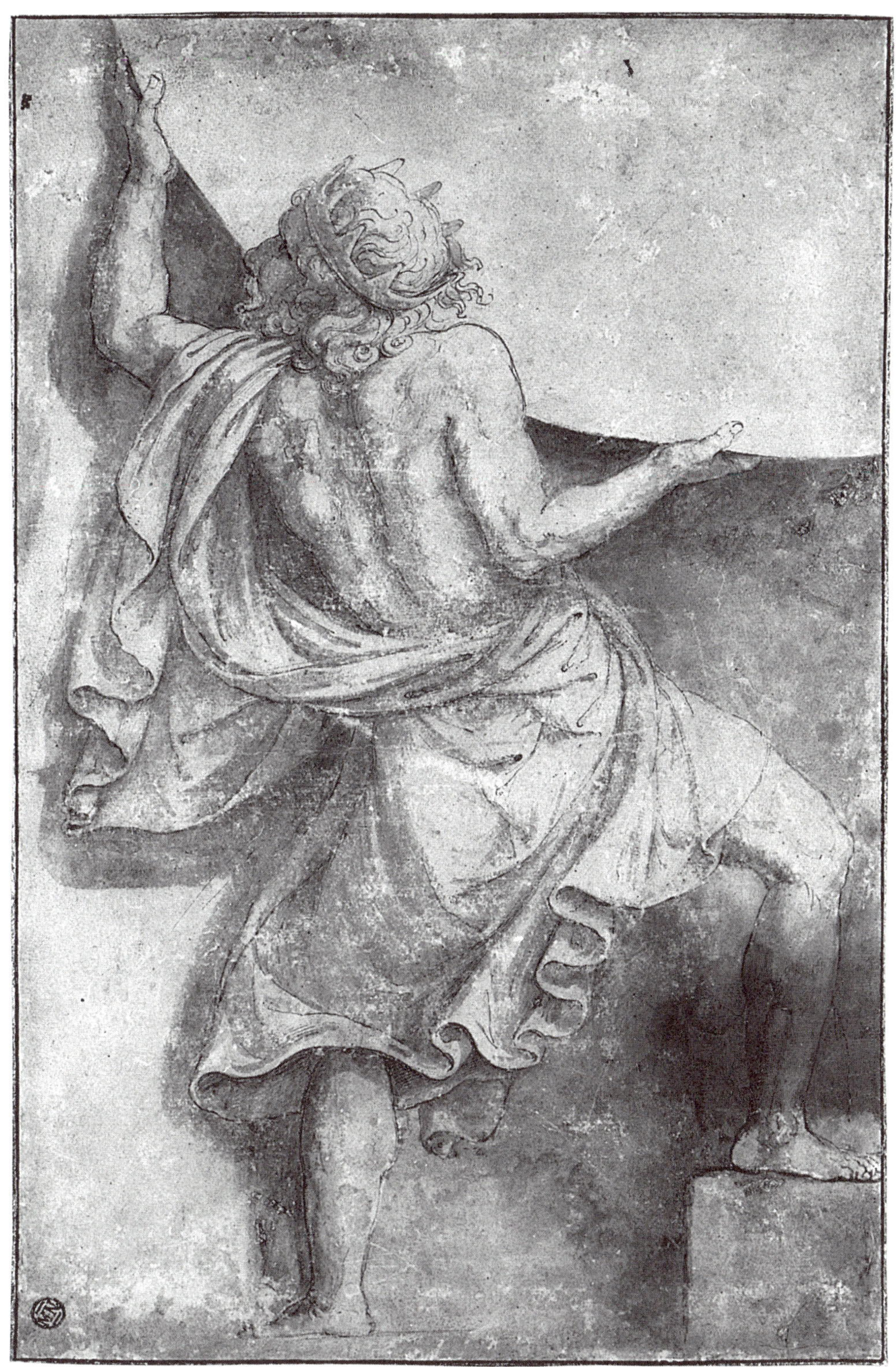

4

5
MONDELLA
The Cortege of Silenus

The subject for lifting this time is no abstract symbol for contemplation, no globe for heroics, and no burden of manufacture and wage-earning. But a body. We are considering not so much a lift-off as a lift-up. And the creature is a mythological human. The weight is all flesh. There is no stitch of clothing; only a wreath of leaves on his head. It's a joke. Grin if you like. Four pointed-eared fauns try hard to lift a grinning Silenus from the ground. Six hands take his arms and the fourth reveler tries hard to lever Silenus's buttocks off the floor. Silenus does not look perturbed. He's drunk. Sitting with squashed buttocks on the hard ground is a commonplace for him. There is a syrinx-player tangling his fingers to drunkenly played notes that also might lighten the cumberous body and set him at least on his feet. But music won't help, nor the threats of a lazy, open-mouthed lion, nor a braying donkey.

Silenus's body of circles and spheres is centred in a square, with some of his companion-figures chopped and cropped by the framing, or has the drawing been cut down? In this drawing of brown on brown on brown—the colours of a beer harvest—all activity and detail is centred on Silenus's head, and most pertinently on his eyes. He has just made a joke, a self-deprecating joke about his weight. Why is Silenus an object to be shifted and hafted and humoured, the tedious embarrassment of yet another self-congratulatory drinking inebriate?

Of course, this podgy lump of human meat is more than a Silenus, he's an allegorical personification of fatness, plumpness, the rotund, his body an inflatable series of ball-like volumes—breasts and belly and head with a double chin. He is like an adult baby, like a maturing version of that child we see in the background. An inflated ballooning comes to mind,

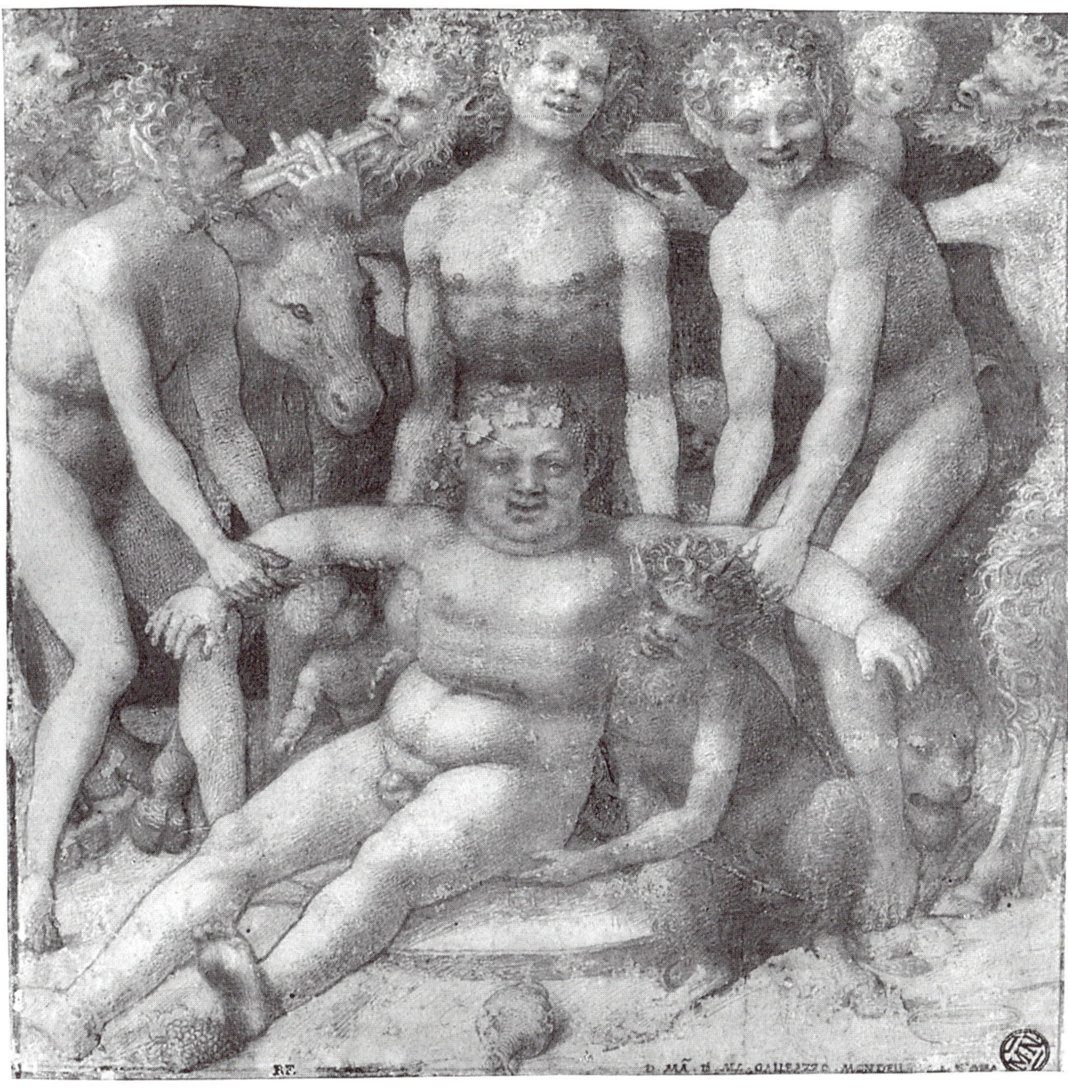

5

and balloons have been known to fly. But such a phenomenon does not come to pass, for these fleshy balloons are not going to be airborne. But if these arrow-eared fauns manage to lift this lump of inebriated meat at least a few inches from the ground, it's a hopeful sign. Silenus probably does not care himself. Alcohol can always be relied upon to make its own flights of fancy.

6

RUBENS after MANTEGNA
Silenus borne by a satyr and two fauns

7

MANTEGNA
Bacchanalia with Silenus

There are three attempts in this Mantegna frieze for a lift-off, and the bacchanalian assistants are more successful. We have bodies off the ground and that is optimistic. The greatest success is Silenus himself. Undoubtedly if anyone is going to fly, who could believe a heavy Silenus would be a candidate? Three fauns have lifted him eight inches. And there are signs of hope also that a female may join him. Then there will be two heavy bodies, male and female, lifted from the ground, potential aviator and aviatrix, in a mockery of levitation. The woman, obese in face and belly, with a modesty-cloth that has slipped to make her more immodest, is carried by a smiling figure whose feet are in water to the ankles. Even too heavy for her carrier's strength, this female drinking companion needs a supporting tree-stump for her left leg. The musician figures on the right are the lightest on their feet, already seeking lighter loads and lighter company, but they are not goat-legged, not capricious jumping possibilities. Gravity, drink, and obesity hold the others to this waterside marshland, despite the straining, but we are looking at hopeful signs already of gravity's release.

The Silenus figure has been copied by Rubens, master of the fleshy body, dead and alive. Silenus has been isolated from the frieze, his trefoil-spouted drinking pot still spilling, and his servants still straining with even greater anxiety and fear of dropping their burden than they were in the Mantegna original. Rubens has rearranged the musculature a little, and variously both hidden and re-invented some more fatness for the legs. The head perhaps is less bullet-shaped, less porcine, less aggressive, and the bacchic servants have increased the Silenus weight by their facial straining. Perhaps they have added nine and a half pounds by physical gesture. But there is no evidence here of the wind that was blowing two ways at once, east and west, in the Mantegna.

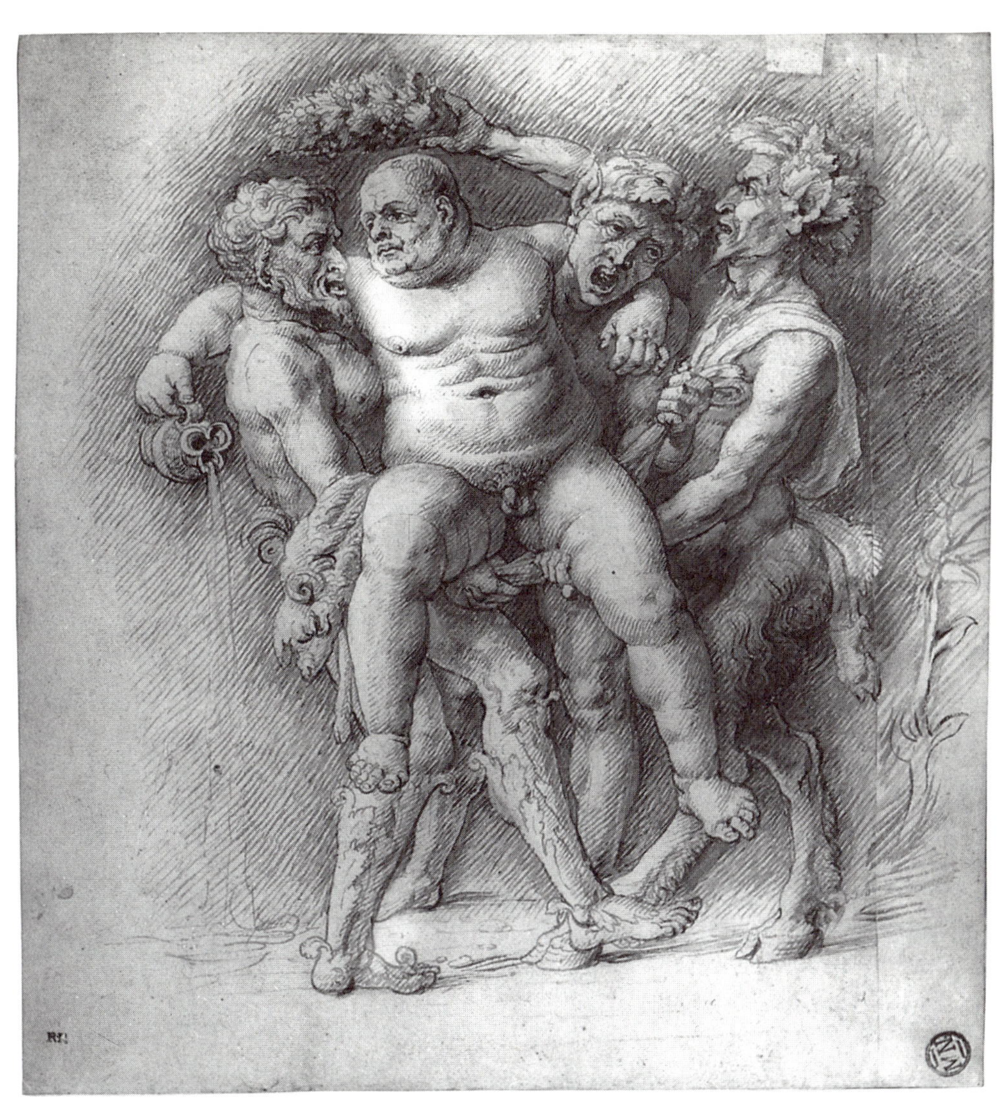

6

7

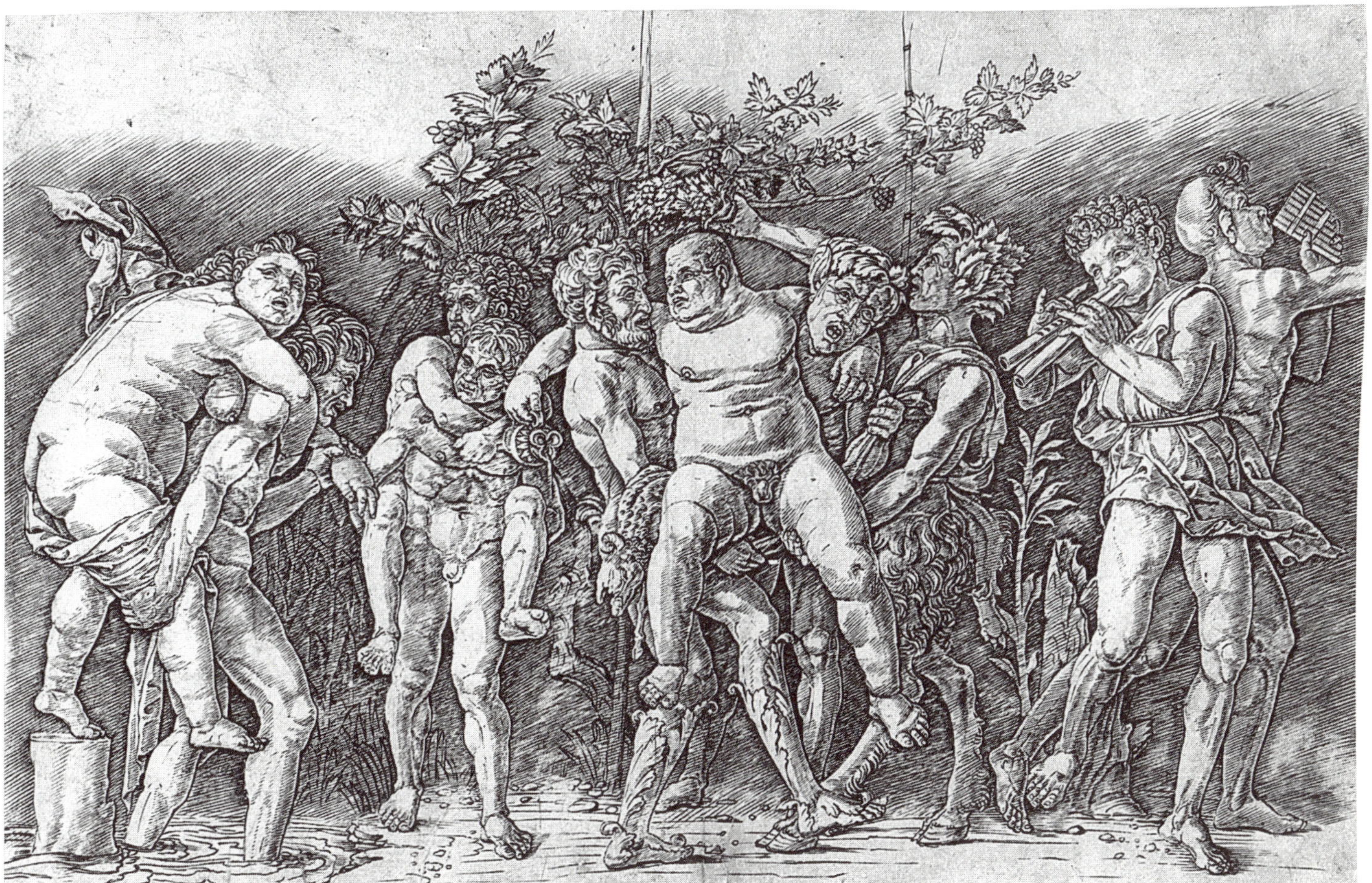

8—9

Giovanni DA BRESCIA after MANTEGNA
Virtus Combusta
Virtus Deserta

An encyclopedia of reference wrapped up in visual signs, some of the canon, some not. But not all for flying. We must search out what is useful.

A double-storey, multi-story drama, unorthodox in its upstairs, downstairs presentation, unfamiliar in the landscape ratio of the theatre, in cinema, more familiar for the presentation of goods for viewing and selling. This is a display case for allegory. Upstairs, on the first storey, above ground-level, the seven actors show precious little energy to fly. Are they the beginners in a flying game? The first creature on the left is from some bestiary of conglomerates, an unorthodox chimera with indecisive animal inheritance. He plays a bagpipe and his long prognathic jaw is tailored to blow long low notes. He is piping his way into a flying state of mind. He has bat's wings, griffin's wings, webbed wings, stretches of skin between five bone vanes. He has sprouting ears of indeterminate structure, antennae for blossoming flight perhaps? Much else of him is jumping goat, long-nippled, high-pricked and curly-shanked, with incipient horns dubious of a real exit on a bald brow. His feet, both webbed and four-clawed, suggestive of both duck and chicken, make him a subject to swim in the sea and walk on the land. Is he blind? One at least of his companions is blinded with a tied sack, and as if to confirm it, he has a leashed dog to lead him. The tightly corded sack also makes him deaf and mute. Is he also disadvantaged with one sandal, making him a cripple to add to his flying disadvantages? Holding the hand of a faun guide, a second companion shields her eyes from the sight below, where the result of pride and hubris are scrambled in a drain before a bolted door. On the right of the image, escorted by females of small flight potential, one blindfolded, the

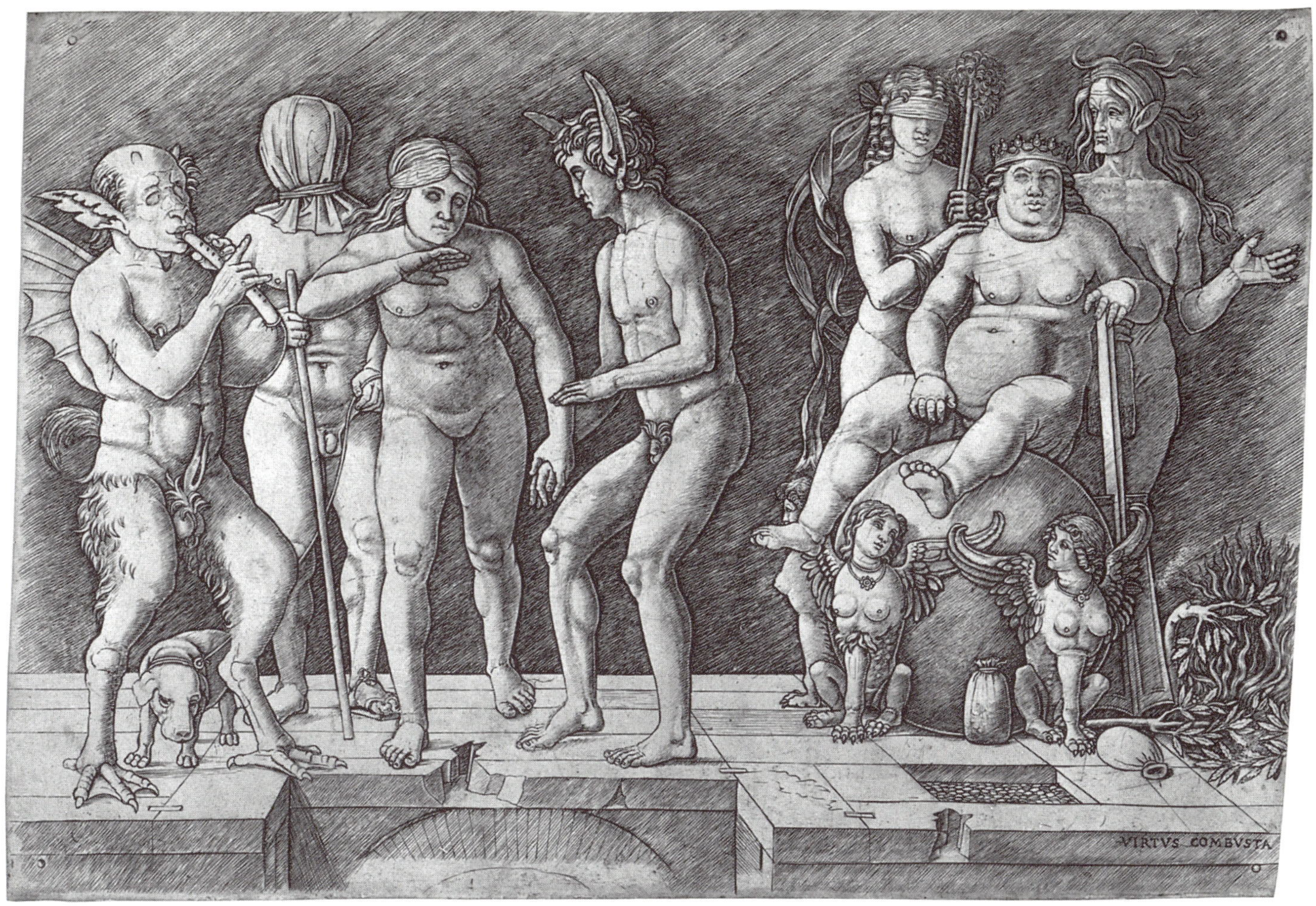

8

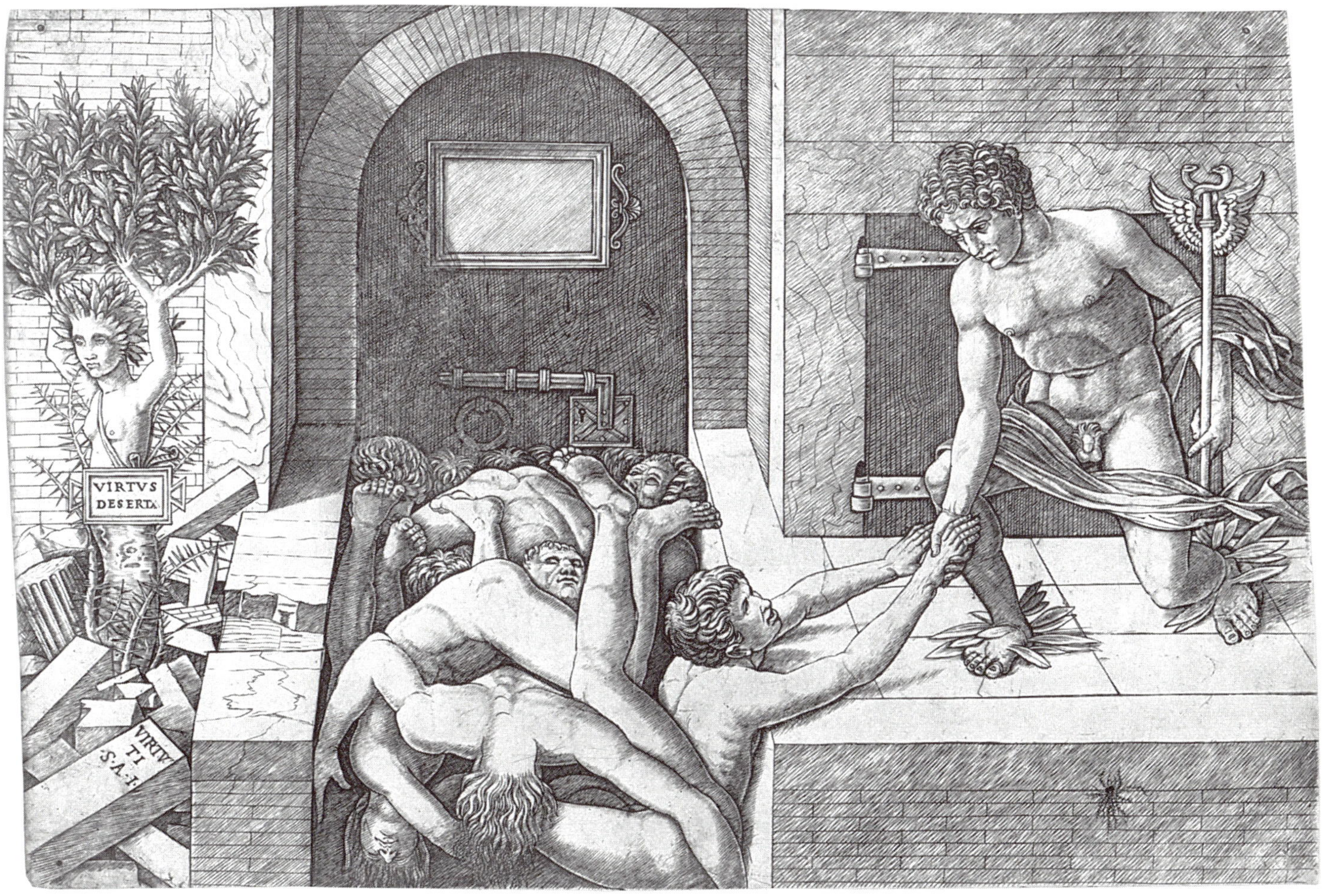

9

other old, sits a fat and breasted king holding for ease rather than support, what could be the rudder or a paddle to a boat, or the vane of a wind-sail, or could it be an upturned noticeboard with flight instructions? He is enthroned on a ball. It could be Redon's ball again, the very presence of unsympathetic gravity.

And at the ball's feet are two three-legged harpies, benevolent by their expression, milkable, conversing with I-told-you-so expressions. They could teach flight. They are fifty percent wings.

Below ground, on the lower storey, is Mercury, avenging postboy and pimp of the Gods, wing-footed in a strange and clumsy way, the feathers stuck into his foot at all and every angle. His staff, his wand, his caduceus, is more efficiently and neatly plumed than his feet. He offers a hand to bring the fallen out of the drain. On his level, on the left, a woman metamorphoses into a tree for crouching birds. Or is it the other way about—the tree has tired of the singing birds and is changing into a woman?

Eight active, solid-bodied characters in search of a flying experience? Whether they are conjured from a private theatrum mundi, or are creatures from a commissioner's instruction manual, are their aspirations for flight limited? Their attributes, in many cases wedded to their flesh and not merely held or carried, are variously and occasionally flight-associated. Will they pilot us?

10
GOYA
"It is her name day"

Two pranksters playing with a woman in a dark corridor, tying her feet together and hauling her up on a pulley. Is it to mimic the death of Saint Peter, who was crucified upside down so that he would not blaspheme by copying the death of Christ? Which makes the fête on the 29th June, a day for fishermen who use lines and ropes to pull in their catch. All circumstantial evidence.

How can you fly feet upwards?

She's scared. So would you be. Is this some excuse to look up her skirts? Some menacing sexual practice? Is she a lazy servant, some cousin they've tricked in a dark corridor, some chattering aunt they think they'll punish? The main torturer has legs like a frog and his companion has a nose like a cod. Their cold-blooded ruse has no ending. The companion pulls on the rope as though he has arms used to bell-ringing. Maybe they think the bells of the fête will drown her screams. Who is laughing? Who will confess to laughing in a Goya capriccio? Does the buck-toothed, bow-tied torturer hold her head lovingly? Has he gripped her by the hair? How did they get her there in that position? Did they leave an open noose on the flagstones in the shadows to catch her as she came scurrying by?

When they have clattered off, laughing down the dark and smelling passageway between two buildings, she will hang there, swinging, her long skirts round her waist, her long hair dragging the dirty ground. This is no way to fly, humiliated in a dark alley, feet pinned together by the weight of your own body. This image is a bad card to deal if you want to learn to fly. It's one from a numbered pack, each one playing-card shaped. Do any of the other cards deal with flying? It's a mocking card.

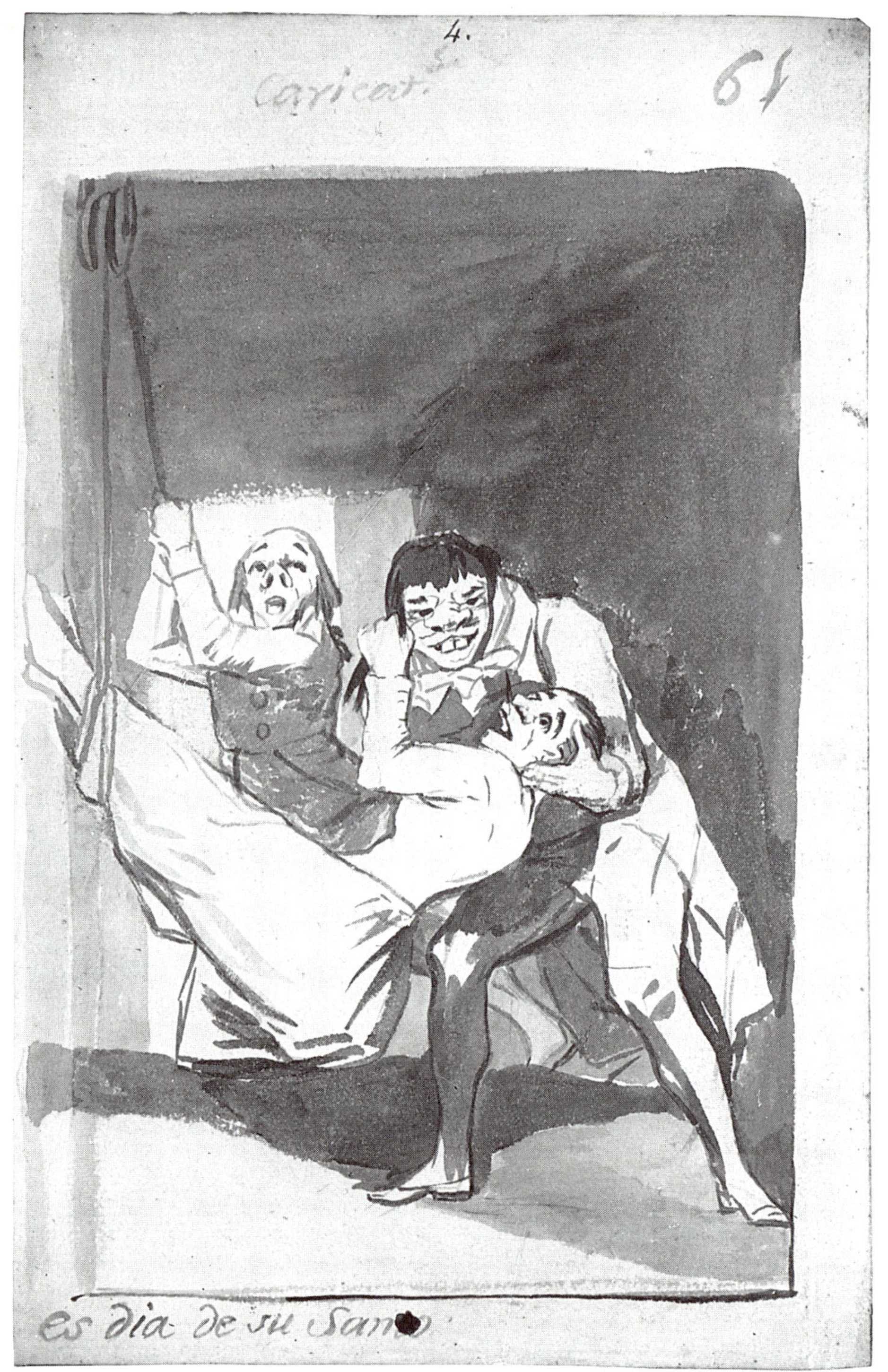

10

11
School of MANTEGNA
Hercules and Antaeus

No amount of on-ground struggling could defeat and kill Antaeus. Only off the floor and separated from the electric touch of gravity could he be de-earthed and conquered. Antaeus, the giant of Libya, son of Poseidon and Earth, was definitely an anti-gravity agent. A definitive non-flyer. Separate him from his mother Earth and he was totally vulnerable. A true case of mother's apron-strings.

This wrestling match is the origin of the wrestling-grip, "Feet off the ground and you're a dead man." Did wrestling need such a myth to get it started? What was the earliest example for wrestlers, this event, or Jacob wrestling with the angel? At least in Jacob's case, there was the possibility of contemplating wings, though the Bible doesn't mention wings in Genesis. But then Jacob was doubly blessed with images of ascending into the skies. He also dreamt of heavenly ladders.

Antaeus being such a deceptively simple case of negative gravity, it took Hercules a long time to work out how to win. Hercules was known for brawn not brains. He spent a good time in conventional arm-locks and shoulder-locks before he caught on. Perhaps it is not so surprising, for from this image, you get the impression they were both small men. If Antaeus was on the ground, he'd be a little taller, though not tall enough perhaps to justify the name of giant. Lift Antaeus off the ground in a triumphal upthrust and hold him there until you could squeeze him to death. We don't get a chance to see Antaeus's face. Whilst Hercules is neatly barber-groomed as befits a winner, Antaeus is a shock-headed nobody with plump buttocks and the indignity of seeing his testicles through his legs. Like you might see a bull. Or a dog. It's not certain what Hercules' right hand is doing, is he grasping Antaeus by the forelock, gripping his brow or putting his eyes out?

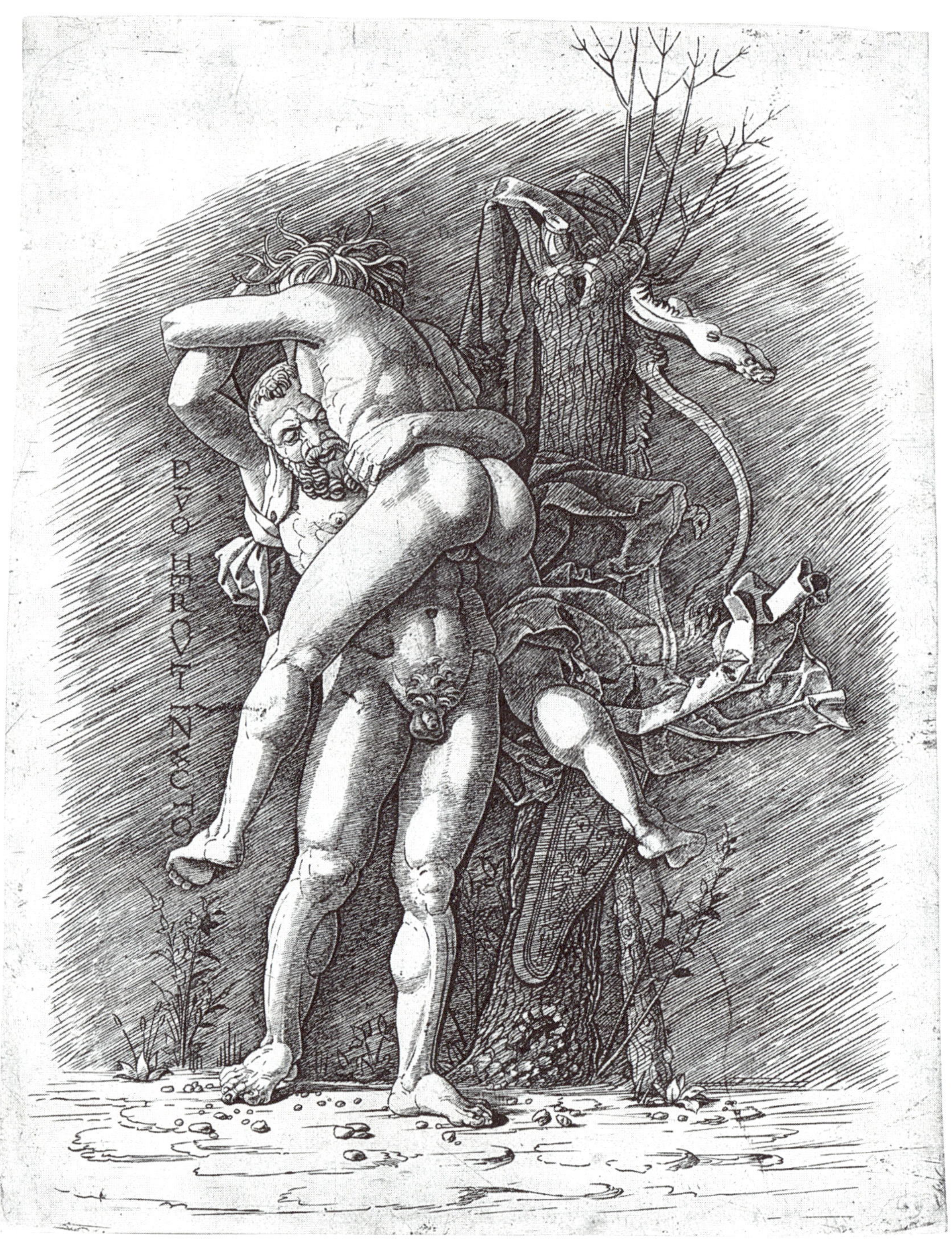

11

If it's certain that Antaeus is never going to fly alive, what of his conquorer? What is his flying potential? His body is his trade and art. Here he has no neck to speak of. Elbow, eye, nipple, navel, and penis make a curve of strength to support his right leg. His left leg has spring-loaded bones. His genitals are at the compositional epicentre of events, the fulcrum of the action, mid-point of the isosceles triangle of Antaeus's legs. Is that where his strength lies? In his sex? Samson is Hercules' biblical equivalent and his strength lay in his hair. Or is the Bible manipulating a euphemism? As allegory, this combat can be interpreted as Lust conquored by Virtue, or Flesh vanquished by Spirit. The overt physicality is reluctant here to separate the moral values in bodily identification.

Mantegna made more than a few variations of this celebrated wrestling match, rearranging the position of the struggling protagonists. Does that make him, or his patron, devotees of ringside wrestling, homophilia, or anti-gravity? For the Hercules and Antaeus archetype, this composition has a novel pose, not so graceful perhaps, but then when was conquoring your enemy in a wrestling match a cause for especial grace? The action is caught in Mantegna's world-style, squashed in a limited foreground to imitate a venerable sculptural ancestry and a truly classical inspiration, though ironically, this story is rarely illustrated in antiquity. The tree may be a tree but it's a dead tree and it's firmly fixed in a glacial marble deposit. There are no clouds because there is no sky. The world stops immediately behind the tree. Though a powerful dissertation on negating magnetic gravity, it is not a promising world to fly in.

12
CAMBIASO
The Flight of Aeneas
13
GIRODET
The Flood

Here are two heroic carryings, two energetic attempts at anti-gravity, two escapes, one from fire and one from water; Cambiaso from burning Troy, Girodet from the Flood. We must trust the titles, for the flames of Troy are totally absent, and the waters of the deluge are little more suggested than an ambiguous wetness on the rocks.

The Troy escape is an image of a family of three generations on the run. It is viewed from a curious angle, from a vigorous top-quarter position to better dramatise the rush of the flight. The heavy body of Aeneas's father, Anchises, is pictured riding high on his son's back, and at our eye-level, to impress on us the encumbering weight, not eased by the old man's dutiful insistence on bringing the household Gods. Or is it God in the singular? The portable hearth-statue is a turbanned figure, maybe from a tradition older still than Troy? The movement of the family down the diagonal of flight is swift and assured, the wife and mother significantly bringing up the rear. We know only too well what happened to Aeneas. And Anchises died honoured in Sicily. What happened to Aeneas's wife? Some say she was lost in the darkness. Some say she was burnt alive. She could not keep up. She fell behind. She had to disappear so Virgil's pious Aeneas could make unadulterous love to Dido. Dido too perished in flames. On a funeral pyre. Aeneas is associated with burning wives.

Anchises is full-bearded like a river-god, much like the old man passenger in the Girodet drawing, whose relationship to the rising water cannot now be cordial. The Girodet pair must surely also be father and son though they have no names. Whilst the son has a muscular torso of flamboyant proportions, the father has two pairs of legs, where Girodet adjusted the balance of weight. The legs hang in a cinematic blur which

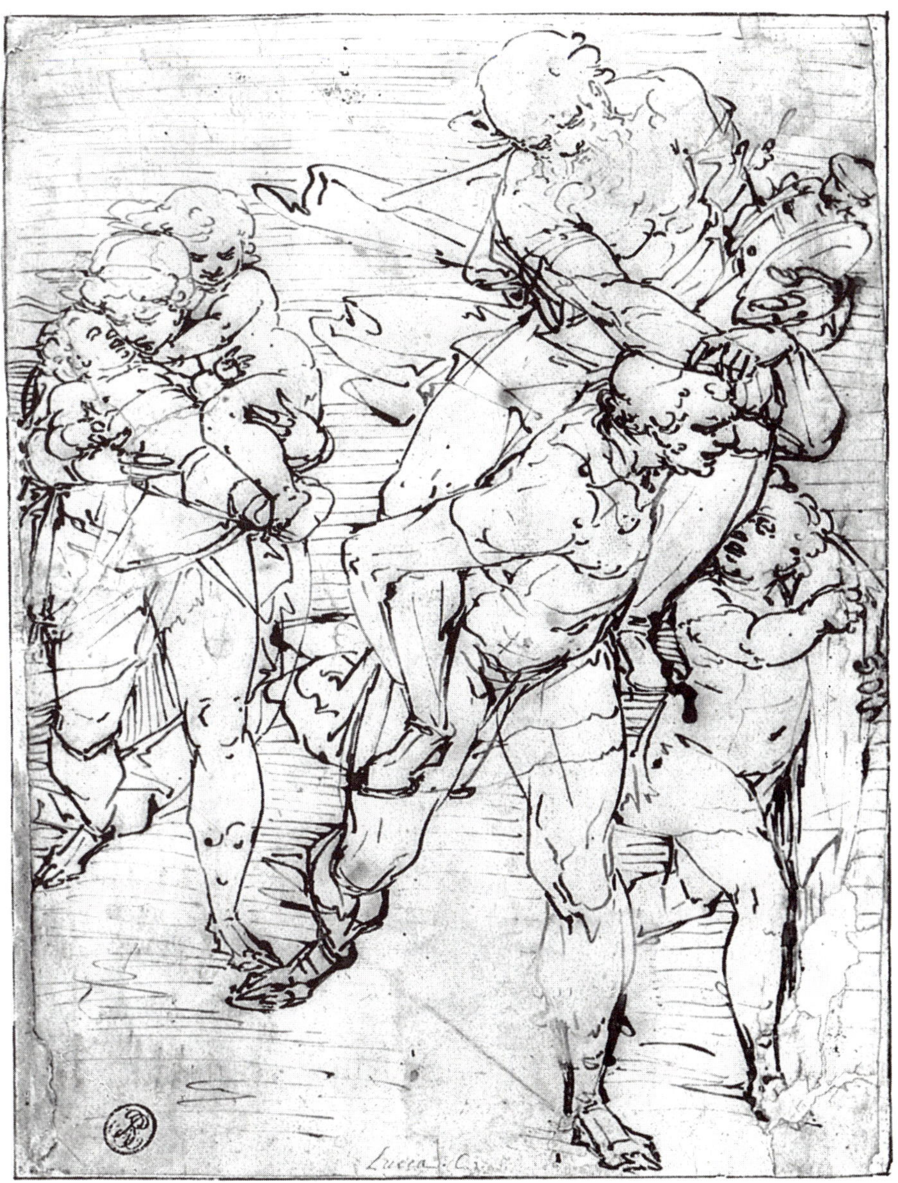

12

gives them a sort of movement, not of life within, but of the sway of paralysed limbs that behave like dead pendulums, increasing the sense of the dead weight that hangs around the young man's shoulders.

The outcome of the flood for all save Noah's party, is well known.

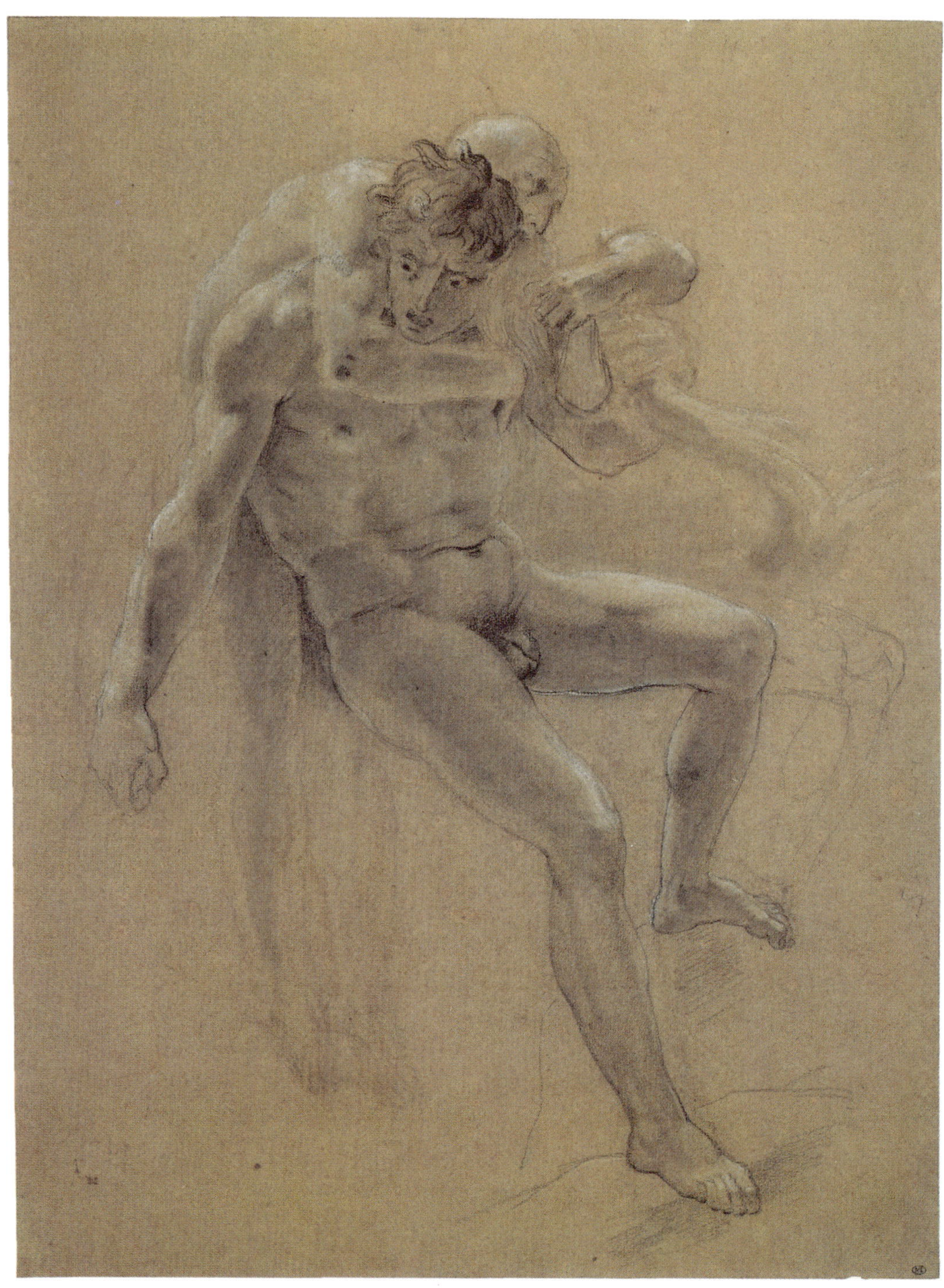

13

Aeneas at least escapes. And to glory. The tens of thousands who did not travel on the Ark are all unnamed. Both these images are images of flight without wings. It is their tragic circumstances that gives them the necessary propulsion. If to flee is also to fly, then here indeed we now have tragic flight.

14
Flemish Shool after JAN VAN EYCK
Saint Christopher

Saint Christopher carries Christ. This is no faun carrying a drunken Silenus, no Anchises being given a saving lift from desperate danger, but a positive act with voluntary passenger, voluntary porter. Sidestepping the particularity of the religious message, we have a child riding on the back of a giant wading across a torrent. Maybe the child is not really a child but a dwarf. Whether child or dwarf, both are perched high enough to see a little further than the giant. We have a new generation seeing further than the last. And if we had a dwarf, then dwarfs make good pilots. Traditionally, of course, they are sympathetic to weight-bearing restrictions, and they are, by repute, wise and wily. So much for orthodox prejudice.

But it is not a dwarf, but the Christ child and Christopher will always be a sturdy beast-of-burden for Christ. By his name, he is required to be. Before he became a walking ferryman, his name was Reprobus, whose etymological sentiments are not entirely unallegorical.

The cloaks are flying. Again there is some wind. Perhaps we can take some comfort that two modes of opposition to gravity are presented here—the charitable act of lifting high a body for take-off and the presence of a wind.

We can see a town on the further shore. Has Christopher carried the Child this far? And there are birds in the sky, at least two. Are they water-birds, or are they birds of prey from among the mountains? The currents are strong, and under the rocks, as the river flows towards us, as vigorous and as rippled in places as Christopher's beard. There is a hermit holding up a lamp. Are we day or are we night? The Golden Legend

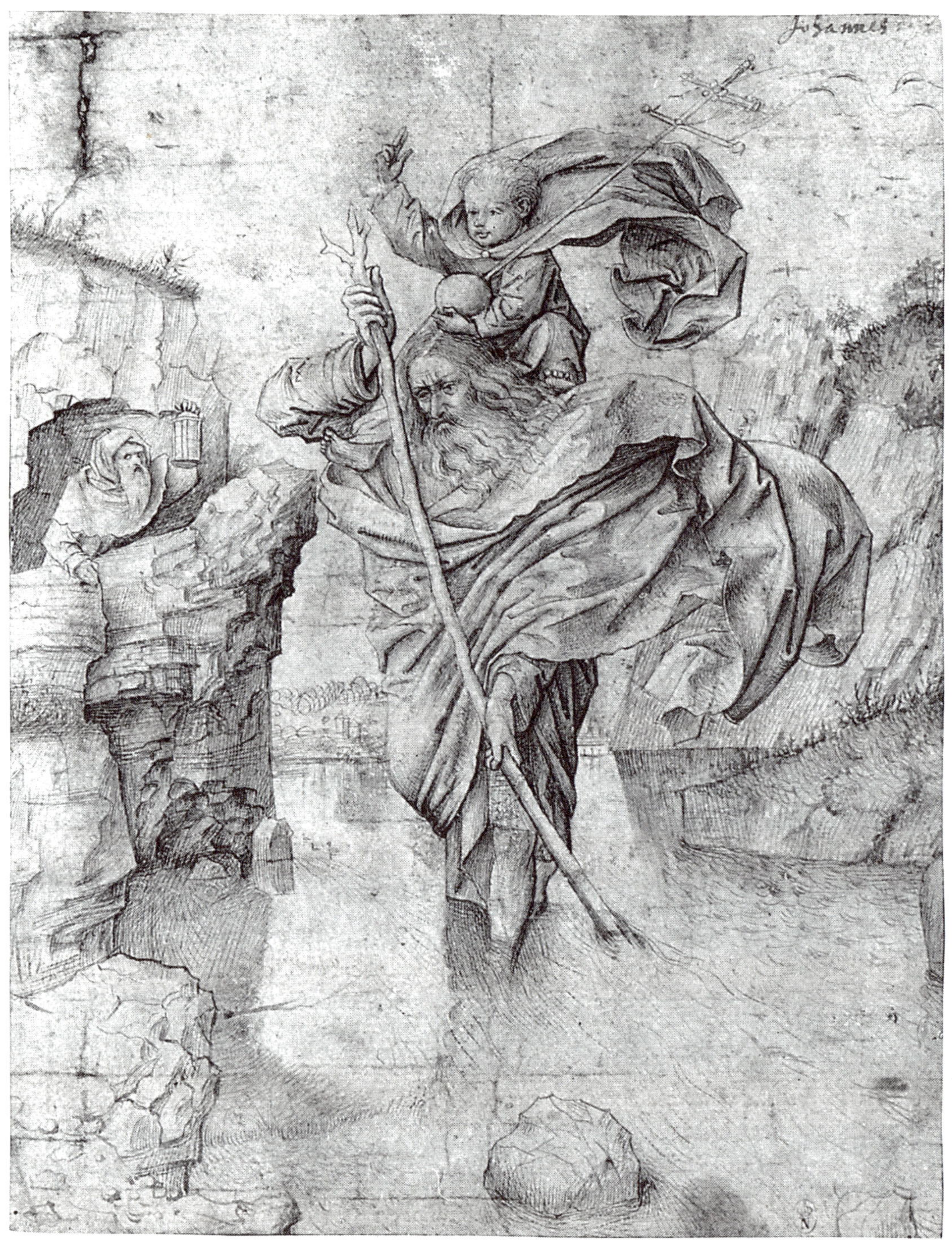

14

would have this hermit as the instigator of Christopher's services. He it was who, on promise to make Christopher the servant of the most powerful of men, enslaved Christopher to the deeps and currents of the treacherous river.

According to Caxton, Christopher with his daily burden of heavy passengers, became a three-call man like Peter with his heavy daily burden of the church. Three times, sitting on the river bank, rubbing his fingers in the dust, did the Christ child have to shout to get Christopher to rise from his bed and proffer him a lift. Every child knows that flyers are three-call people. "One, two, three, go!" is the password among children for those about to jump, and rise, and fly. It was no easy crossing. Despite the sturdy curved staff, and the apparent small weight of a child, the river rose and the child grew as heavy as lead and Christopher was not so certain this time that he was going to reach the further bank. He was to find out the identity of his passenger when, ordered to stick his water-staff in the desert sand, he saw it flourish into a palm tree with birds singing in the branches, a hopeful sign for us of flying possibilities. Later, Christopher was arrested by a monarch who made him the target for forty archers whose arrows were diverted. By divine intervention, one arrow made a sideways turn and drove straight into the eye of the troublesome king, blinding him. High carriage, dead branches into live trees for twittering birds, diverted arrows, Christopher is more than just a patron saint of travelers, of pilgrims. Can he be the patron saint of flyers, aviators, aviatrix, airmen, pilots?

CHAPTER TWO

Possibilities of Flight

We have encouragement, now we need examples. All who follow in this chapter intimate lift-off and suggest flight, although the flying might only be in the mind, in wish-fulfilment, in spirit. We should be optimistic.

15
After MICHELANGELO
Leda

A mating with swans. A dynastic move. "If I cannot fly myself then my offspring shall." But alas, it did not turn out that way. Leda's four off-springs were all human, though born of eggs. What can you expect, for the swan was Jupiter and Gods make mortals in their own image. This drawing, in all traditional probability, is a copy, and who knows what particular subjectivity guided the copier to sway Michelangelo's meaning this way or that? Some small line, some stray shadow, can persuade us to different interpretation, but the intent is indubitably carnal, if ornithologi-cally so. But even if we doubt the copier, we cannot doubt that Michel-angelo had considerable erotic purpose in birds, as we shall see with Ganymede and the eagle, another incident to make Juno jealous. The darkest part of this drawing is at the point of anatomical consummation, and the twist of the Leda body makes no compromise on its intent and on our concentration. This is a copulation on a bolstered bed with a swan. The swan's neck and head snuggly share the same line as Leda's belly and breast. Beak and lips meet in an ornithological kiss.

Was Leda modelled on some goosegirl? Is that how her mythology arose? Some voyeur down by the river, watching goosegirls, seeing much familiarity between girl and goose? Guano on Leda's pink feet, green grass smudges on her knee, white feathers stuck to her leg? What was the particular model for this Leda gossegirl like before aristocratic writers borrowed her away from village greens and put her in a palace? For our purposes, whatever the pleasure, she is a cul-de-sac, a false end, for it is we who want to fly, not some hypothetical offspring.

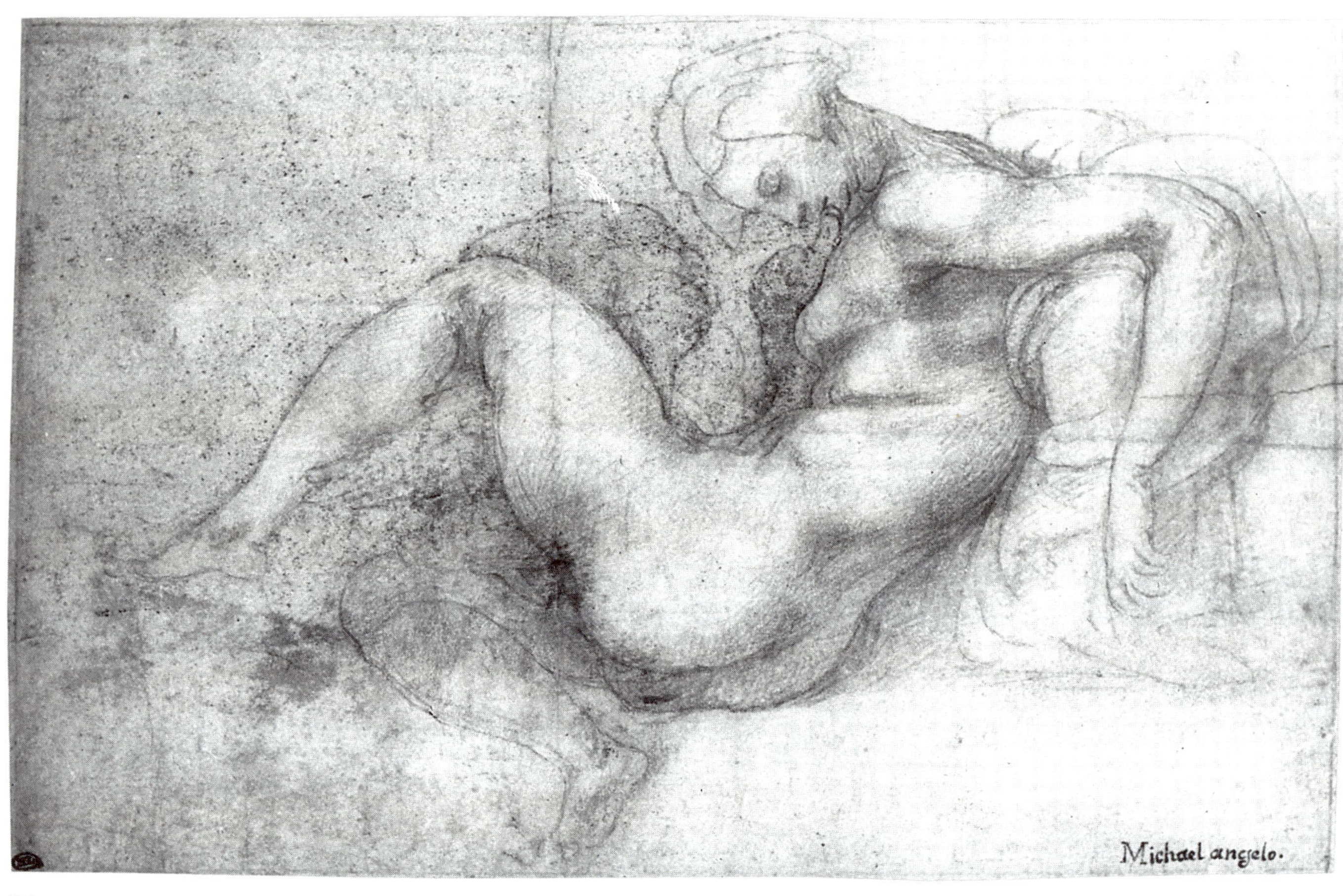

15

16
VAN DYCK (?)
The Stigmata of Saint Francis

From the carnal to the spiritual, though the flesh is still at issue. Francis receives his stigmata. The wounds that nailed Christ's body down in order to let his spirit fly, are transposed by intense identification to a monk surprised at prayer before a cave. The identification is made with conventionalised graphic language. Slanting diagonal light-rays travel across the space between Christ and Francis to support the transposing supernatural energy. It is a curiosity that Christ's feet, as well as being nailed to the foot of the cross, also seemed nailed to the picture-frame.

We should take pains to note the details that have been scrupulously drawn in this very detailed image. A list of the pictorial events is of pertinent interest. For attributes of mortality, Francis and his companion are surrounded by gnarled vegetation and venerable tree-roots and there is a skull in the cave-mouth. For attributes of voluntary poverty, there is a dwelling of ragged wood behind the trees, and the monks are flanneled into brown serge habits which are bound around with rope. For attributes of service and humility, a rosary lies abandoned on the ground. Saint Francis's shoes are off his feet before the Lord, though his less reverent companion is sandaled-footed. For attributes of the burden of pain, the wounds in Francis's hands and feet are not just the marks of nails, but seemingly the nails themselves, lodged there deeply. And the mark of the spear in Christ's side has, in its transference, ripped the Franciscan habit and bloodied the body and the cloth. These are all the detailed canonical records of an artist fulfiling his obligations. The list can continue to note evidence that might emphasise, not simply the Francisican reputation as a lover of Nature, but, dare it be said, attributes of flight?

There is a lizard standing transfixed before an open-winged butterfly upon the ground. Is the lizard predatory? A second winged creature,

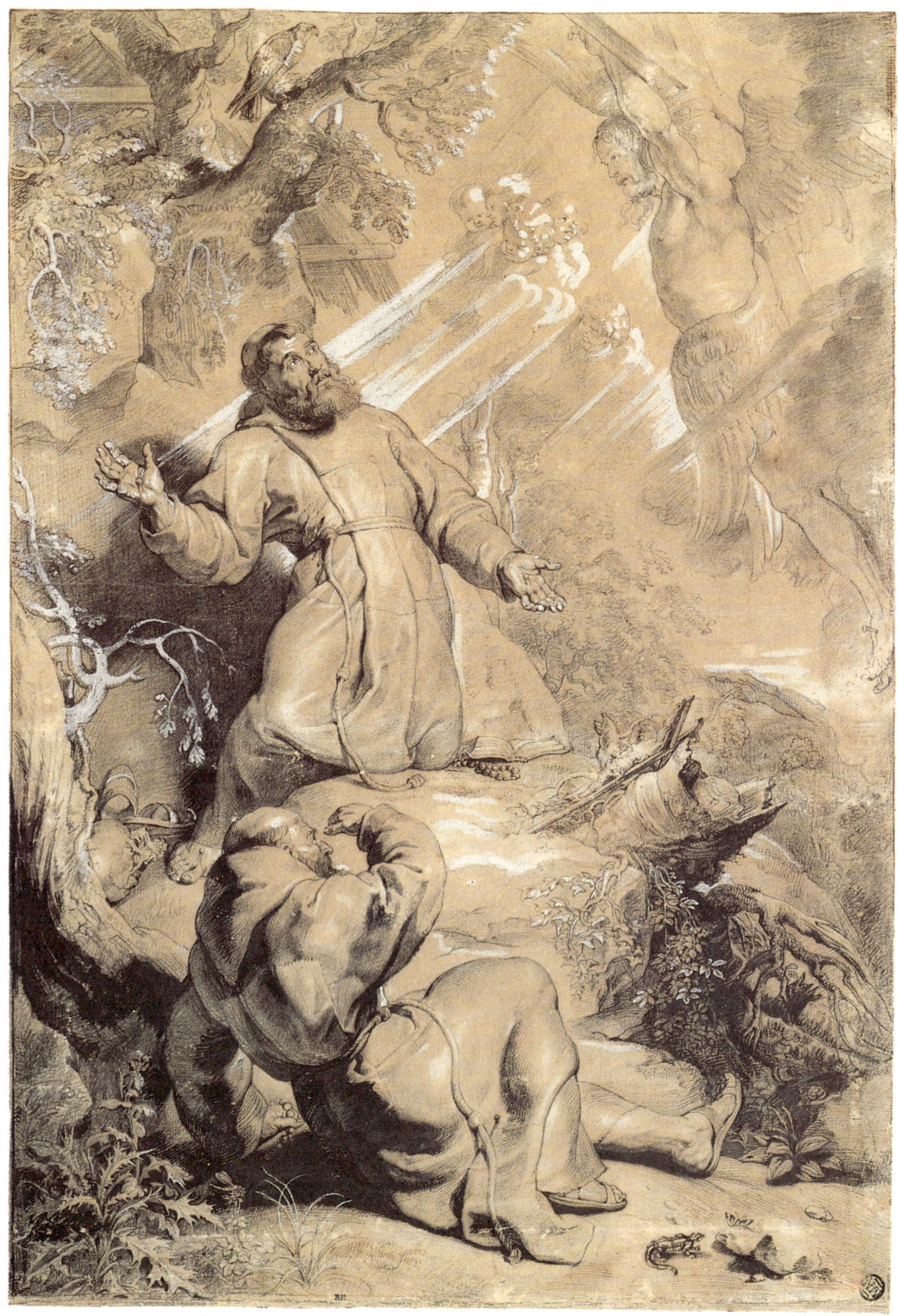

16

another insect, a dragon-fly or a damsel-fly, is perched on a single-stemmed plant by the foreground thistle. There is a bird of prey in the branches above Saint Francis's head, a falcon, a buzzard? We and Saint Francis are situated on a hillside. Maybe the hillside is important for us. We and Francis are elevated by the vision. We need elevation. The heads of the cherubim have wings. Which leaves us most significantly with a very particular vision of Christ. He is most extravagantly winged. The vision acknowledges the small conventional crucifix leant against the broken tree-stump, thus making the demonstrative departure from source iconography most emphatic. Christ is a vision of some omnipotent bird. He is both nailed and flying, at one and the same time, on the cross. His wings are ornithologically detailed with primary and secondary feathers, and they grow from Christ's back, from a space between the vertical post of the crucifix and Christ's spine, but one is placed under the other so that all Christ's vertebrae must be judged to give them support. Upper and lower wings are held in alternate positions, opened and closed, to demonstrate the mechanism of flight. Is there such a record, biblical, canonical, or apocryphal, of Christ having such literal wings?

17

SERAFINO DA VERONA
The Expulsion from Paradise

Has the flying curve left the ground yet? Even birds, who despite the necessary equipment also have an instinct to fly without especial training, need examples—their parents. They watch whilst waiting for the necessary moment. We need examples too. Images that will give us hope that flight is possible, even probable, and then, centimetre by centimetre, we must see about the prospects.

After the false example of Leda, and the spiritual example of Saint Francis, why not begin at the beginning, at the time of man's first taste of his inadequacies, when he also had to include in his disappointments, the realisation that, unlike the angel, he could not fly. Leaving Paradise might also have meant losing the power to fly.

With pointed finger and body aslant, this well-dressed da Verona angel of dubious sex is riding a cloud. The angel's side of the picture is indeed an essay of the etherium, one large dusty vapour excitement densely obscuring the garden. The upper air has descended to Eden to give Adam a taste of his earthiness. Yet the angel, however sexed, is mortal-shaped or is that a blasphemy? If God made man in his own image, then surely he made angels likewise. Which means if we are angel-shaped and they can fly, then why not us? Perhaps the real punishment in the Garden was to be de-winged. Are there signs of banished wings on these poor souls, some scar or blemish that, in pursuit of Darwin creationism, we could resurrect and say this is how we were punished? Where, when God-given, could the wings have been fixed to the human frame? At the shoulder, at the waist, at the ankels, at the ears? Eve's fleshy body leaves little room for further anatomical alterations, but her long tight curls could hide possibilities. Adam is a bent man already. He shows us his back and there is nothing there.

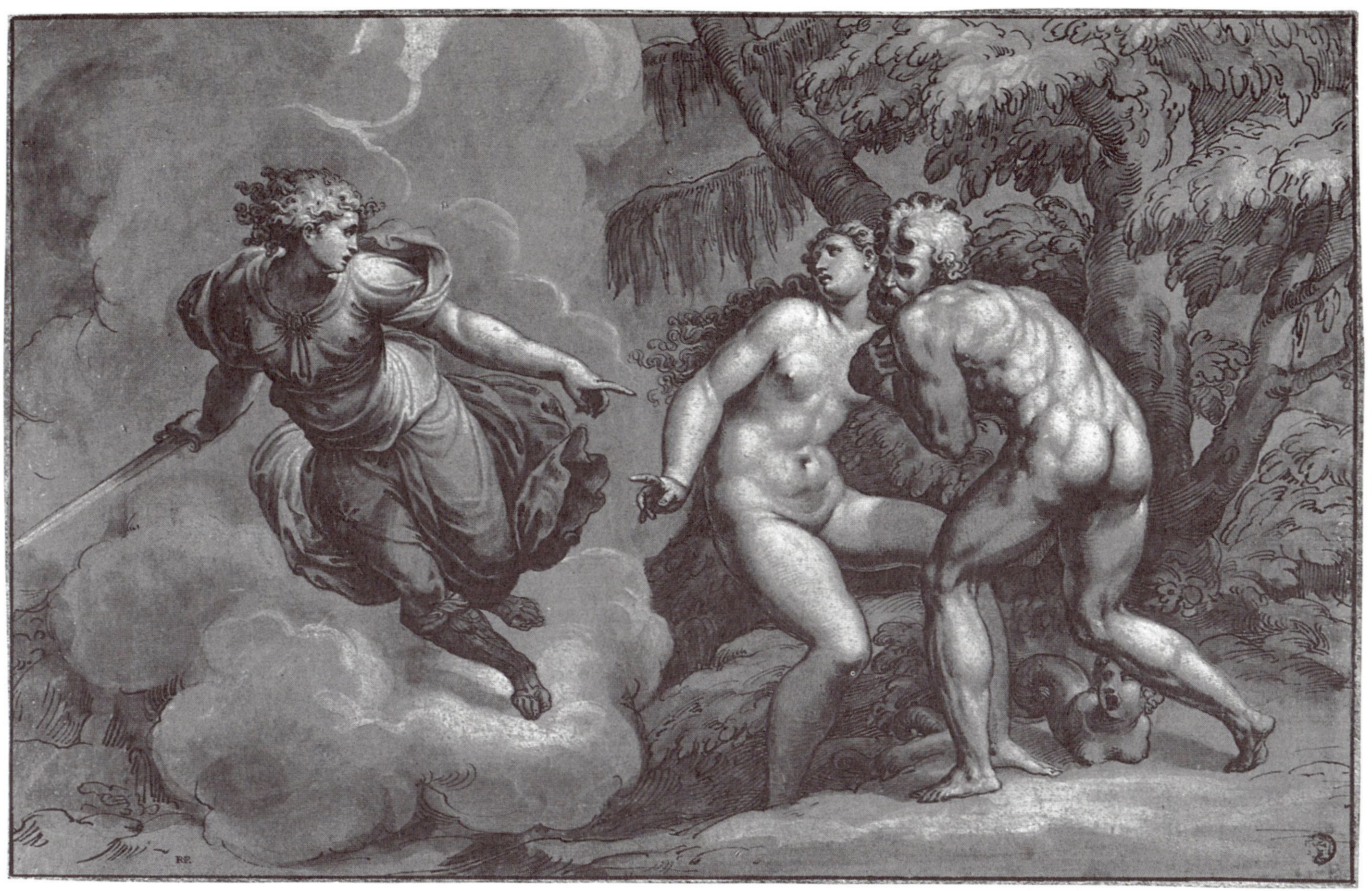

17

The picture's ratio is conventional, but it is a two-part scheme. There is rushing movement in the first half that is devoted to the element of air, and frozen stasis in the second, the element of earth. Left and right, first and second, air and earth, cloud and vegetation. And to join the two separate worlds are the fingers of the angel and Eve. They miss contact, and a line drawn between the two out-stretched fore-fingers splits the picture. The possibility of contact is broken forever.

Looking at them both, Eve and angel, surely both are female. The breasts, the belly, the hips and thighs suggest so. And does this suggest complicity, an electric charge between females? But this charge did not contact. A false reminder of a famous electric flash between God and man? This one is not permitted to happen. And why? Because there is another woman on the ground—the serpent. If Adam and Eve have no air borne potential then what of the serpent? She is female too, her breasts drag on the earth. She has no arms or fingers to point any electric charges or receive one. Her mouth is squarely open in dismay. She will never ever fly. Snakes with wings? Impossible?

18
Annibale CARRACCI
Ulysses before Circe

The Carracci *Ulysses before Circe,* an unprepossessing story of man into imminent pig by poison, offers us a mechanism for flight, though the wings in evidence are small and anatomically associated with the ankles. There are also wings attached to Mercury's helmet, but a helmet is detachable. Could the helmet achieve independent flight? A helmet can be hung on a peg in the closet or the cloakroom. It can be lost or stolen. It is the anklewings that should attract us. The story is admonitory. Ulysses, picaresquely returning from the Trojan Wars, has arrived on the island of the seductive resident Circe who offers sailors hospitality. However, she has poisoned the wine or the soup with a substance that will surely change the visitors into pigs. Mercury, patron of travellers, flies in to dissuade Ulysses from drinking. The efficacy of the poison is already apparent. On the marbled flagged floor, a sailor has succumbed. His head is metamorphosing. He will soon be grunting. His flying days are indubitably finished. Pigs never fly.

Mercury's timed arrival is essential. Some seconds more and the nobly accoutred Ulysses too would be snuffling and eating roots. Three hands meet around the poisoned bowl. Circe invites, Ulysses accepts, and Mercury, hovering in the air, appears to drop an antidote into the offering. Is he therefore invisible to Circe's eyes, for she would surely antidote the antidote. Despite the variations on the iconography, it is Mercury's wings that interest us. By all accounts they are inseparable from the ankle, though the anatomy is in dispute. Carracci himself thinks so too, for the ghost of two pairs of wings are fluttering there on the right foot. Indeed the foot itself has moved, imputing illusion of movement. Are the wings attached to the ankle-bone or to the lower calf? The left leg has securer and more substantial wings but the anatomical exactness is vaguer, for they now appear to sprout from the back of the heel.

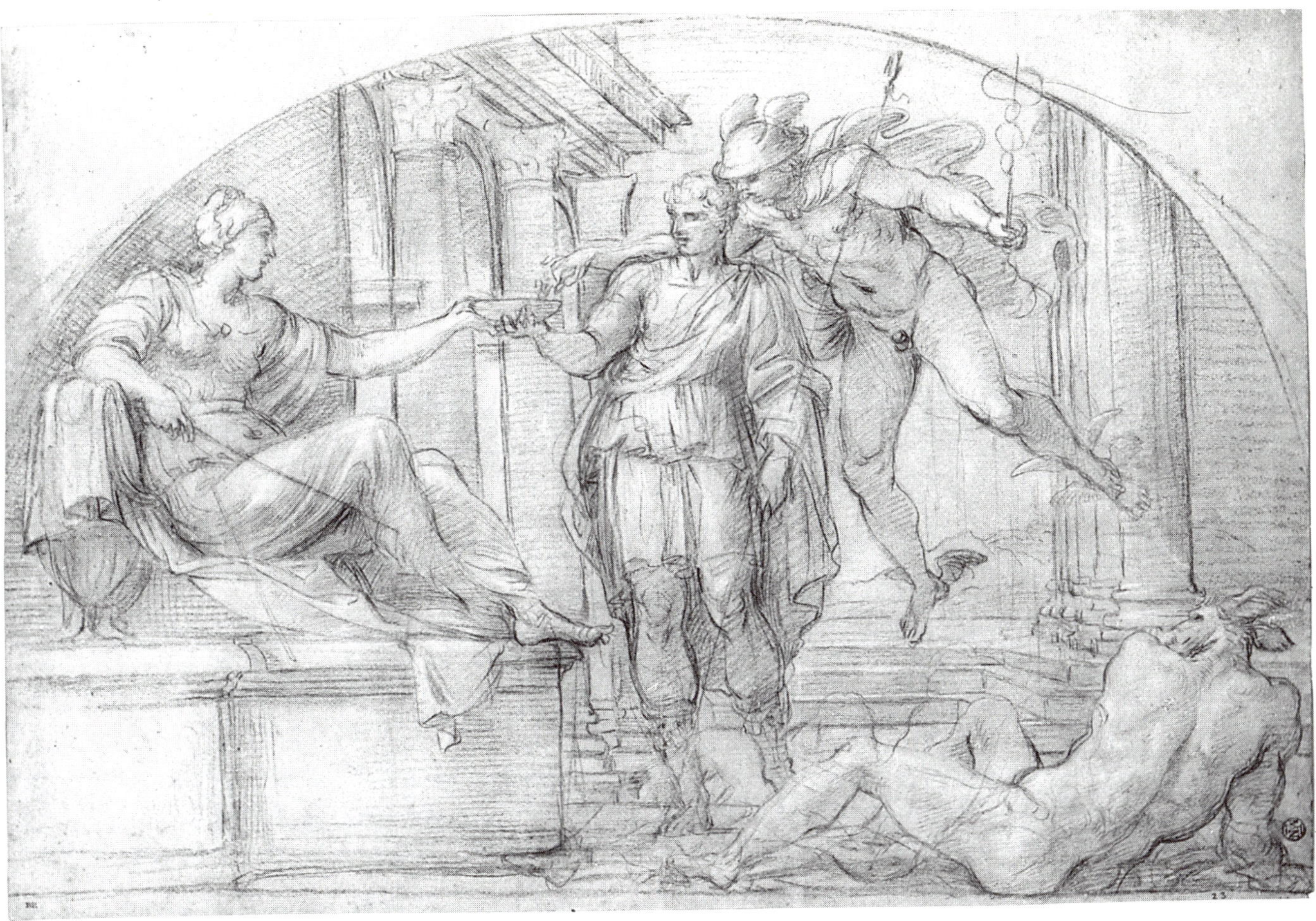

What other evidence is there? Is nakedness a prerequisite to flight? Mercury is surely naked. But so then is the pig-transforming sailor, and he is incorrigibly earth-bound. Both the identifiable mortal protagonists are clothed, copiously and heroically so, though their clothing would not hide ankle-wings if they should be there. Is there a whisper from Mercury to his acolyte that we could identify? If we doubt the strength of those mercurial ankle wings, is the means of flight the Mercury magic wand? It is a mere sketch of a caduceus, but we know it should be two serpents bounding in two entwining circles regularly frozen and usually winged. This caduceus, though it can be suspected of having the power to induce sleep, may be the conducting rod that powers the messenger-boy Mercury himself. Circe too has a wand, a straight and unelaborate affair, but doubt-less capable of much damage—damage to flight? The whole drawing is circle-topped and cuts out much of the sky, bedding down the space and truncating the columns to seduce us into a tight shallow perspective-space. The agile Mercury fluttering among the architecture suggests that if we too had wings on our ankles, we too might have flying maneuverability among our own man-made architecture.

19

BOURDON

Saint Roch and the Plague-stricken

With Bourdon, we are climbing higher. Saint Roch flies in, in preparation for a painting on a stairway. Before his striding entrance, the plague-stricken victims either lie or flee. Dying, dead, or escaping, they are much gravity associated, their heroic bodies are broad and heavy to keep them mortal and earthbound. Also perhaps to keep their suffering dignified? They bear no especial mark of cholera or the bubonic plague. Bearded Roch, not as heroically conceived as his victims, issues out of high doors raising a two-fingered salutation, a blessing accompanied by cherubs intent on keeping him afloat. One assisting angel, with a protective gesture, appears to shield Saint Roch's head with a floating cloud-borne cloak, or more suggestive still, appears to unveil him, this precious healing saint. It is a gesture complemented in the left-hand corner by a fleeing plague-victim who appears to unveil himself.

Like Saint Christopher, Saint Roch carries a staff. In this case, a long pilgrim's staff, not for wading torrents, but to identify his intent. However, he wears no cap with the pilgrim's shell, and, in this image of himself, he does not lift the hem of his cloak to show the purple bubonic sore on his inner thigh, a gesture that disturbs for its intimacy. Nor does he show his faithful dog. The dog that fed the plague-stricken Roch on stolen bread when the saint dragged himself off into the wilderness to avoid his contamination affecting others. This dog makes more than one Saint Roch image a sentimental icon in a side chapel shown to children in the candle-light to distract their perplexed attentions on that exposed thigh with its mysterious purple bruise.

Saint Roch stands upon a cloud. How easy that sounds. How difficult that is to perform. The cloud's underside is darkly and diagonally shaded to give it a little forward drifting movement. This cloud is like a rock, the saint's namesake, a promontory of water vapour and tufa jutting out from some celestial strata. It is a geomorphic, saint-bearing material. In this catalogue of flying instructions, we may be wise to pay great attention to the substance of such clouds.

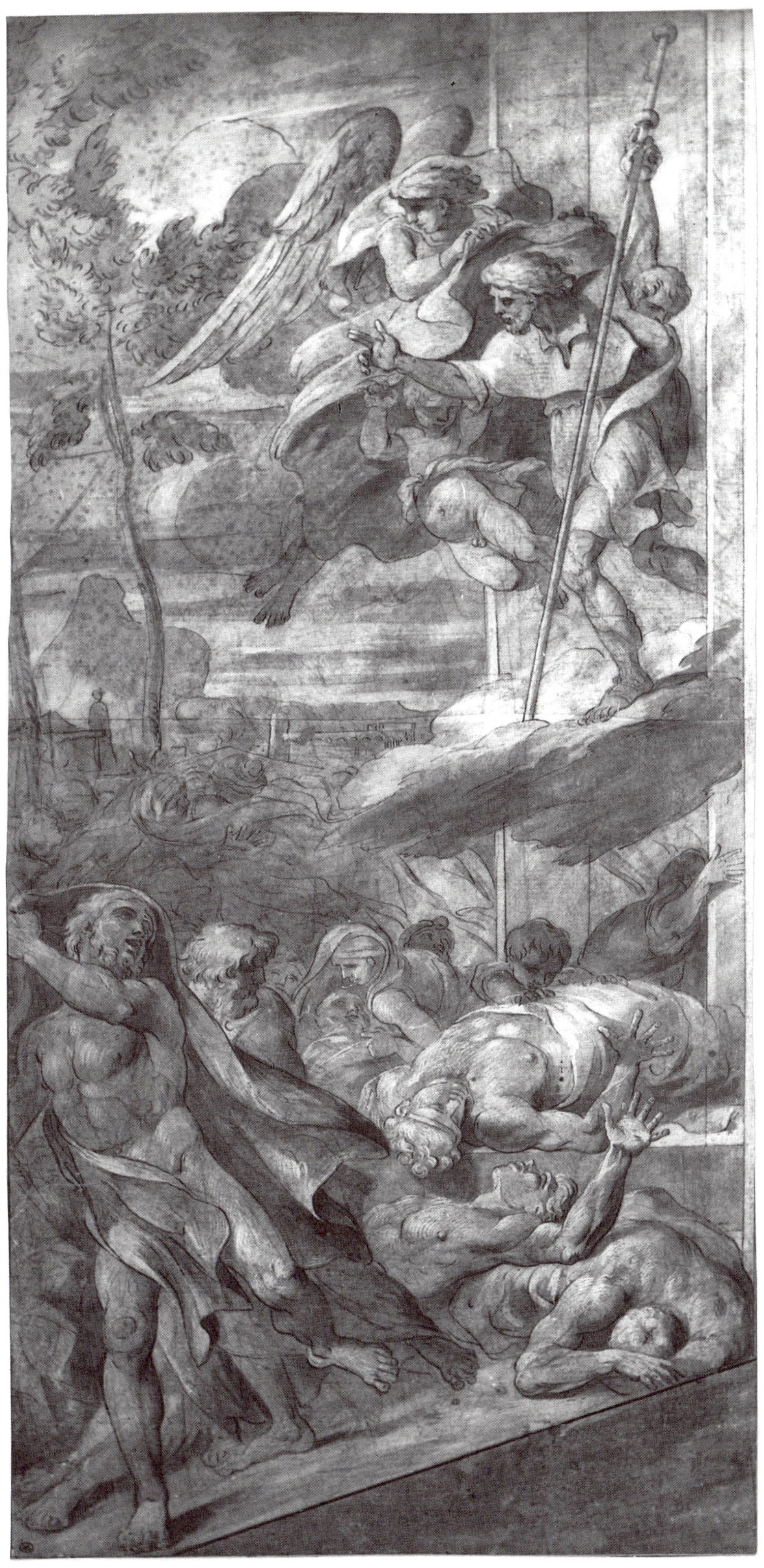

20
CAMBIASO
The Annunciation

From a two-thirds over-view, the sort of position that is difficult to assume
without standing on the furniture, an angel visits Mary. He swoops downward to the Holy vessel of the future Christ whilst she kneels at her
devotions beside her bed in her sky-opened bedroom. Without doubt,
she cowers, hand over head, as the angel points straight upwards. Is this
a metaphorical invitation to ascend through Holy pregnancy? The angel
is under orders from the long-fingered God established in the clouds
above. He is accompanied by a host of children, seraphim, cherubim,
putti at play in a bed of clouds, at least eighteen of them cavorting, some
of them swiftly drawn in quickly receding lines of startled heads. If children like this can fly, then why not us? Does age, as well as the naturally
increasing corporeal heaviness of adulthood, break the spell and then
out-balance the necessary lightness for flying? Or is it all a question of
innocence? Perhaps we might more pertinently say it is a question of the
necessary suspension of disbelief, for this swooping visit is like the opening
event in a piece of grand theatre.

The angel has a precursor, the dove, who is the first harbinger, easily
and familiarly wide-winged. Why should God be manifest as a dove, a
white-feathered domestic pigeon with homeing instincts and a predeliction
to fuss its females? Antiquity often makes the white dove a companion
attribute of Venus, love of another sort.

The downward rush of the angel is exaggerated by the vertical speed
lines, traces of the rushing air he has left behind, indicators of the brief
vacuum in the air his falling flight has formed. His flight is fast and abrupt,
no wonder Mary fears a violent contact. His wings are long and broad,
the first active, large-winged phenomenon we have witnessed.

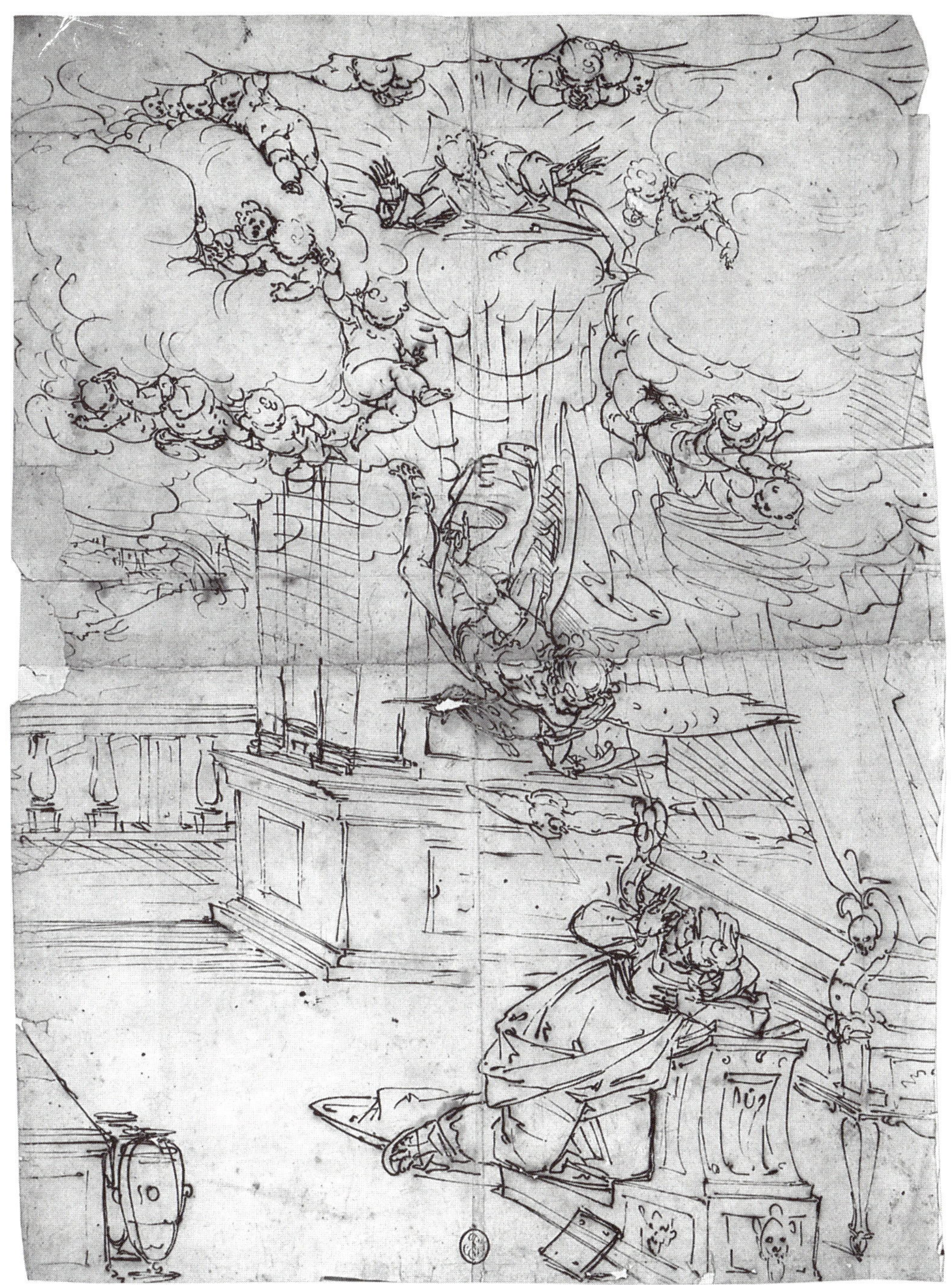

20

21
RUBENS after RAPHAEL
God and Noah

Here comes God flying around the corner, his heavy body inches from the ground, held aslant by two cherubim whose chubby arms strain to hold Him up. God points his fingers left and right as if to emphasize that flying is one and the same thing as a blessing, which perhaps it is. God's body is heavy and with that loose, wide-spread gesture, languid in its heaviness. How can such deified material float so low in the firmament? This is God down among the domestic buildings, guiding his way between the cowshed and the barn, scattering the straw among the chickens as he passes. Such powerful low flying gives us great confidence. All the figures in this image are heavy. Man, God, cherubim, and mortal children are made weighty. Is this a prediluvian weightiness? Perhaps before the flood, flying was not such an unexpected possibility. What is the lesson offered? Perhaps the hope that it must be possible to fly if such heaviness can be accommodated.

So curiously intimate are the familiarities between God and Noah, that not much in figure and physique separates these two patriarchal sages. It is all in gesture, and the relative positions. And is it the knowledge that one can fly supported by children, whilst the other must kneel and hold his struggling child, that makes one God and the other his subject? They could be brothers, these two, cousins. So is this really God with Noah? And does convention traditionally make Noah's children, Shem, Cham, and Japhet, so young? In more familiar depiction, these sons saw the timber and hammer the nails alongside their father as the dark clouds roll by above the Ark shipyard. Japeth here might still be fed at his mother's generous breasts.

If the cherubim and Noah's children are made of the selfsame flesh, does that make them interchangeable as potential flyers? God flies, Noah

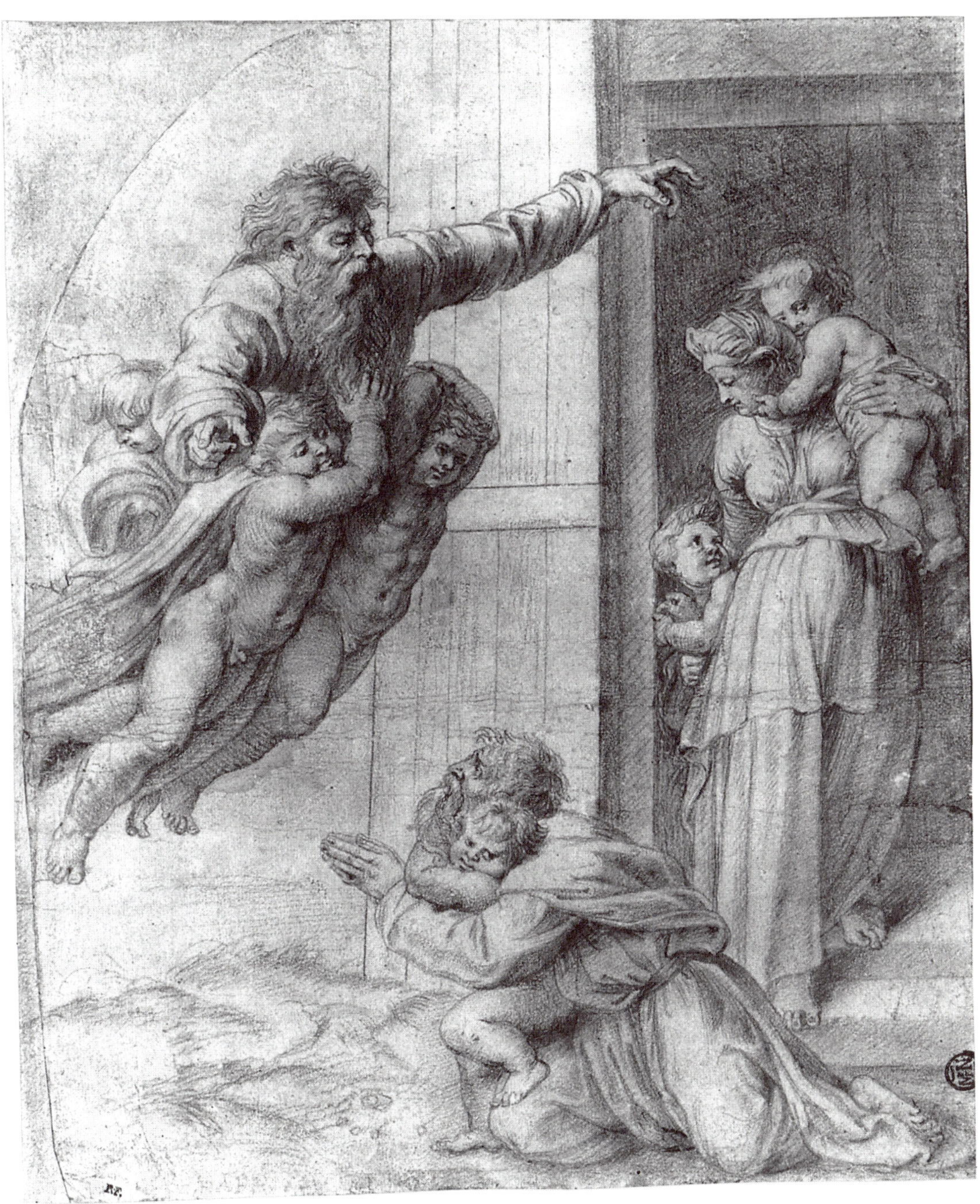

21

kneels, Noah's wife descends. Her nonchalance on the stairs makes her appear oblivious of the holy visit, as though God has dropped by like a familiar neighbour who is free to use the latchkey, make use of the garden. Given Noah's easy reputation for familiarity with his God, that perhaps is not so inappropriate.

In the timber-framed entrance of the Ark, the standing child, Noah's first-born, holds—guess what—a bird. Is it one of those first two birds in the Bible, the raven and the dove? Which is this? For all time these birds are going to fly in opposition to one another, one flying one way, one the other. They are always going to be called the black bird and the white bird, and we know how those birds behaved, demonstrating that even flying suffers a black-white prejudice.

22
POUSSIN attributed
The Burning Bush

A flying example by vision. The low angle makes no compromise. God floats. He soars in the hot air rising from the burning bush, a modest piece of vegetation, a juniper perhaps, certainly some sweet-scented plant. God's arms are outstretched and the outstretched fingers are pointing east and west in intimation of the crucifix. Moses stands in risk of singeing his face and burning his hair; covering his eyes, he kneels low. He hides his eyes and therefore cannot see this example of Holy flight. The drawing is oval and squared-up for transference, so God and the bush that burns so fiercely is going to be larger. Much larger. Does Moses look after sheep? Does Moses have a crook under his left arm? Or is it his sometime attribute, a wand? But the bush does not burn, that is the miracle.

God undoubtedly flies, though his feet, especially his left foot, do not read as magestic supporters of that heavy frame.

After God has departed, the bush will flicker with warm lights, then smoke a little, then a small wind will blow away the suggestion of ash and there will be the leaves and the branches as same as ever, for goats and sheep to nibble, and for Moses to rub his eyes from the woodsmoke and pronounce himself, like us, the recipient of a vision. A flying vision.

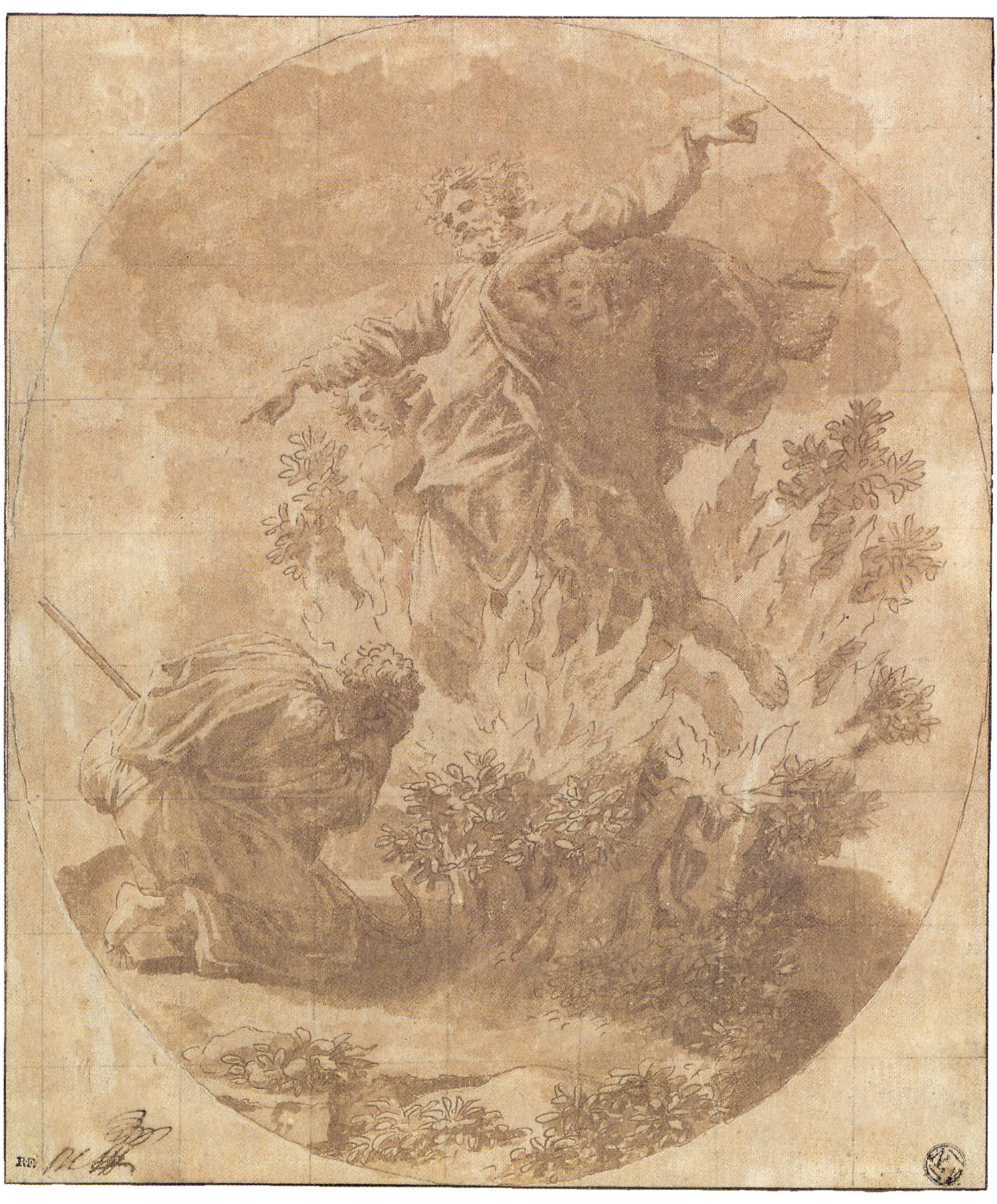

22

23
ORSI
The Conversion of Saint Paul

God and a horse. On a dark night on the road to Damascus, somewhere between Stalmyria and Esalipson. Near the junction of two highways the locals call the Geese-Fork because the disposition of the roads is like the long, taut V made by flying geese. The first creature to hear God flying down from Heaven was the horse. Saul, in his impressive Roman armour that was so apposite for persecution and putting the fear of Rome into Christians, was thrown. Saul had witnessed the stoning of Stephen, he should know about violence that arrives by air. Reputedly short, bald, ungainly, and black bearded, Saul fitted the archetype for a prosecutor. With those characteristics, God would see him easily on any road in the dark. When the horse fell, Saul was fortunate his left leg did not become trapped, and he could add lameness to his unattractiveness. The grooms and soldiers were too worried about the temporary disarray of arms and supplies to look much on God. The two most significant grooms look to Saul, already half way to becoming Paul. And to his horse, its rump thrust high, forcing its tail into the air and making it the picture's central visual flourish under the light of God. Is this a message for flying horses? Already, not liking the untidy indignity of fallen mounts, the groom is urging the horse onto its legs, pulling hard on its tackle, making a strong V of its reins that mirrors the road-junction where all this extraordinary event takes place.

The only person to guess the true significance of all this was Saul, now much closer still to becoming Paul, and he was blinded. Shaken out of his dogmatic, self-appointed aggressions with the world, either for or against Christ, not only does this man not have a seat on his horse, he has no eyesight to see God and how he flies down out of his heaven. His knowledge of flight is darkness and the smell of the damp road near his

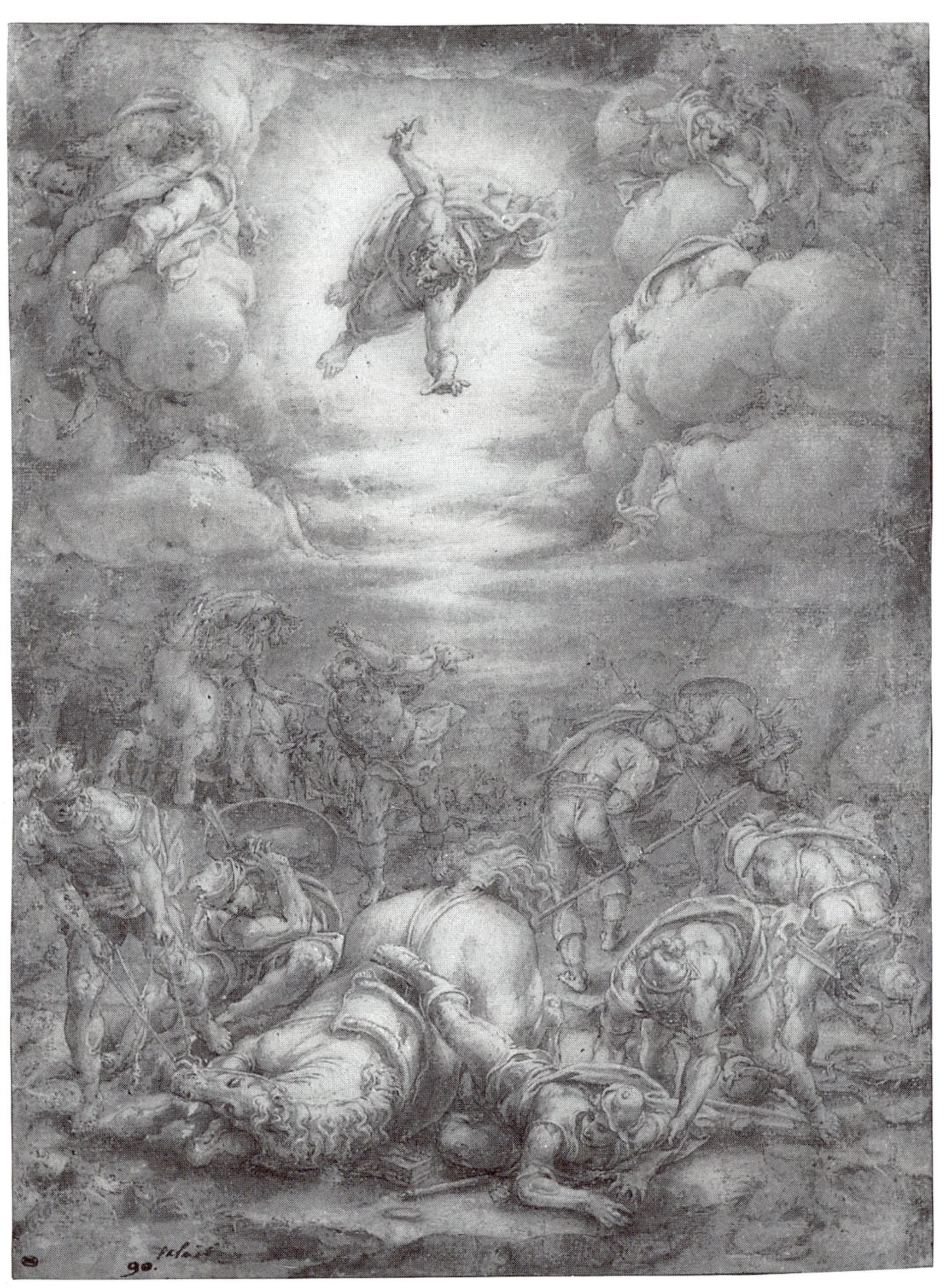

23

face, and much noise and much confusion. Besides, being a Roman, he knows the allegory for Fallen Pride is an unseated horseman. This whole event is arranged to fit the mould. There is no mention of horses in *Acts, Chapter 9, verses 1 to 9.*

What is curious from this record of the event, is a time difference. God's visit and the events it precipitated seem more than several moments apart. God has just arrived, but the horse and Saul, now certainly Paul, are already on the ground.

God is no flying goose somewhere between Stalmyria and Esalipson. His body here has five points like a star, though it is not seen at all by the blinded Paul, but by us, and from the most unexpected angle. Caught up in the problems of the draughtsman's particular depiction, God's head is small, and though we are very willing to read the image as we are invited to, the unfamiliarity of the flying position asks something of our knowledge of the human shape, for here could be a figure whose head grows out of his chest, companion of the anthropophagi out of Mandeville. Is this no idle observation, but a significant factor in our search for flight? The swiftest birds have the most negligeable necks.

There are swiftly flying figures in the clouds about God, secreted in cloud crevices like roots in a rock face, and making the visitation of significance for Saul, by now indisputedly Paul, and, indeed, for his perse-cution-soldiers, his horse, all the pagans and unbelievers in Stalmyria and Esalipson, and soon, all Christendom. And a warning. He who can make you fly in spirit, and perhaps in deed, can easily throw you down, even from a horse's back, and in the bargain, for a life of errors, blind you so that all your negatives become positives.

24
GOYA
They rise up joyfully

Looking at Goya's dancing figures, is music the clue for elevation? Does dance do the trick? We may think with dance we might fly. These two creatures have no doubt. Are they witches, are they devils? Their feet are tucked up. Hanging on with two tight fists, to his, or is it her, tambourine, the lower figure is in some paroxysm of pain or pleasure, and fears no crumpled fall. Why? Because etymologically a tambourine is also an African pigeon? Without this knowledge, his or her crash to earth would be substantial. Flight is a passage of linguistic ambiguity and double-meaning.

You can tell by the body posture, with the limbs not at all prepared for disaster, that here is confidence. It is true perhaps that their pose, and even their physiognomy, may look oriental, even the rapid watercolour brush-strokes may reprise in our imagination, the slippery ambiguity of genies—better spelt jinnies—escaped out of stoppered bottles. We see the foot's underside in the lower figure, and he, or she, has black heels and dirty soles. These feet have touched earth at some time. Yet we cannot see that earth now, and we have no true earth-bound perspective on either of these creatures.

The quality of fine flying is not to know, or care, which is up and which is down, just grip onto your talisman, your tambourine, or your castanets, (whose origin may be the Latin for chestnuts which does not help) and you might be away. We could follow their example and use music?

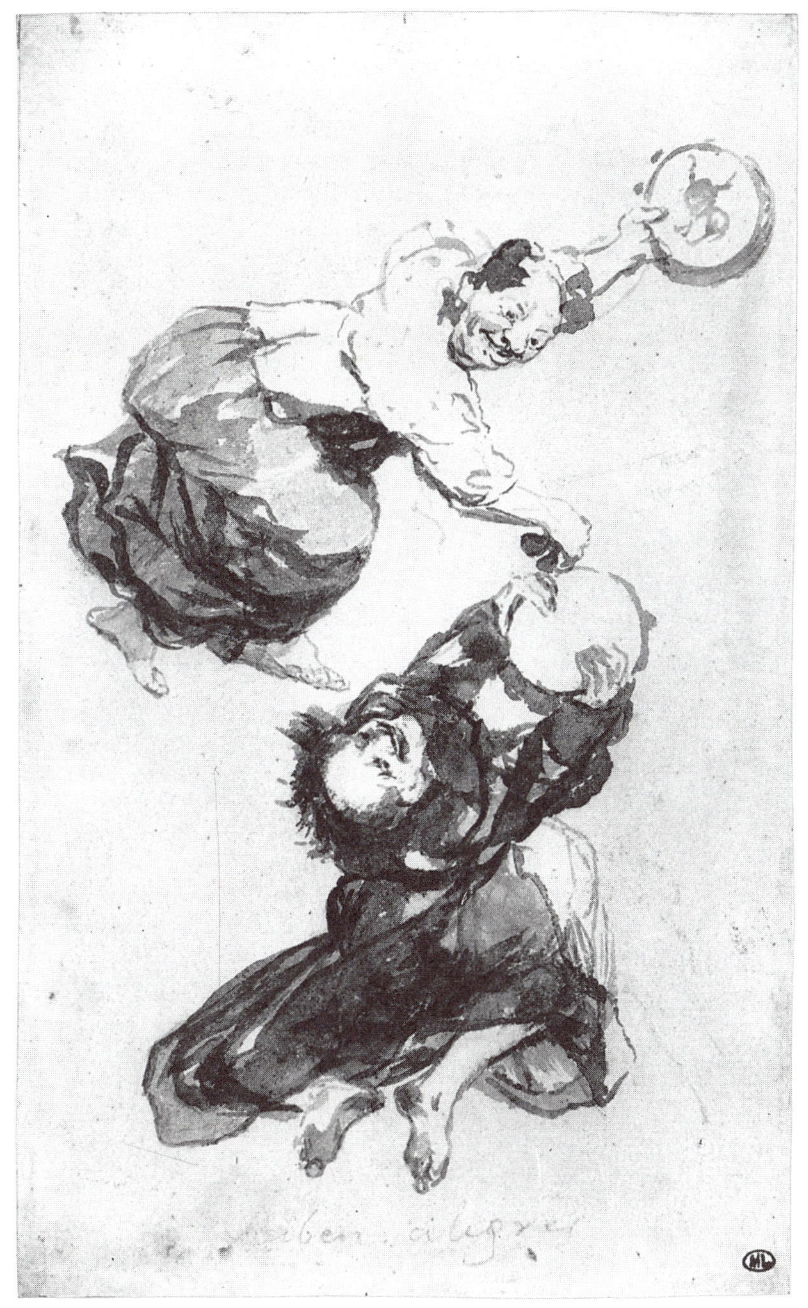

24

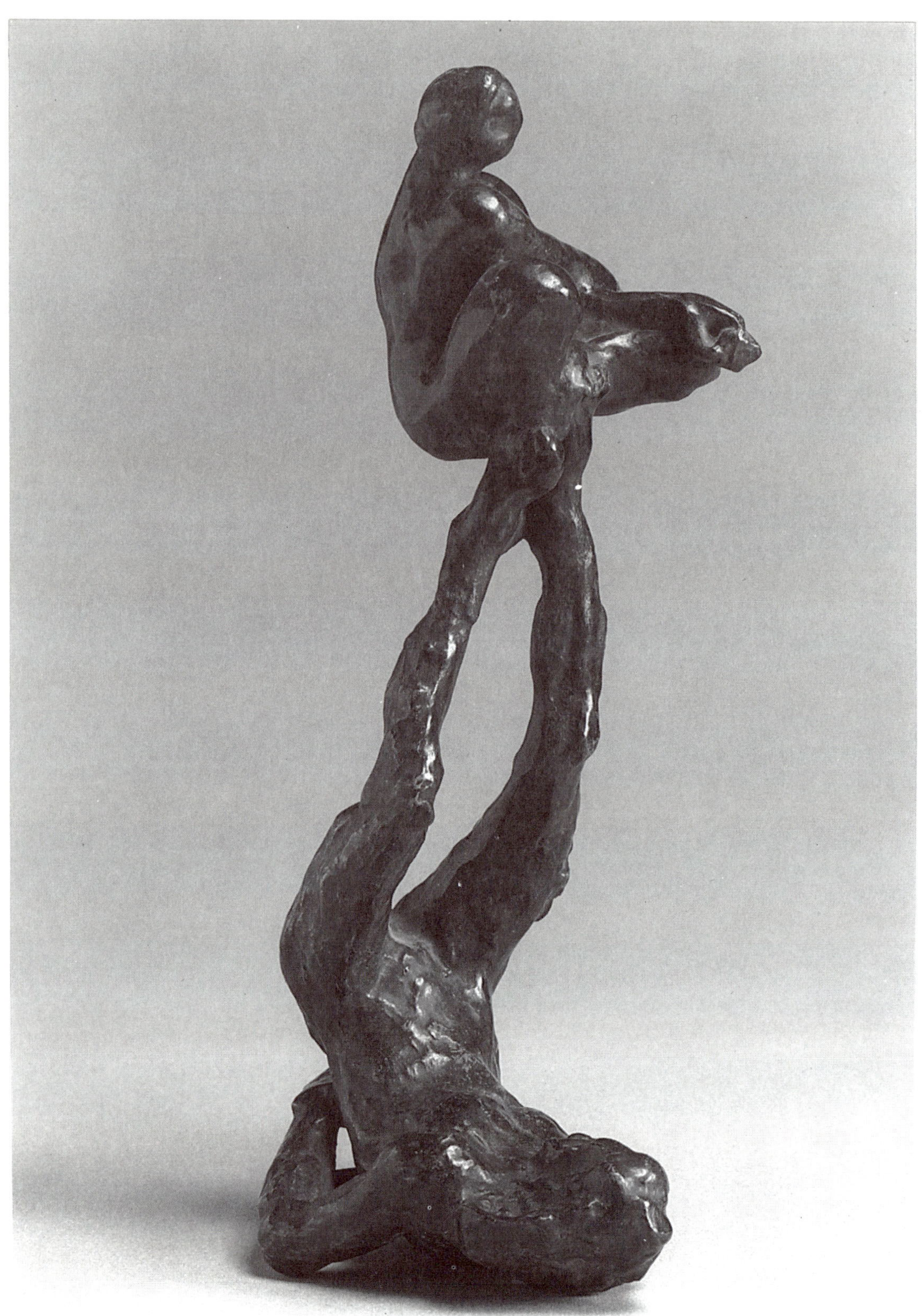

25 RODIN, *The Juggler,* or *The Acrobat*

Flight Begins

The forces and pressures of flight begin, the chains and bonds strain and are unloosed, ladders for ascent are readied, and winds examined. A tendency to flight begins though the ground is never out of sight.

26
SUBLEYRAS
Force chaining up Time

27
HEEMSKERCK
History shackling Time

With Subleyras, Time, bearded old man, is not so much about to fly as to be swept away in a strong cross wind that has whipped away his feet. He has wings muscularly affixed to his shoulders, but they are not empowering him. And he cannot fly far. Like a tethered kite, he is mightily chained to an Ionic-capped column. As a Titan in dotage, he has been severely down-graded from ferocious child-eater and sometime King of The Golden Age. Now his protagonist and would-be keeper is helmeted History. She guards the heavily-linked chain that tethers Time to the earth like an errant dog fastened to a stake. She rests her foot on solid foundations, and in the case of a link-breakage, she has a lion to offer chase, though the beast is wingless. If Time should escape, however, then he will surely bump along the ground in the earth-hugging wind and be easy meat.

Time has a beard and a scythe, though the scythe's blade is so deeply foreshortened it looks too broad to adequately cut through the years. It is reminiscent of a paddle, and we should consider the years being wet and watery, oceanic, needing to be ploughed by a sternly held rudder. History does not look at Time, she looks steadfastly away. Maybe she should be more concerned, for Time will always flee History and the chains must surely break.

The angle of vision is steep, above our eye-line, making the vertigo more spectacular and maybe, for the faint-hearted, making the image a check and a censorship on our longing to take wing.

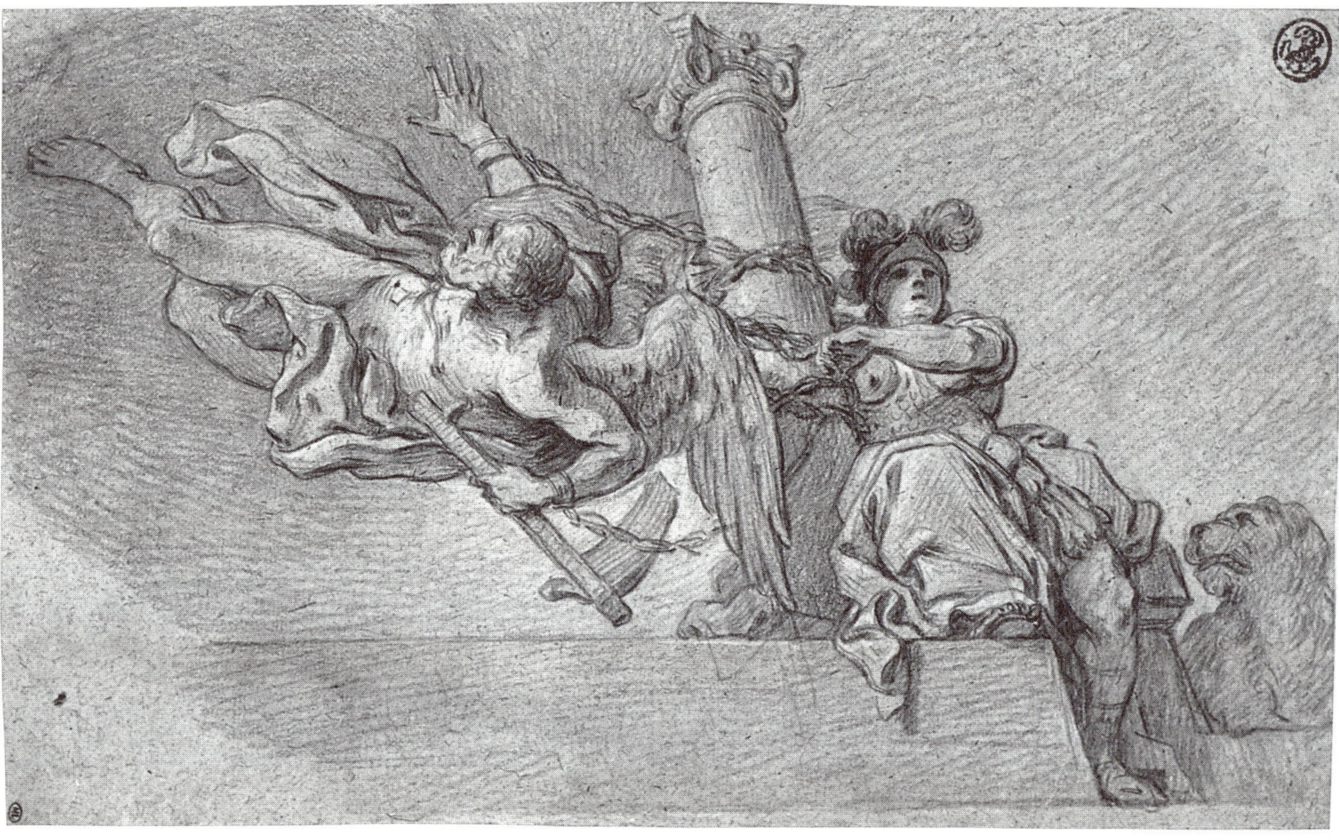

26

In the Heemskerck drawing, less bravura, less accomplished, less classi-cal, the allegory is surely more significantly managed, for the illustration is of the present tense, and tense is wholly significant. History, temporarily dropping her book to the floor, is in the process of binding Time, but with a feeble bondage—a ribbon, a cord, scarcely a rope, and certainly not with chains. Though History knows that tieing Time in knots must be a temporary thing, there is no confusion of Heemskerck's sympathies. He is a partisan for History. For his History is civilised, Time barbaric. History stands for law and reason and has taut, smoothed, regulation feathers. Time has only a drazzle of bent and crumpled plumages. History is clothed and wreathed and stands like Classical Victory or biblical arch-angel. Time is the beast, naked, hirsute, muscular, kneeling. History is booted, and laced at the knee, and modestly necked and coiffeured. His-tory is a woman. Her robes are a maze of expensive energetic folds, but

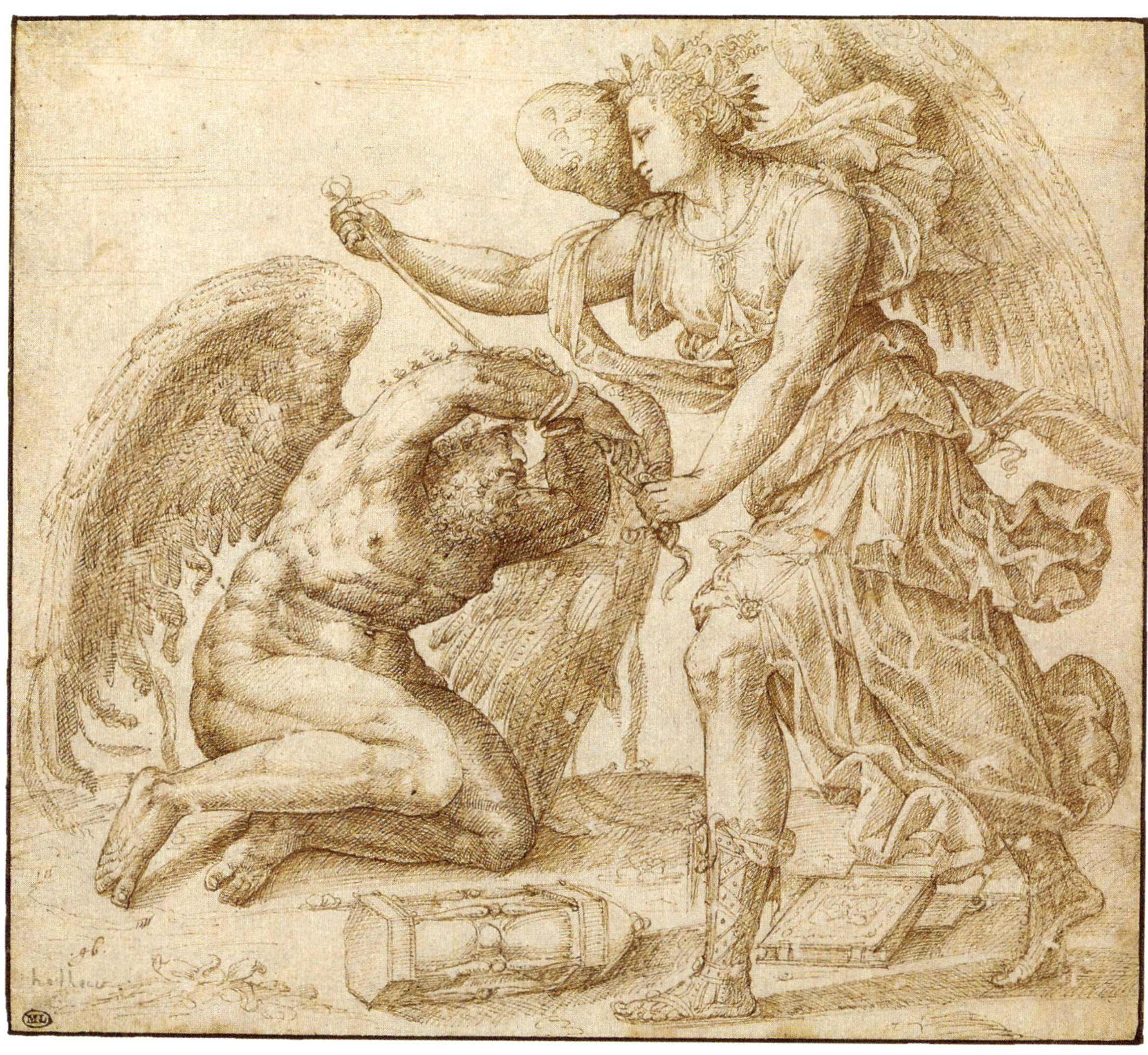

27

she is not unduly martial. There is no evidence of helmet or lion. Time is male.

The allegorical reasonings are confident, the draughtsmanship less so. Close unto touching at the arms and hands, the figures are at least a meter apart at their feet. But why this fear and dread? Surely Time is neutral? What hopes and fears for flyers are there here?

28
DUBREUIL
Prometheus unbound

A scene of release after so long a torture, Prometheus, man's champion, is freed by Hercules, man's champion. Two champions together. The eagle that daily savaged Prometheus's liver lies dead on the rock, now no more than a dead bird speared by an arrow like a spiked chicken. With the eagle dead, then Prometheus's liver will be renewable no more. Hercules unbinds Prometheus, having dropped his cloak and armour. And his quiver. There are flighted arrows in his possession, epitome of swift (if limited) flight. A bold revenge and one to attract a God's vendetta. Early christians made no difficulties for themselves in cross-converting Prometheus and Christ.

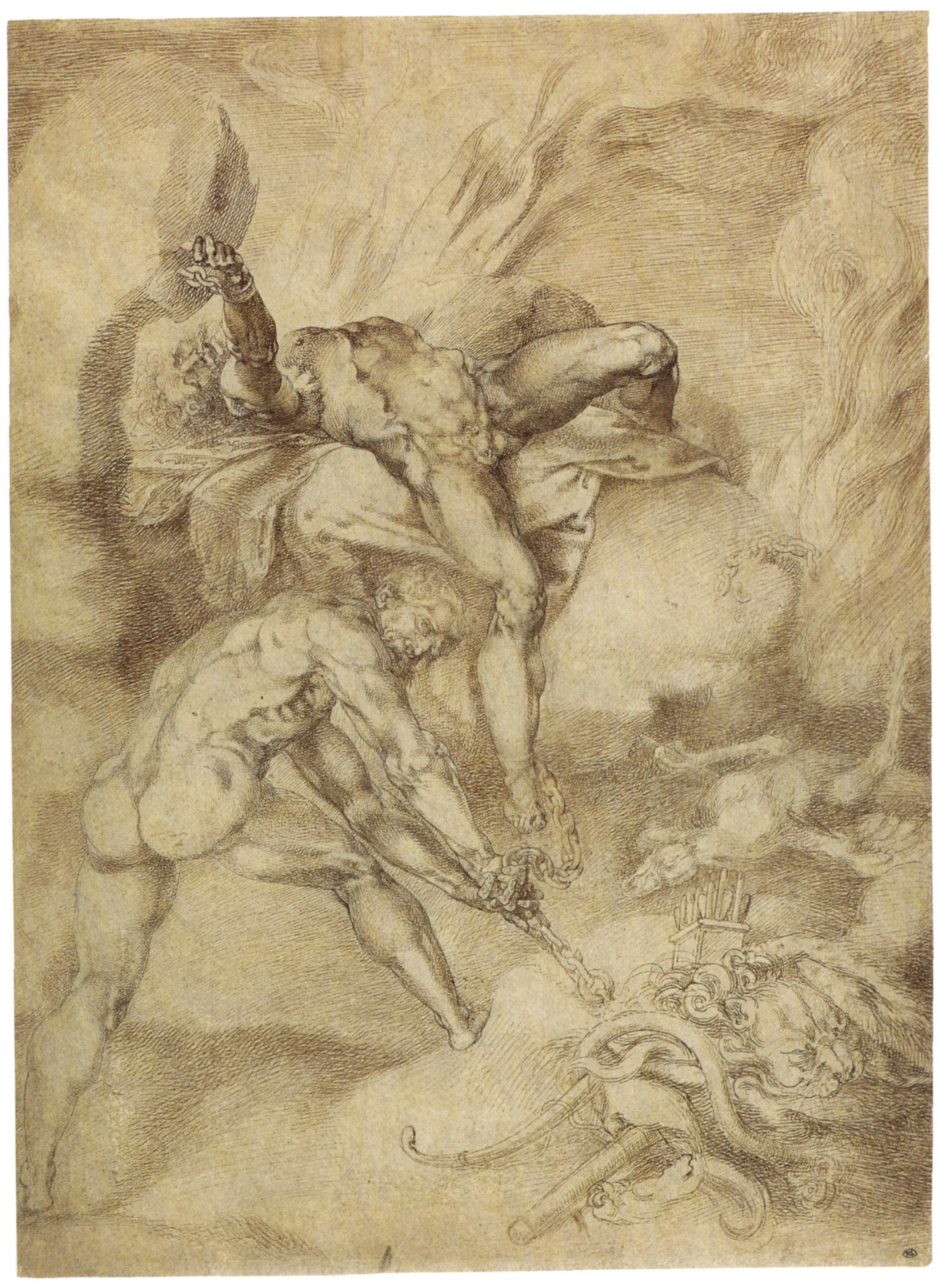

28

29

STEINLEN
Shipyard

30

CANUTI
Apotheosis of Saint Dominic

Ladders to heaven or ladders merely to the deck of a ship? Jacob had a ladder with which privilege he could whisper in God's ear. A ladder is one of the instruments of the Passion. Ziggurats and pyramids are staired and stepped, reaching God and his kingdoms by engineering and manufacture. The architect and master-builder could provide the best way to heaven. All people are interested in looking at the view. "And Satan took him to a high place." "And they built a tall building and called it Babel." Ladders to reach Christ on the cross, to storm Jerico, to storm Massada, to take Troy.

Steinlen has his ladders in a boatyard but he is more interested in the ladders than in the boats. The boats are invisible, a mirage. The ladders are not parallel in their verticals but pointed over a great length, each rung getting shorter as the ladder gets higher, their construction adding a sensation of false perspective that suggests they might stretch further than the drawing indicates. A steepledore, a dockworker, a navvy, is levered out of contact with the ground, using his weight to spring-fly, and on the left, a worker stretches high, presumably to catch a load or furrel down a rope, but his stretched image is of a man in an upward dive, arms thrust forward, head up. Turn him ninety degrees and he will be flying horizontally in a fast swoop. Turn him another ninety degrees and he will be head-diving into expectation of deep water.

Canuti has other and more ethereal problems. His Dominic travels skywards accompanied by those who don't need ladders to ascend to their rightful domicile. Look closely and even Dominic does not grace the rungs with his feet, but is supported on a pedestal carried by an angel. Christ supports one ladder, the Virgin the other. Angels on clouds swirl in music around Dominic's pragmatic ascent, and, bursting ahead and above him,

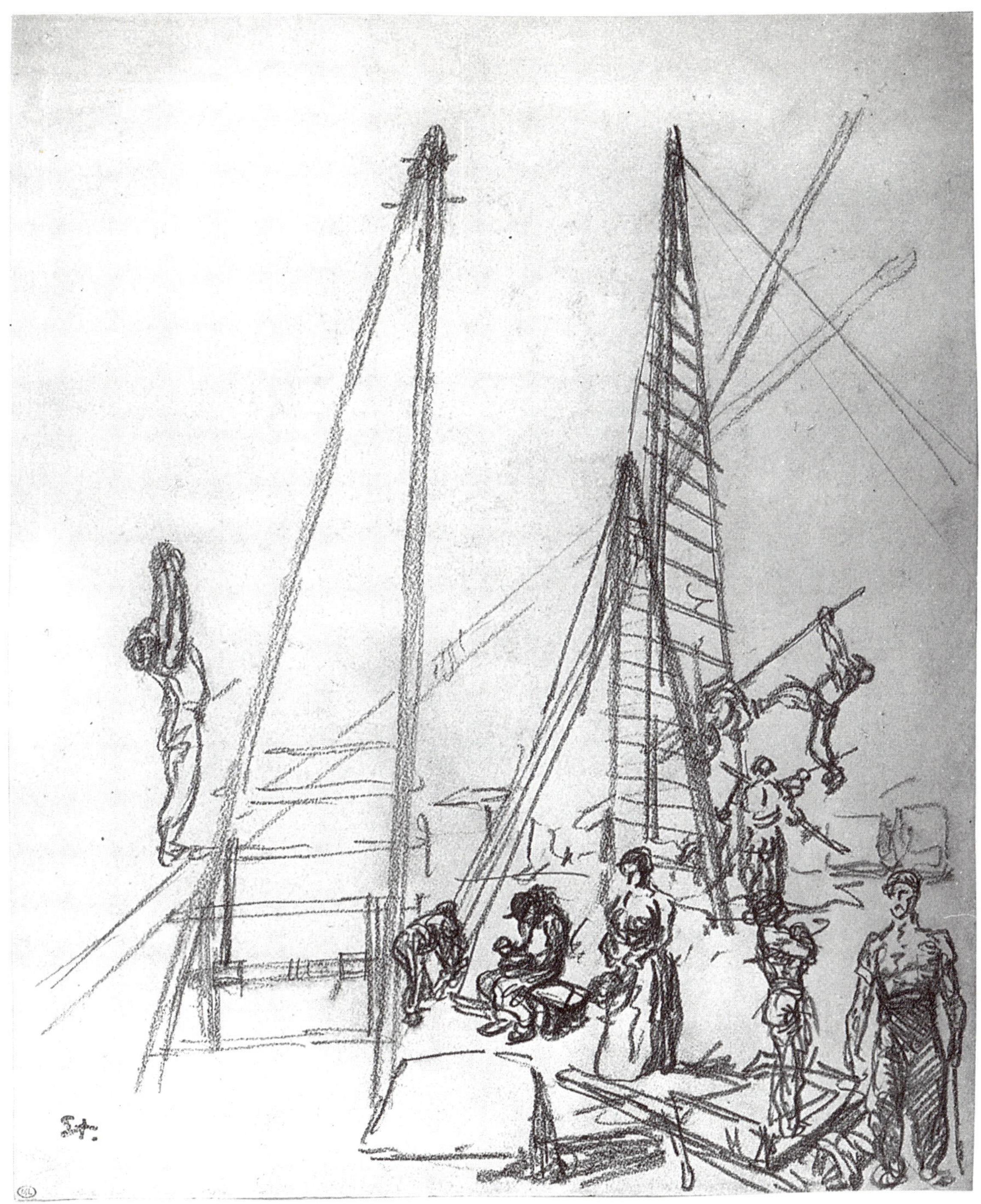

flowers and putti explode from a bank of vapour. It is like a summer-outing in the apple orchards. The flying company mock Dominic's mortality and winglessness. They have wings held at right angles, offering him courteous service to remind him that he has not their means of quick and easy propulsion. His cloak has to stand in for wings, flying out at right angles. He is caught at ladder height in a blaze of light between clouds with shadowed bases. Leaving the earth is to understand its baseness, its underclouded shadow.

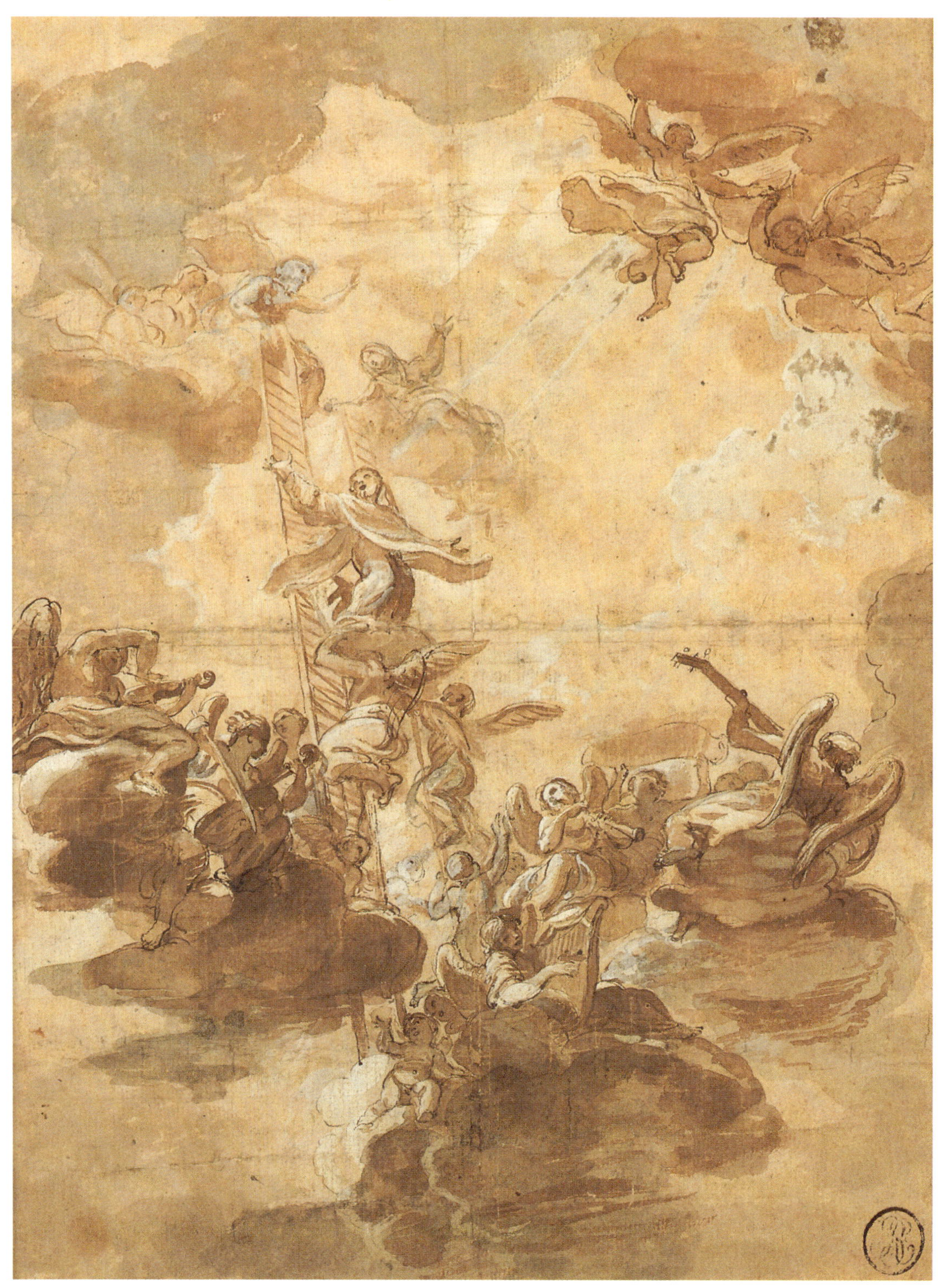

30

31
FARINATI
Boreas and Oreithyia

Wind and gravity, a mixture to fly kites. This entire image is kite-shaped, only needing a tail. We can give it a tale and call it "Holding Down the Wind." Under a blowing Zephyr, Boreas, the north, or north-east wind, is abducting Oreithyia, daughter of an early Athenean king. She is wrapped in clothes against his coldness. Is he carrying her up or letting her down? Are they taking off into wind-blown abduction, or are they landing back in his kingdom? Is he about to swathe her in dark thunder-clouds on a high ledge of a rock in the river Ergines and ravish her surrounded by lightning and thunder? Which ever way, they make an example of practical gravity, for Farinati has placed them precariously on a ledge high above our eye-line, a deep perspective point to rationalise the spaces of the ceiling or the upper wall from the vantage-point of the ground. They are drawn to fall or fly. The clouds begin to puff and swell beneath them. Her coiffure is in place, uninterrupted by the wind that blows her clothes and his. She looks deep downwards to the ground far below. Yet she has some purchase. His face is deeply shadowed with a band of blackness that cuts across his cheek. The embrace is intimate, her breasts near his face, his hand holds her buttock. Her weight is cradled in his arms; though her outward steadying right hand is none too sure of safety in his ability to hold. They are caught in a moment of shifting weight. One second later and the pose will be all over or all changed. Both cannot stay frozen like this. The flow of antagonistic air from the zephyr's mouth is triangular shaped, and catching the light in a wide span of spittle-wet air, causes excess havoc from so small an orifice. That is a strange thing we accept. This singular small head is capable of sustained fierce breath. What licenses we permit without even a shrug of disbelief. The couple stand in a spider's web of grid lines in a rhombus for enlarge-

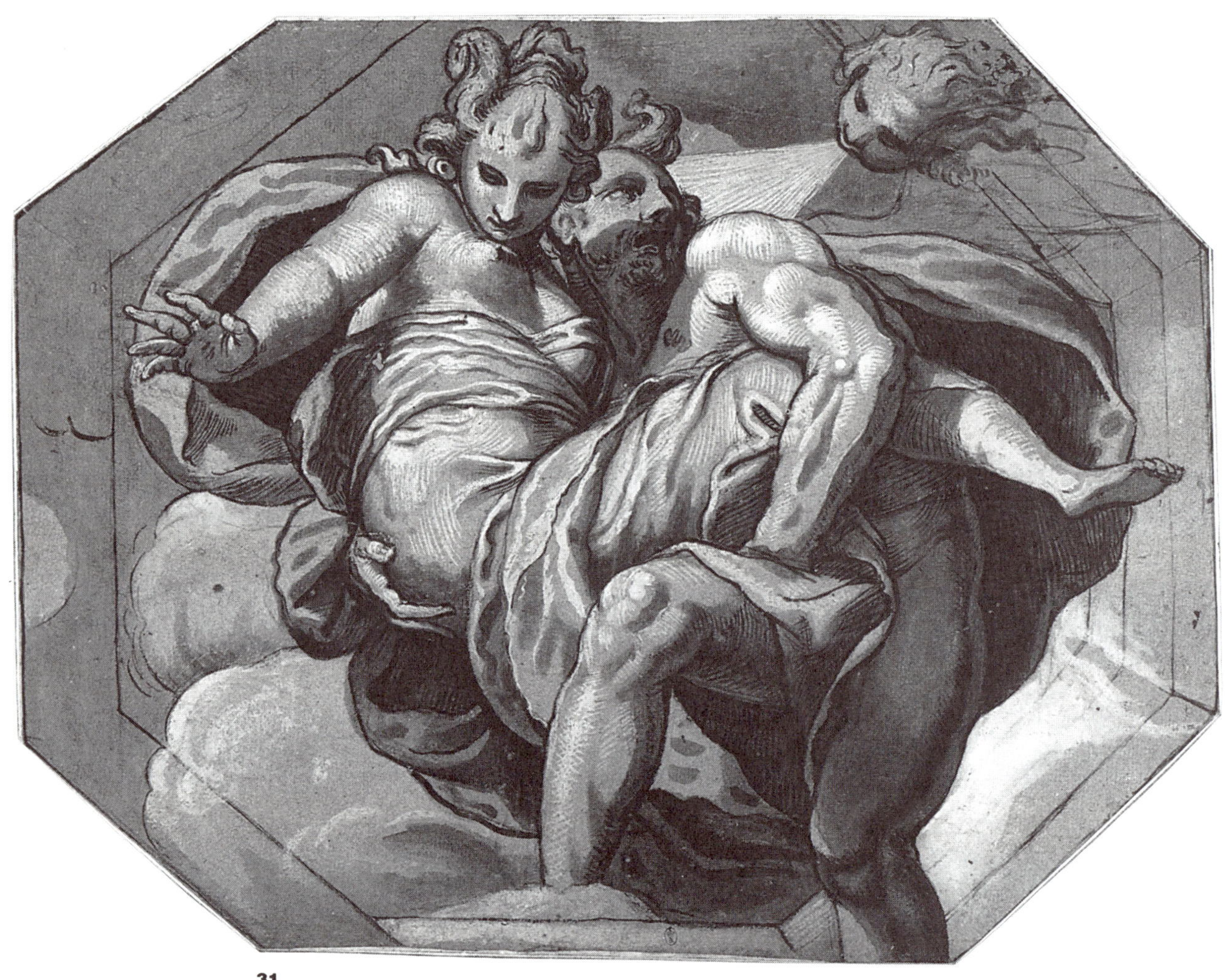

31

ment, when the wind, like all else, will grow bigger and the bodies grow heavier. Wind and gravity, some special mixture, some radical essence, to fly kites.

The result of this union, forced or not forced, willing or unwilling, was twin sons who grew up to sprout wings, and a daughter, whose future husband fell victim to the Harpies. Oreithyia was jealous of horses for Boreas was a horse-ravisher. It was believed that when mares desired offspring they persistently turned their hindquarters to the north-east when the Spring wings of the boreal were at their mightiest.

The Skies

This is the chapter that examines the sky. Having gained some confidence that flight is possible, we should need a medium, the skies themselves.

The sky. Not so much an empty space, but a soup. A soup of myriad impediments. Water vapour, birds, high-flying insects, dust, gases, flying ice, thermal risings, pollen grains. And on very especial and portentous occasions, a meteor racing itself to extinction. Or frogs surprised by a cyclone. Or a passing soul. Or a falling angel. Or an aviator.

You can scarcely draw or paint the sky, only its impediments. You can paint only the semi-solids in the soup. The blue that steadily pales or darkens, as it bends over towards the horizon, is a trick of light. It is a mixture of low angles of the sun and shifting water vapour, a complexity of risings and fallings of heat and cold that make the ephemeral colourings of dawn and dusk.

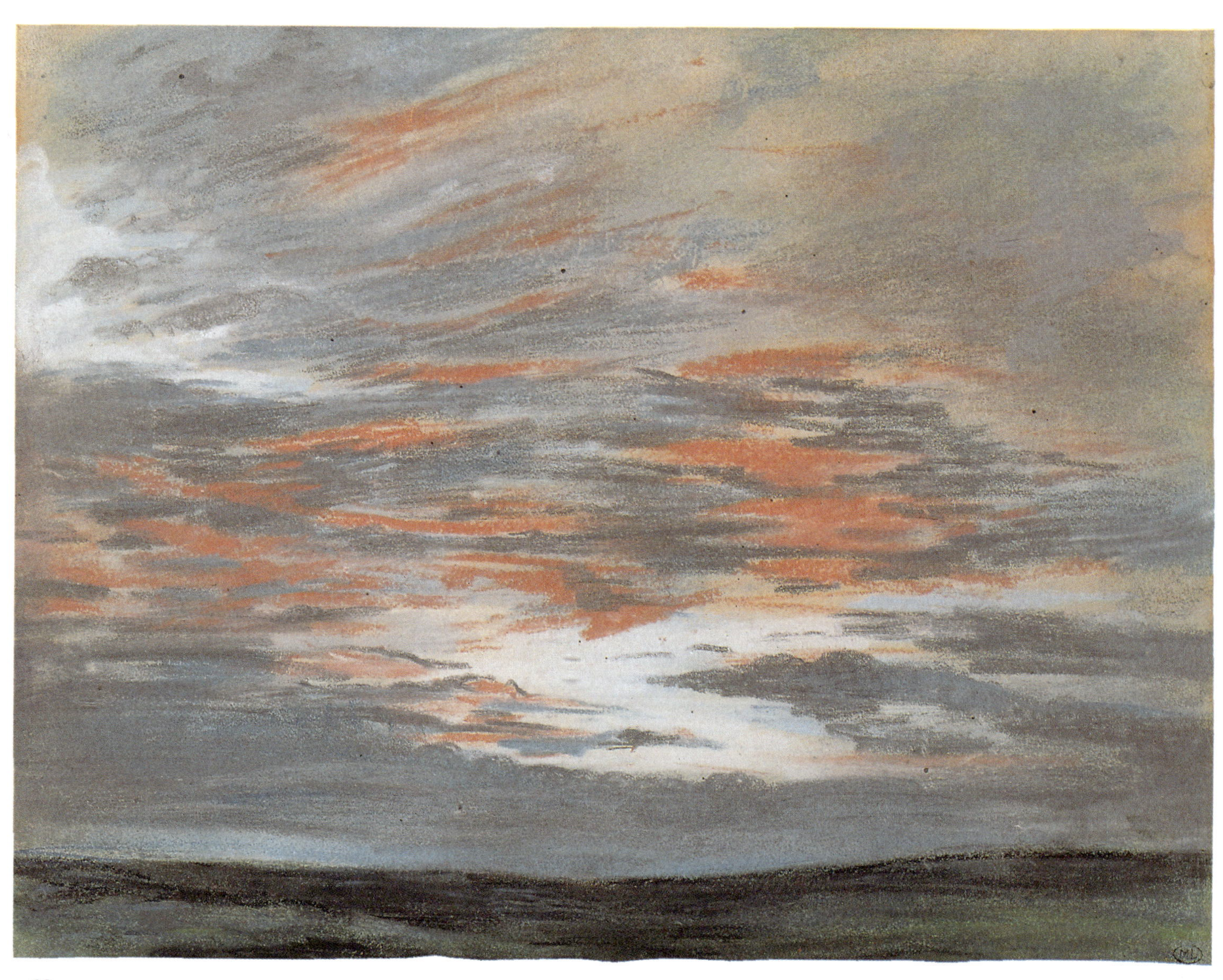

32

"There is no such colour as blue, blue is an illusion, for the sky is really black. And the blue of the sea is merely the reflection of the blue of the sky which is a provable illusion."

What are we left with? Blue eyes, irises, forget-me-nots, plumbago, woad, flax, cornflowers, lapis lazuli, a bruise on the body, the blue whale? Enough blue to discredit any blue-disbeliever. Prime interruption of the carefully graduated blue skies are the clouds, and when painters paint the soup of the sky, they paint clouds, they paint no more than water vapour. Though da Vinci once sketched a sky of precipitating pots and pans, nothing so recognisable or so material is normally anticipated. Stratus, cumulus, cumulus cirrus, stratus cirrus, a mackerel sky, a hunter's sky, red sky at night is a shepherd's delight, red sky in the morning is shepherd's warning. Enough blue to make a sailor's jacket. A black sky back of Bill's mother's.

In the twentieth century all of us can watch the clouds at first hand with great intimacy from the comfort of a window of an airplane. We can watch the cloud mountains from close-up and find them, as we must have always found them, to be as insubstantial as the mist that occasionally covers the ground, and as insubstantial as the steam coming from under the saucepan-lid. And yet with no embarrassment, no apology, no special pleading, the cloud, in two thousand years of use, could effortlessly support the rumbling and crashing of armies of angels and the pounding heaviness of Gods in transport.

Painters painting water vapour. No surprise so many water-colourists delighted in the splash and puddle of the skies. Water to paint water. Anticipation of twentieth-century freedoms to take a line and a splash for a walk. No one to make a spot-check. A cloud changes shape every moment, from a camel to a beautiful woman, from a peacock to a snail, without any real necessity for Mantegna to force the issue in the skies above Saint Sebastian.

Into this mixture of water-vapours there is an opportunity to fly. With Constable as meteorological map-maker, we could examine the flat skies over East Anglia, the nearest in England you can get to the flat lands and open skies of Holland. There is indeed a suggestion of a windmill on the wide horizon. Though English and Dutch skies after the Reformation are not likely to spawn clouds for heavenly host, they will come by sea or cart-track. There is the suggestion of heavy cloud shadow on the flat fields, racing left to right, perhaps west to east, the prevailing direction of English

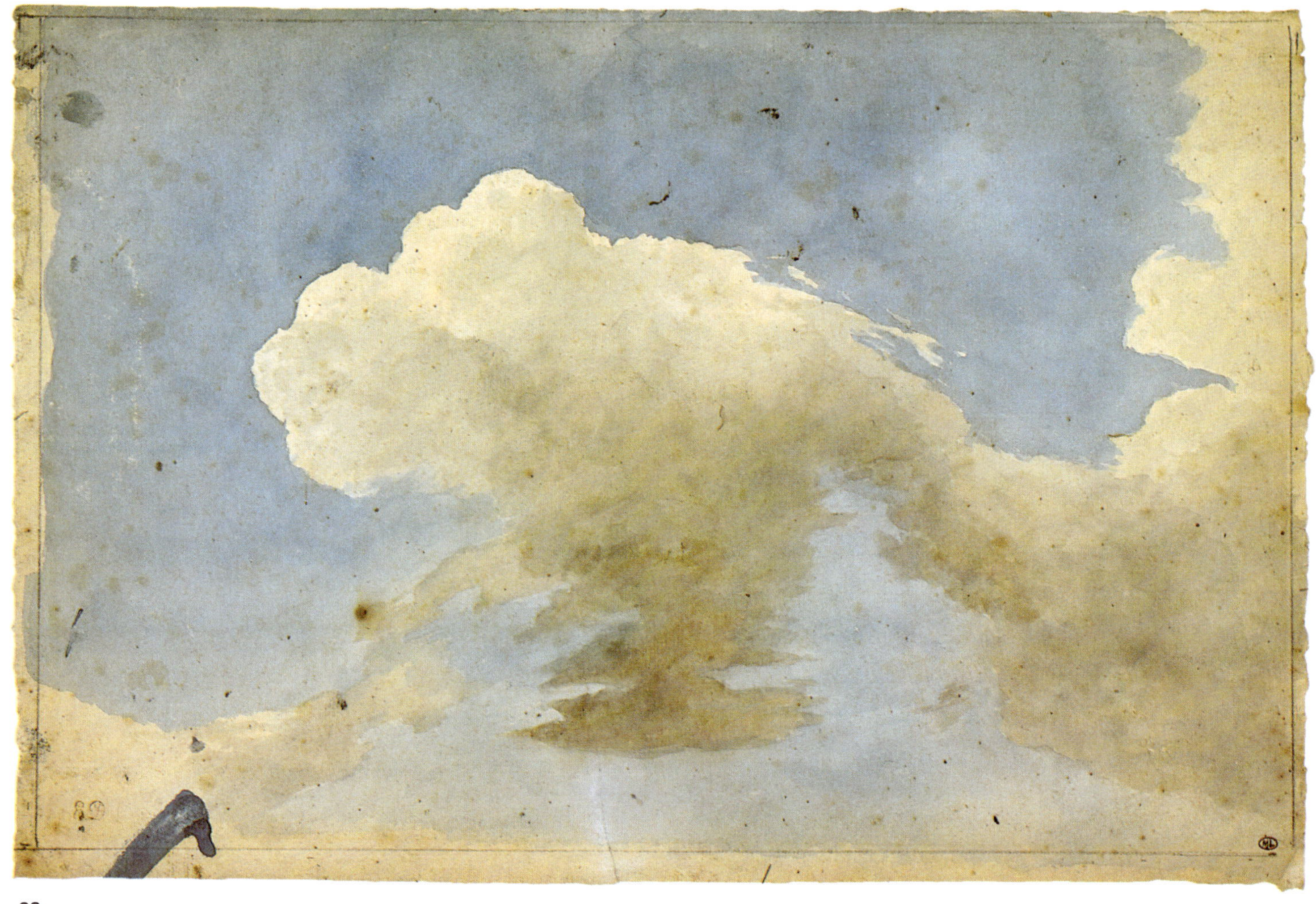

33

winds, bringing water from the Atlantic Ocean to drop on England. The change of the landscape colour with such a racing light is extreme, it is nothing to measure twelve tones of green-ness on a light meter, with the edges of the cloud-shadow sometimes so sharp it is comparable to the switching on and off of an electric light.

Constable's flat, dragged, and brushed strokes are as much characteristics of the brush and the water, as they are of clouds, the paper's inherent occasional greasiness interrupting the water-scumblings.

The Delacroix sky is a more self-consciously dramatic affair. Hammer-headed cumulus cloud, foretaste of summer storm, shaped like a bullfrog, an embryo, a white head of cauliflower, an immature iguana fresh from saltwater? Open to your subjectivity. A true example of bringing privatised knowledge to an image of which the author had no cognizance.

There is no land in this Delacroix, we have no scale, but then is scale ever possible in the mountains of the sky?

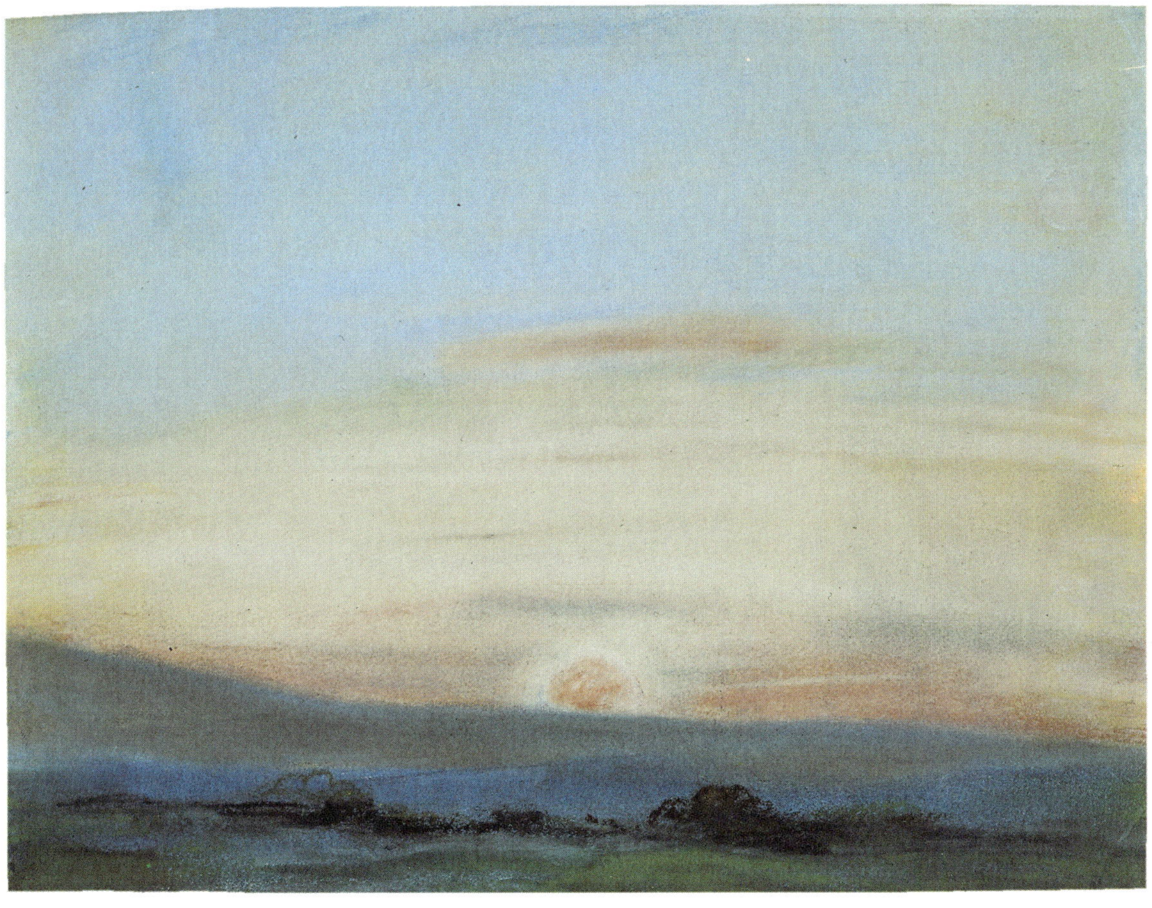

35

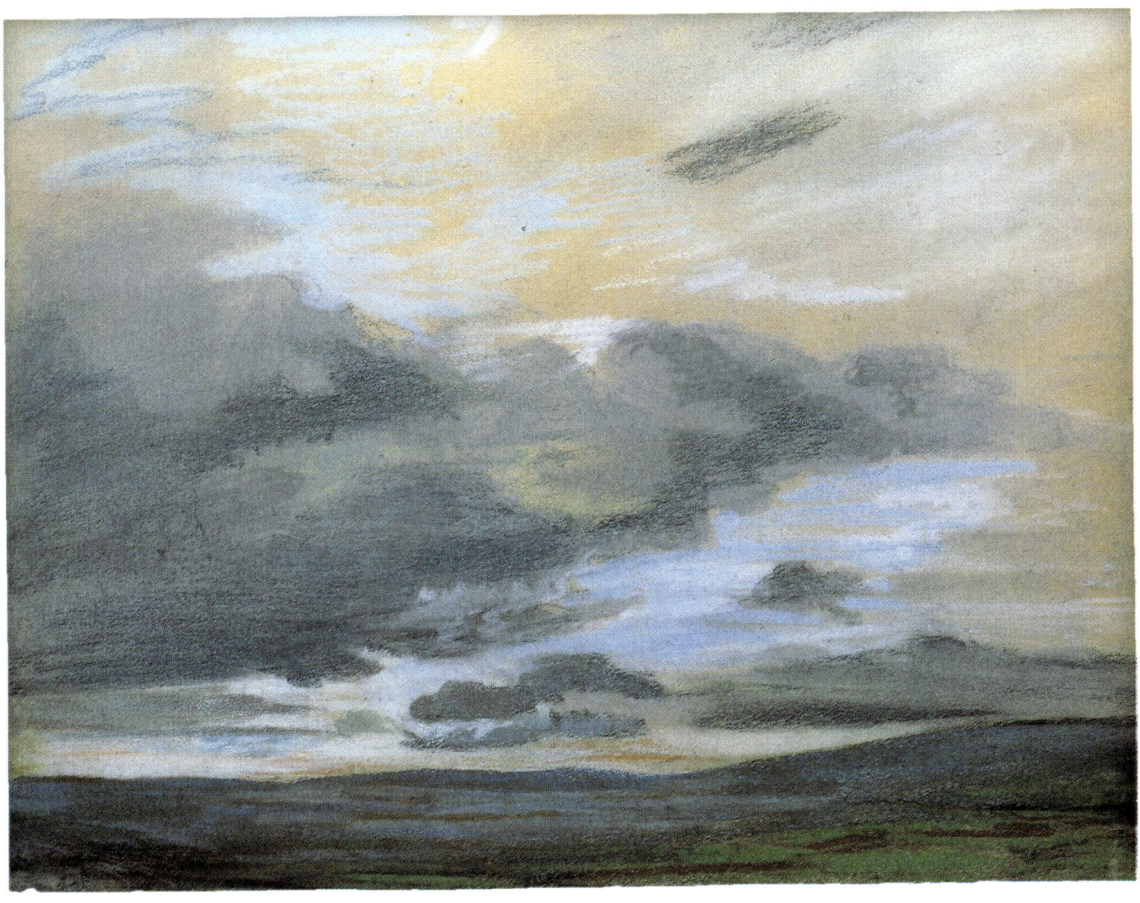

34

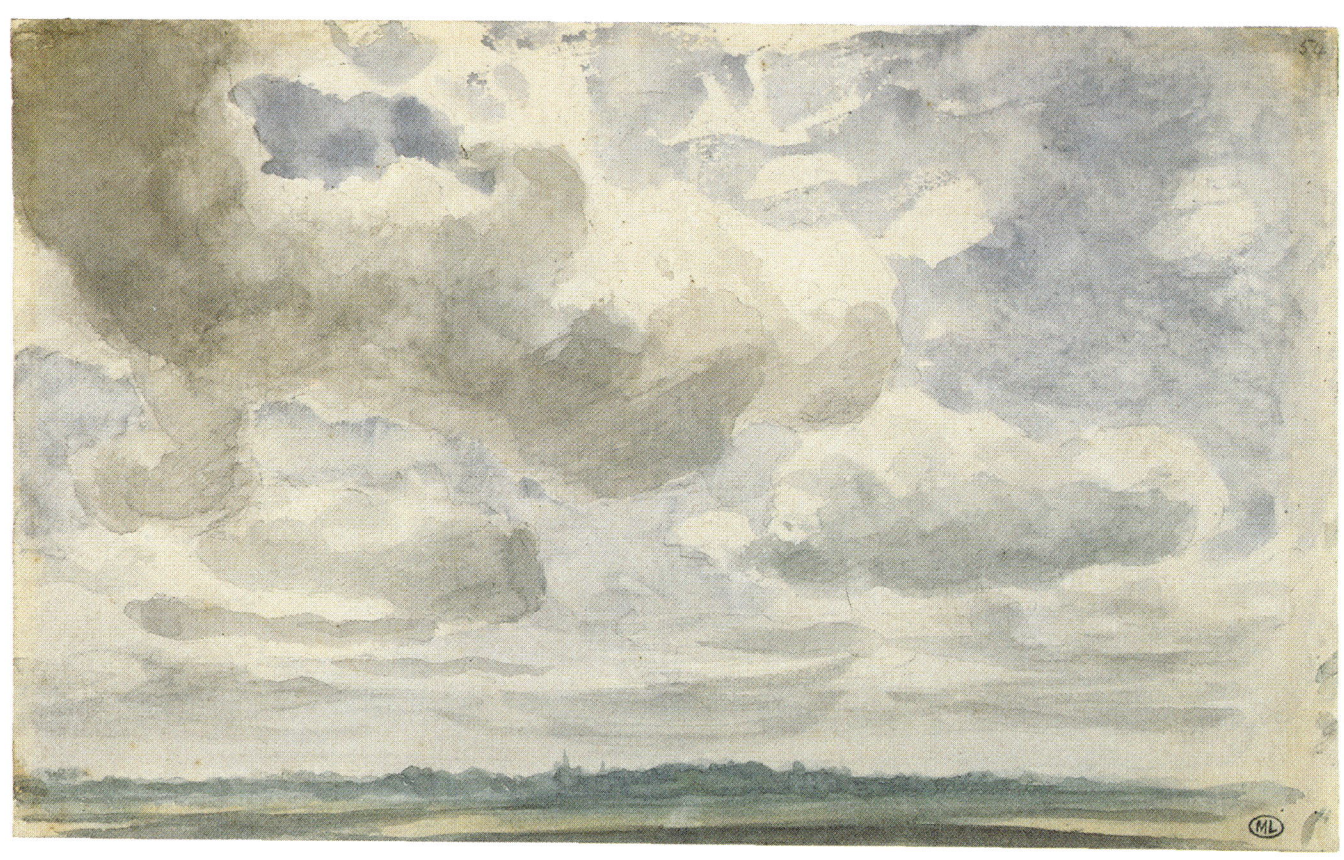

36

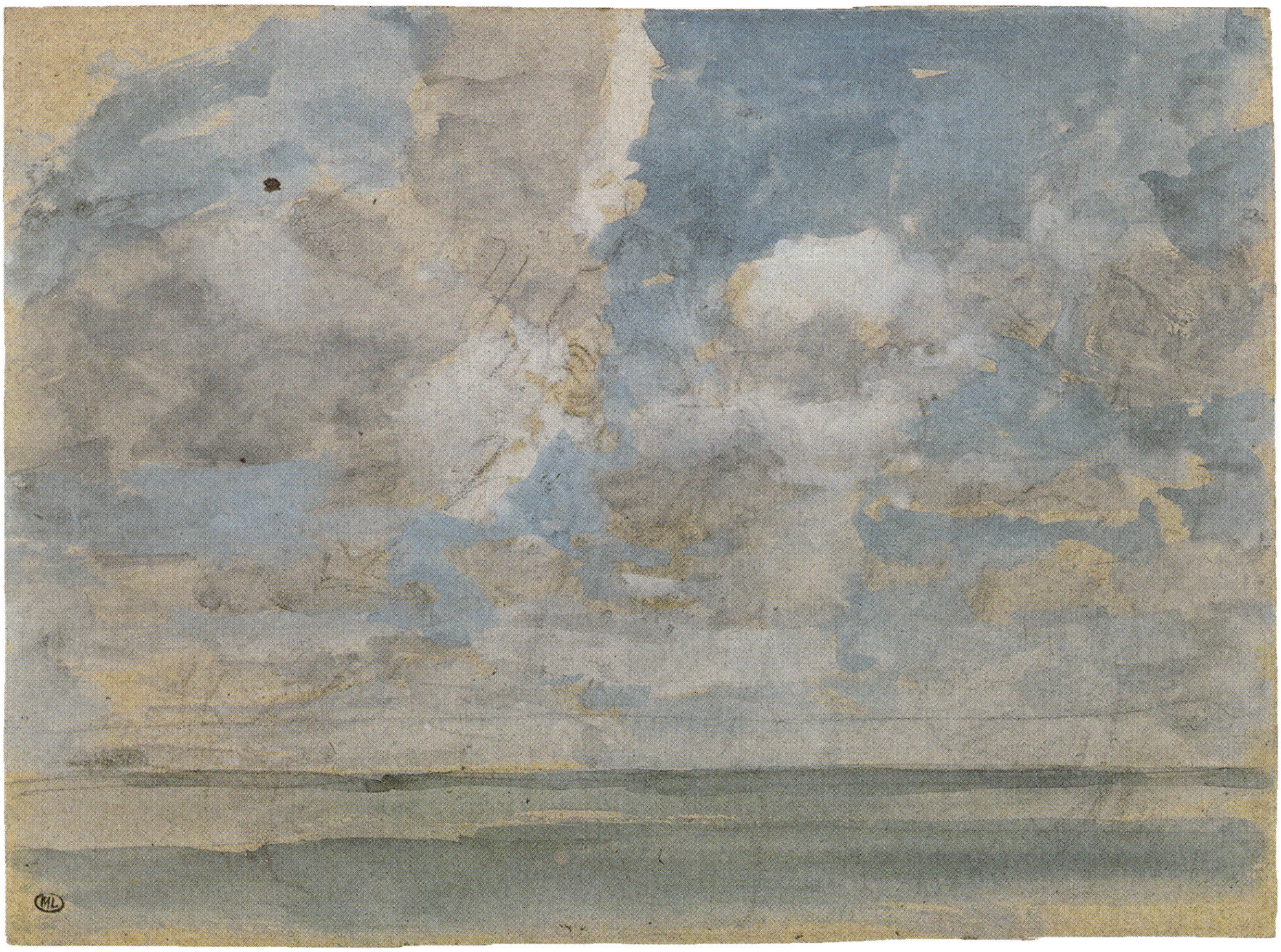

38

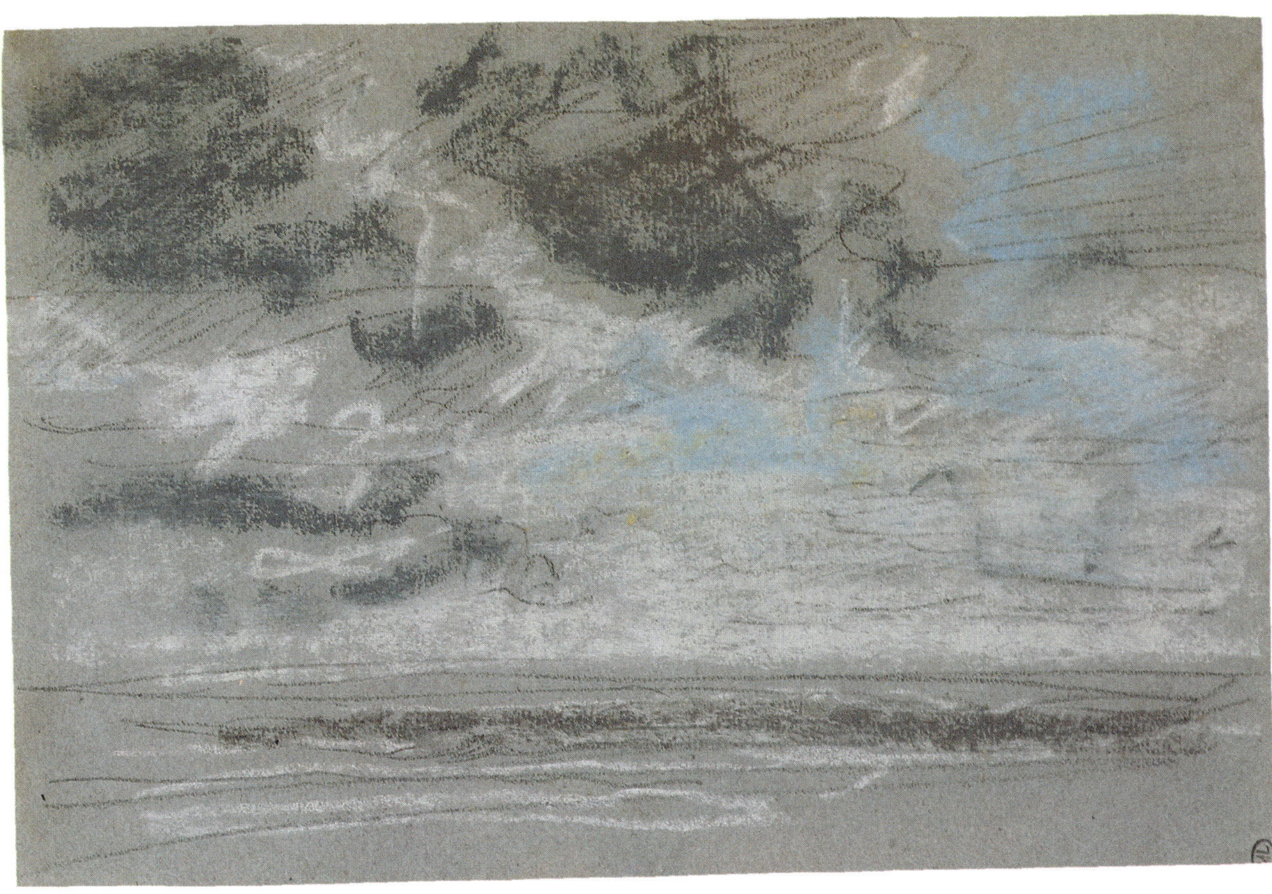

37

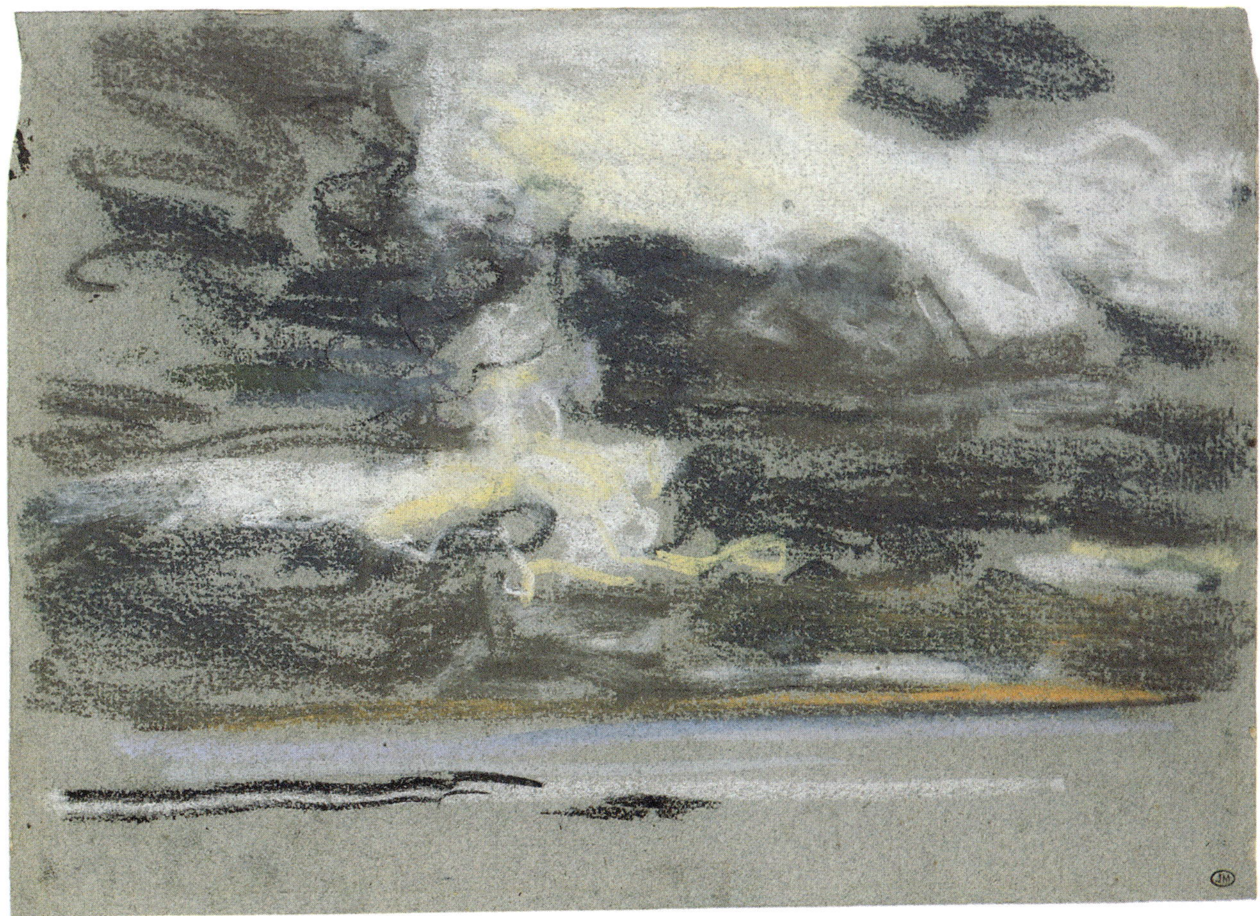

39

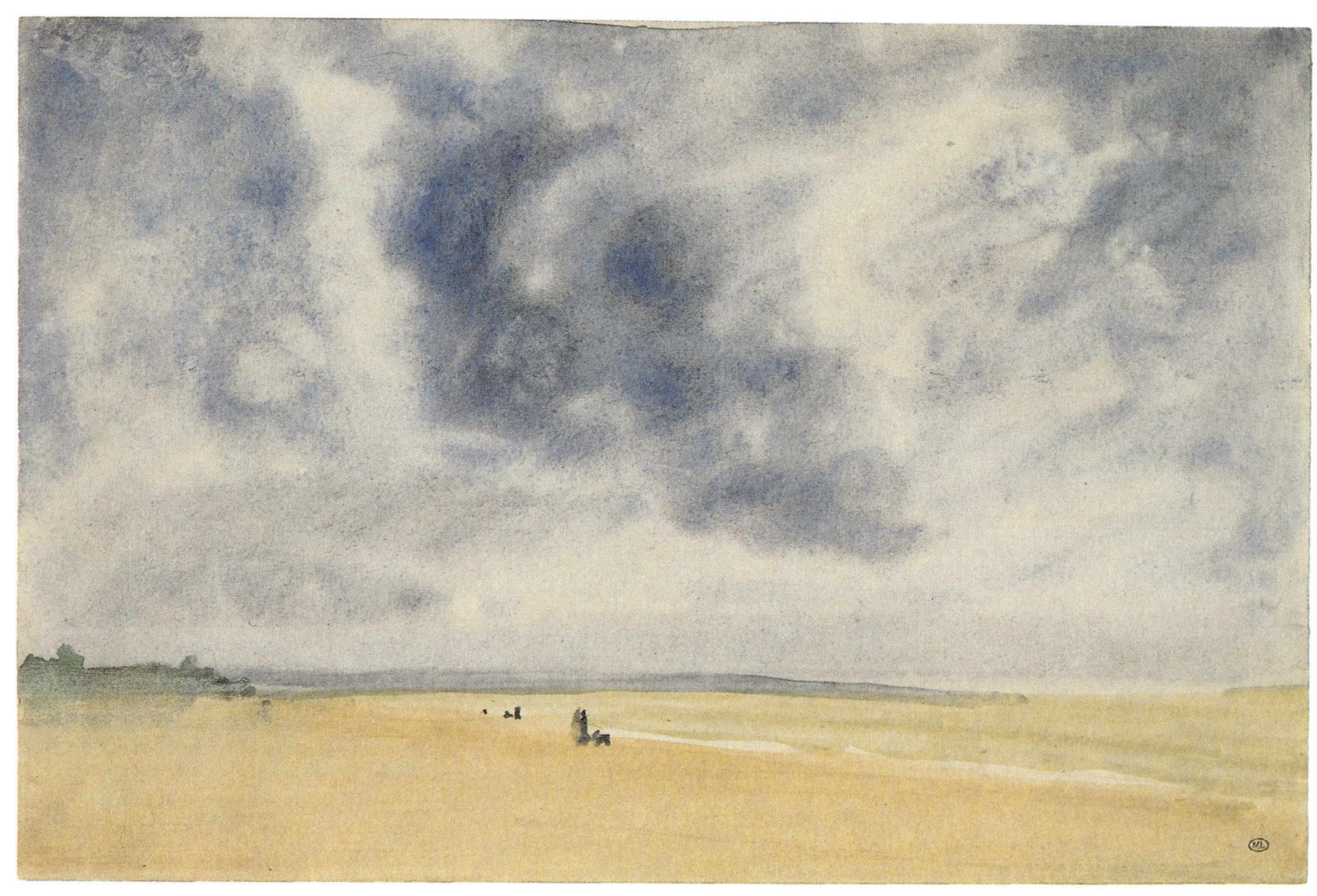

40

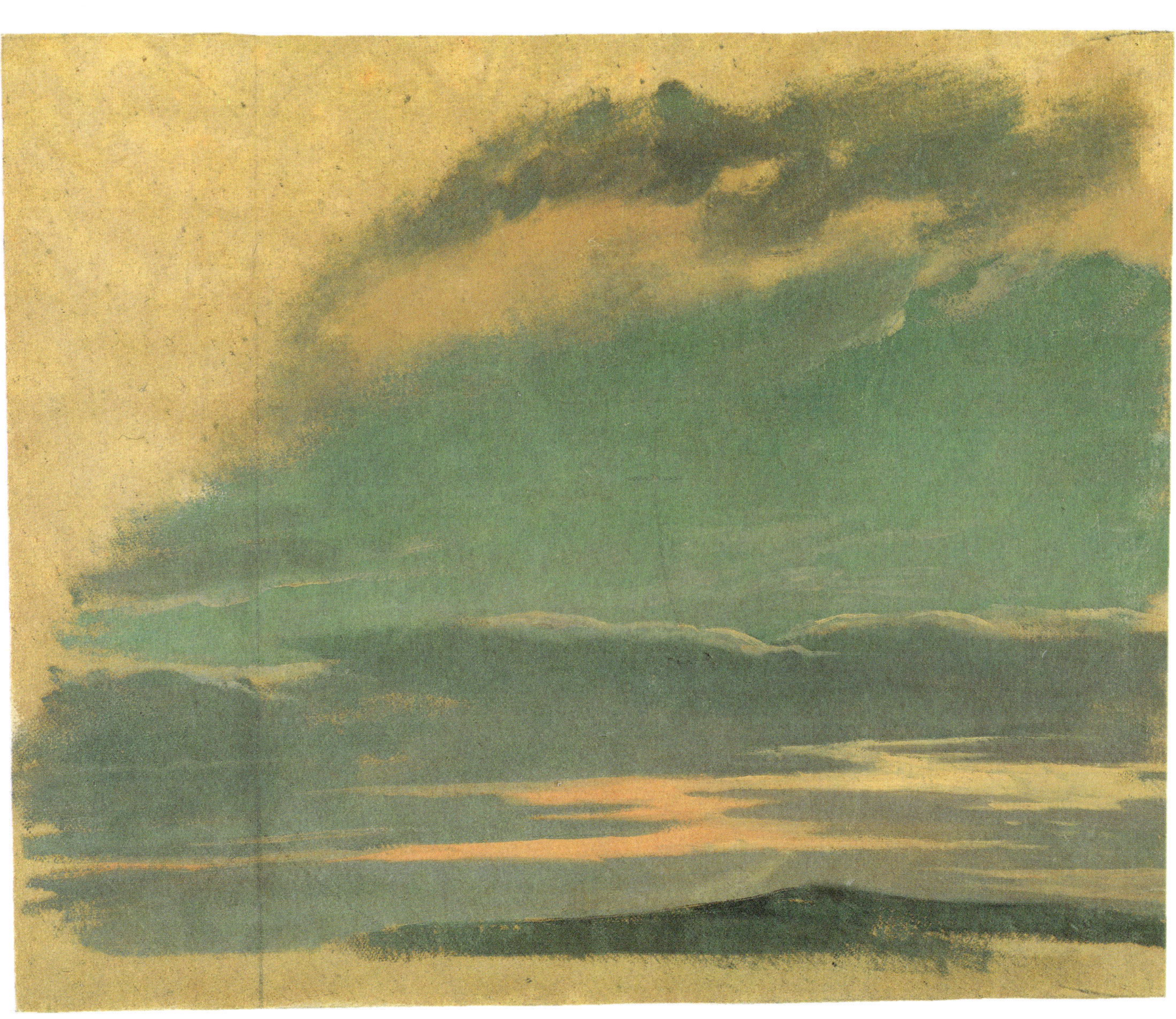

41

42
VLEUGHELS
Studies of wings

To fly we shall need a mechanism. But strictly no machine. The power of this present dream of flight must be self generated. Wings are an obvious possibility, wings of sufficient size to hold the weight of a human, making them at least the size of the wings of a swan or the wings of an eagle. Perhaps there is a choice of bird? Swan or eagle, pacific and predatory, vegetarian and carnivore? No swan ever soars. Every swan flight from water, its most natural habitat, is a great effort. There is much noise and much beating of wings, and the subsequent flight is low. More than a few incidents of dramatic danger have been caused by low-flying swans unable to change course without much foresight, unable to gain much height without a forward plan. And the beating wings make a noise like a creaking row-boat allied to heavy breathing.

The eagle has no such problems. It is seriously believed that dinosaurs, those serpent monsters, did not die but became transmogrified into birds. Scales became feathers. On swan and eagle, the reptilian scales are still there on webbed and clawed feet. Can we imagine that the Eden serpent and the dove of the Holy spirit are first cousins? And archaeopteryx is the exchange mechanism, that reptile into bird caught to fossilize in the Haberlein limestone? A natural history experiment that succeeded in whitewashing the reptilian serpent to make it an image of grace.

Vleughels has presented a winged template. Even his name sounds an invitation to some sort of flight. Are these wings strictly studies for ornithological examination or could we believe them to be studies for the wings of angels?

If we have gained personalised wings as implements of flight, how do we use them, and, most importantly, where do we go? Do we exercise

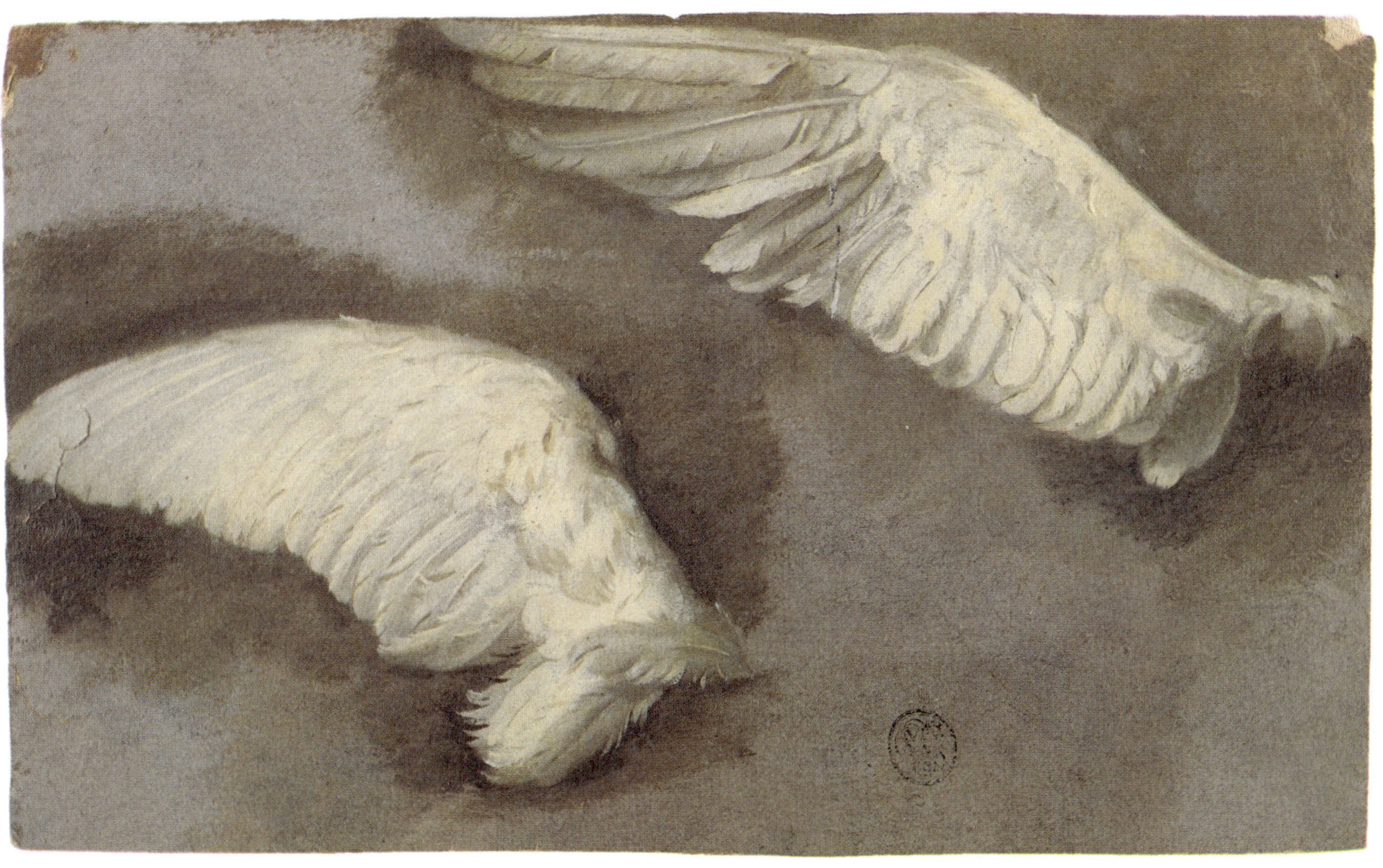

42

flight for its own sake, to experience just the language of flying, or is there a journey to be had? And if we have confronted the challenge and mastered the craft, what is the medium? Two hundred and fifty-three percent less resistant at sea level when the temperature is fifty-nine degrees Fahrenheit. Yet air will flow through your fingers in the same way. Keep your fingers closed. Air will drive itself into your mouth and nostrils at speed. Just like water. Keep your mouth closed and breathe through your nose. Air will pin your ears back to your head and press hard against your belly and, if you are male, blow your genitals back through your legs. However it will not wet your hair unless it is raining. And droplets of the stuff will not cling to the hairs of your arm, or glisten on your feet. You will not be able to catch the medium in the wrinkles of your palm, or trap a small quantity of it in your navel.

What about muscle strain. There will be the use of unaccustomed muscles. Certainly the shoulders will suffer from the repetitive beating and frequent changes of steering. Certainly the muscles of the belly will suffer from the effort of keeping the legs outstretched. How severe those aches will be. Try practising before you attempt to take to the sky. Lie down, face down on a bed. Not the floor. The floor is too hard and you can't look over the floor's edge. Besides, you are too vulnerable on the floor, too much like a worm, a snake, a serpent liable to be trodden upon. Lay on your belly on the bed. It is not going to be necessary to turn over on your back. What bird ever turns over on its back? A partridge perhaps, trying to trick its flying predator. An immature swift perhaps, practising aerobatics? You are not a partridge or a swift. And a swan could never fly on its back. As you lie on the bed, try looking forwards and consider the possibility of the pain in the neck and shoulders if you hold this position for a long time. An equivalent earth position is to walk the ground looking directly at the sky over your head. Not only do you wonder what your feet are doing, your throat feels unacceptably vulnerable. You feel you are facing the world with your throat which is not an organ that can protect itself. It's an offering to a blow, a thump, or worse. If we intend to fly, we should develop a neck carapace.

With these characteristics in mind let us approach the medium, the sky. What is the sound of the sky? Is it echoic? In an anechoic chamber you can hear two sounds, a deep rumbling which is the noise of your blood pumping down the arteries, and a regular whining, which is the noise of your pulses. Will we be able to hear these inner sounds when we fly in the silent sky? What noises would you be able to hear from the earth? Do the clouds make a sound? What is the noise of the clouds?

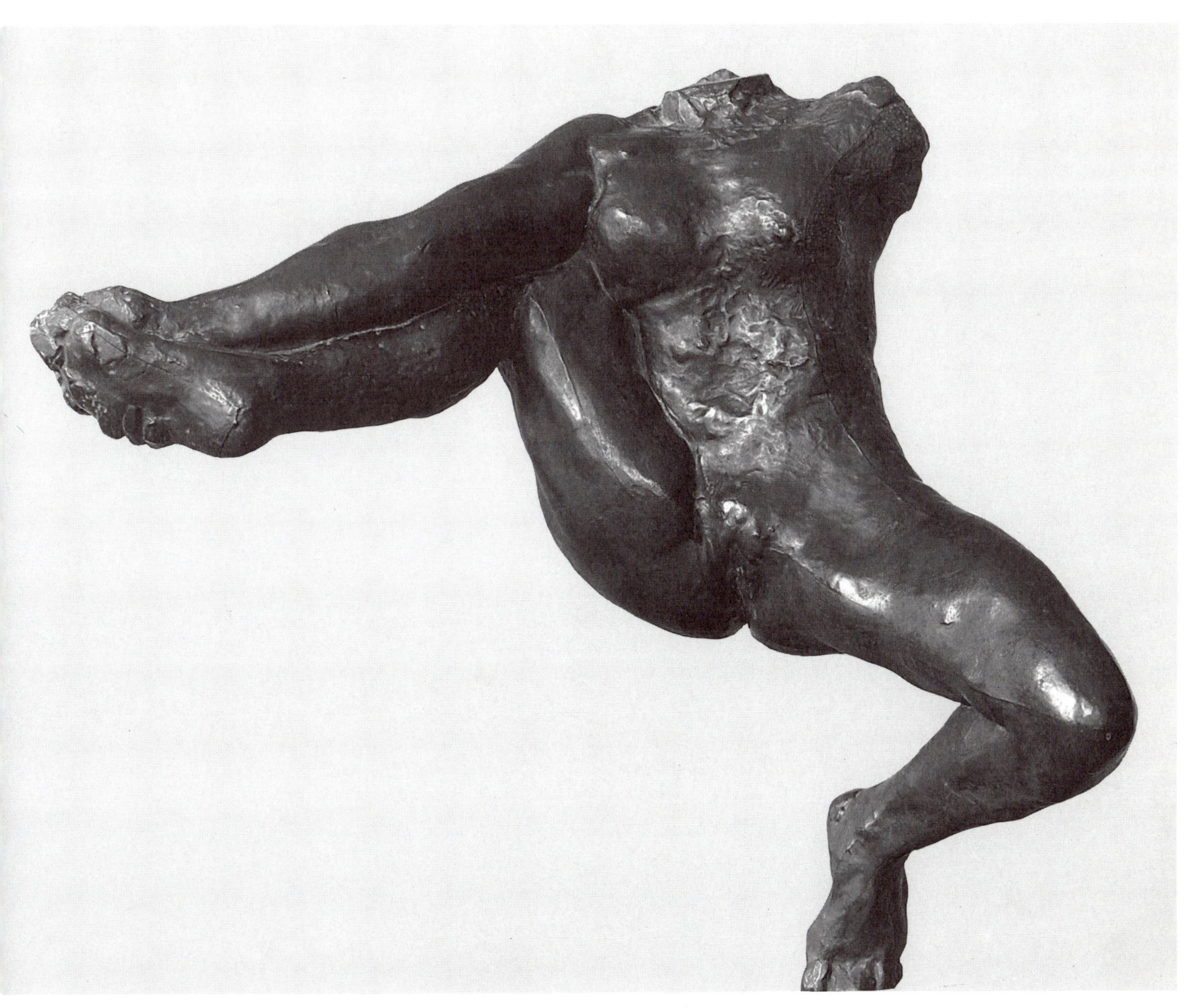

43 RODIN, *Iris, messenger of the gods.*

The Lower Reaches

Now we can be truly airborne. At first, just above the earth to get our bearings and appreciate how fortunate we are. And then in ever-increasing confidence to lift completely away from the Earth's surface and ascend towards Heaven.

44
REDON
Winged old man

Is this an old man with a long white beard or is it a bird? It is certainly not a plane. The forward edge of the hooded cape is the throat of a bird and the beak of the bird is the hood's peak. We can read the image either way. We are, either way, in an act of contemplation in a sanctified space and the ambience is spiritual, suggestively Byzantine. The architectural space is limited by a heavy curtain, or is it a massively girthed column? The old bird-man is winged, and if it is a man-bird, then the bird is eyeless, blind. We are shifting in areas of ambiguity, much like flight itself. If we take this image as encouragement, for the moment we must take it cautiously, for, the creature is presently earth-bound. We can see a single foot, rooting the tree-trunk of his body to the flagstones. If the figure is about to move, it will slowly exit to the left. The figure is so oppressively near to a left exit we could resurrect that ancient theory that left-directed exits are negative. Should we take this monkish figure as a serious guide if he is walking the wrong way?

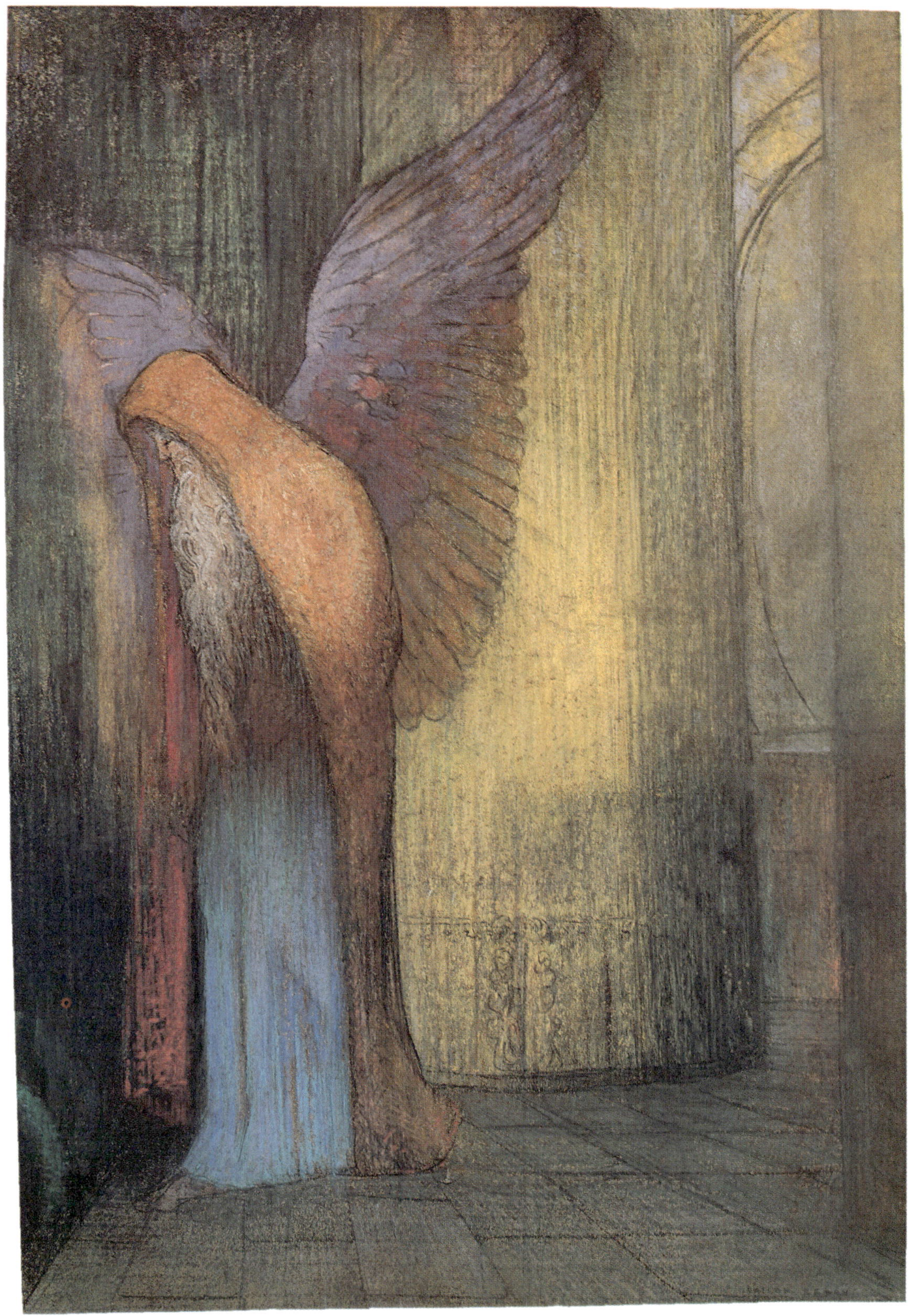

44

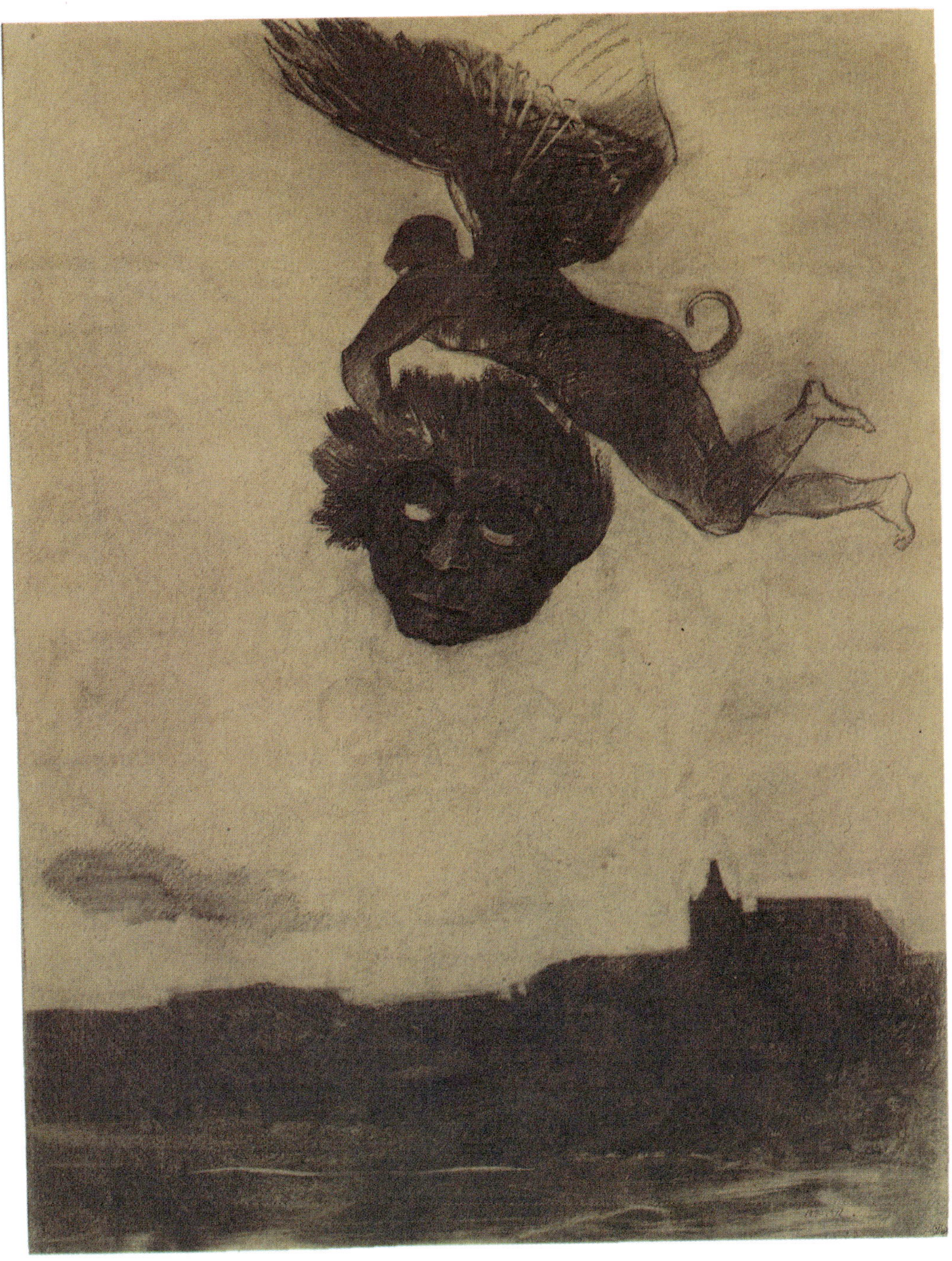

45

45
REDON
Winged demon

Redon has a black angel, scouting at dusk, carrying a large mask whose eyes hold the sky. This flying figure has a curled tail fixed to a fleshy anatomy. This black angel is on devilish business. The mask is heavy and awkward to hold, a dead weight forever dragging downwards. It could be dropped. It would fall like a stone into the streets of the town. Or do those white glints and glimpses below him indicate that the angel flies over water, some river rushing beside the basilica on the far bank? Is this picture suitable for our future experiences? Do we need to know how to carry a heavy object on our flight, how to transport our own baggage? I would suggest that this apparition flying in an evening light is useful. We can be made to feel the cold evening breeze and wonder how we can navigate once daylight has left us. How is our relationship with the ground when the lights go out? Will we meet creatures like this in the twilight?

46

REDON
Winged woman

Another Redon, enigma abounding. We are flying. Gently. The breeze is imperceptible. An angel, almost certainly a winged female, is playing with the clouds. One cloud is her footstool. That clouds should have such substance as this. It is an apprenticeship flight close to the ground where the cloud shadows are small and neat, and cast from a sun directly over-head. If the clouds misbehave then the angel-figure can step to the ground and no harm will befall. A calm and fair beginning for a flight-adventure.

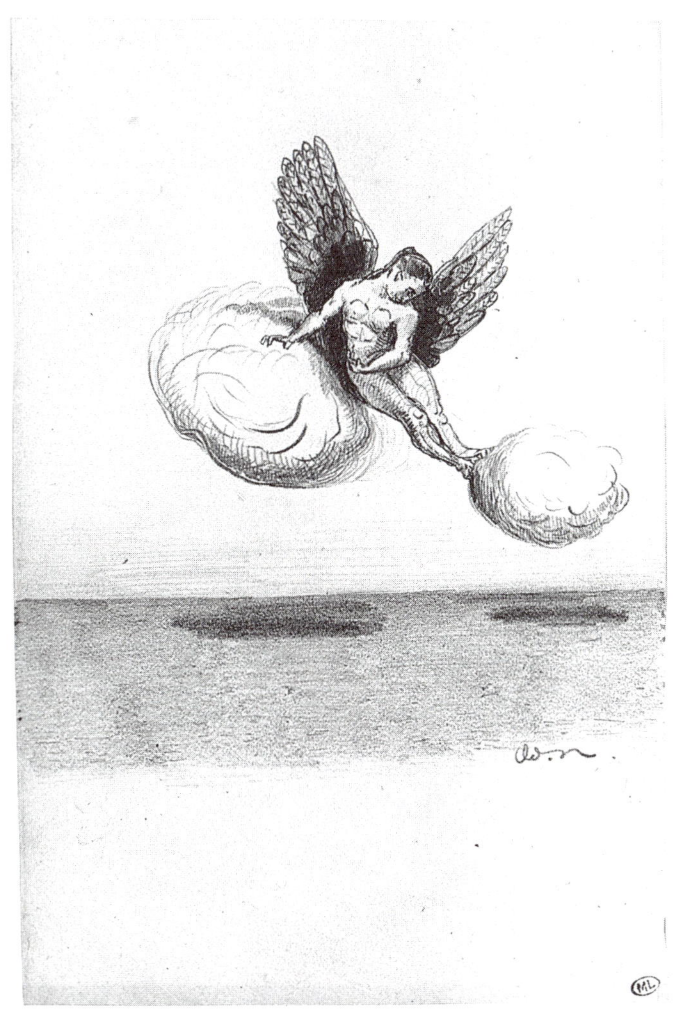

47
RENI
The Separation of Day and Night

With sudden noise, here we have an energetic angel who divides Day and Night. Like a determined prospector, this angel has two crossed sticks, two crossed wands. Like the apparatus of a diviner, it has the semblance of a divining rod, and it is artlessly manufactured in such a simple way for such a sundering of opposites. Maybe that cross-arms gesture is masonic, it appears ritualistic, making a force-field for violent sundering. Day and Night bounce vigorously apart. To a European, if the angel is arriving like a hurricane from the North, then Day bounds suitably to the West and Night arcs to the East. All three are caught in a regular panel made of four touching circles in a rectangle that is not far short of a square. Certainly all three figures are not responsive to gravity, but the angel of separation has feeble wings. With classical canon nicety, but not absolved from an accusation of coyness, Night and Day show their sex. Why should Night be female?

The Allegory of Day and Night. Are they flighted? Do they have wings? Why should Night be feminine? Because the moon is female? Females and lunatics under the moon. Are they the same age, these two? Are they like twins from the same mother, made in the same womb? In Ethiopia, Night is male and has a mirror in which Day's sun is feebly reflected as the moon. By day, this Night was kept chained below the Red Sea where he buried his head in his mirror to hide his black face. This Reni pair, so recently sprung apart, have faces destined to look both ways. At least Day has. Night looks over her shoulder at him, regretful at his brightness springing away. Emnity seems inevitable, though Day and Night ought to be lovers passionately meeting like a couple on different working-shifts;

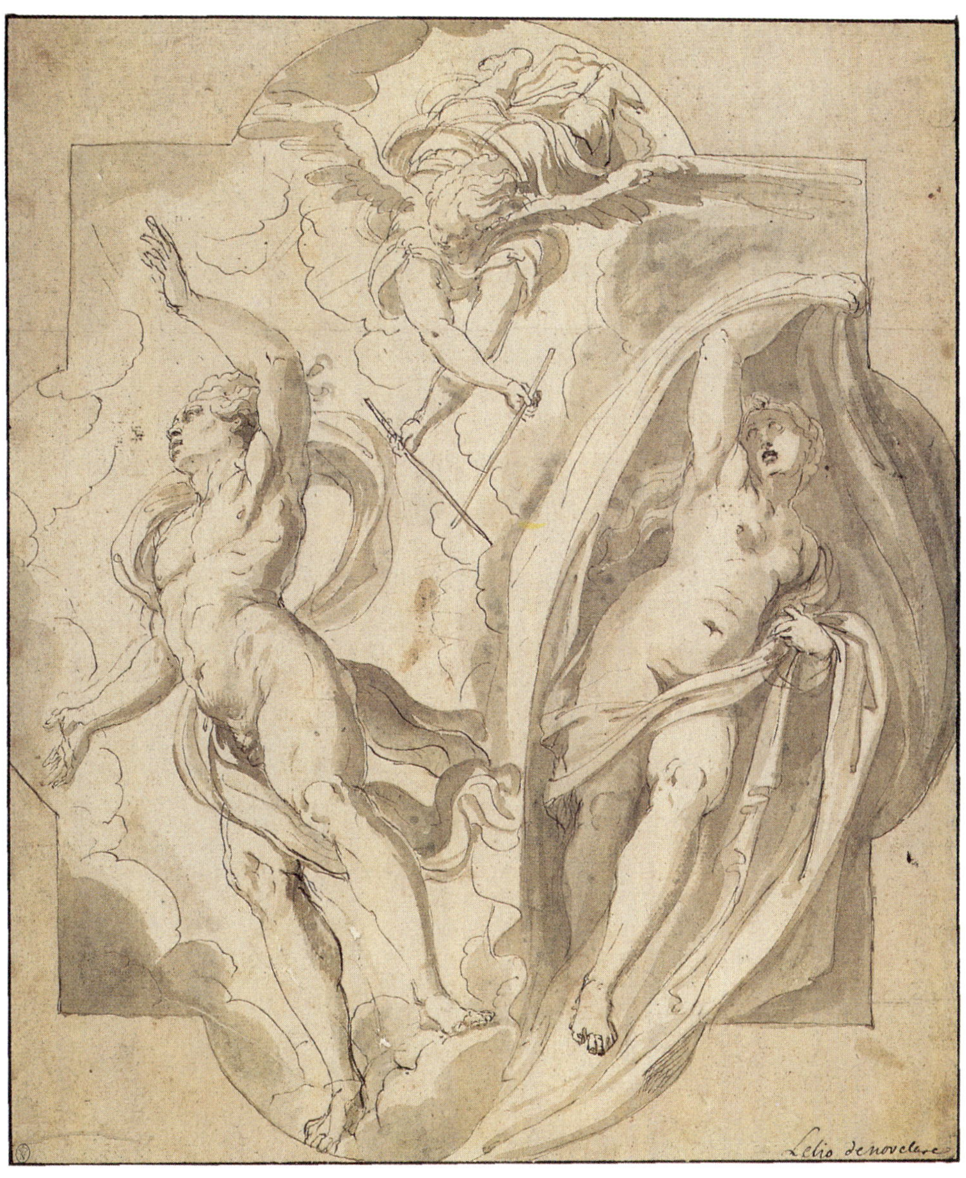

47

at dawn and dusk getting into the other's still-warm bed-sheets. Night flies lazily. Day flies with excessive energy. He'll be inventing new strokes, pushing out his chest, confident of night-times's admiration.

48
CECCO BRAVO
Flying figures

Two angels rise in an interior, up among the ceiling lights and the pelmet boards. This is a curious Peter Pan affair, almost domestic—with a suggestion of a catch game. The flying is well-nigh crowded out by interior decoration. Will the swish of the wings creating draughts, knock the ornaments from the walls? Is the lower angel attempting to catch and support the legs of its companion? Neuter gender is intimated, because again the sex of these participants is insubstantially suggested, but if it reprises a Peter Pan world of sexless children, then the gender ambiguity could not be more accurate.

Dashed lines make a bright circular aurora to illuminate the head of the superior angel. This one is the catcher, but both protagonists will continue to spiral in upward flight, and eventually take us through the ceiling into the open air. That, or else we will come up flat against the ceiling, bumping like a hydrogen balloon against the stucco. The upper figure is wingless. Is he or she a fugitive, a child, diving upwards to escape pursuit? I think not. The pursuit is too beneficent. There is the faintest suggestion of a further figure holding a curtain drape and outstretched hand, but more like as not, this is a painted creature or an architectural statue, a caryatid putting aside her heavy business for a moment to re-arrange the upholstery.

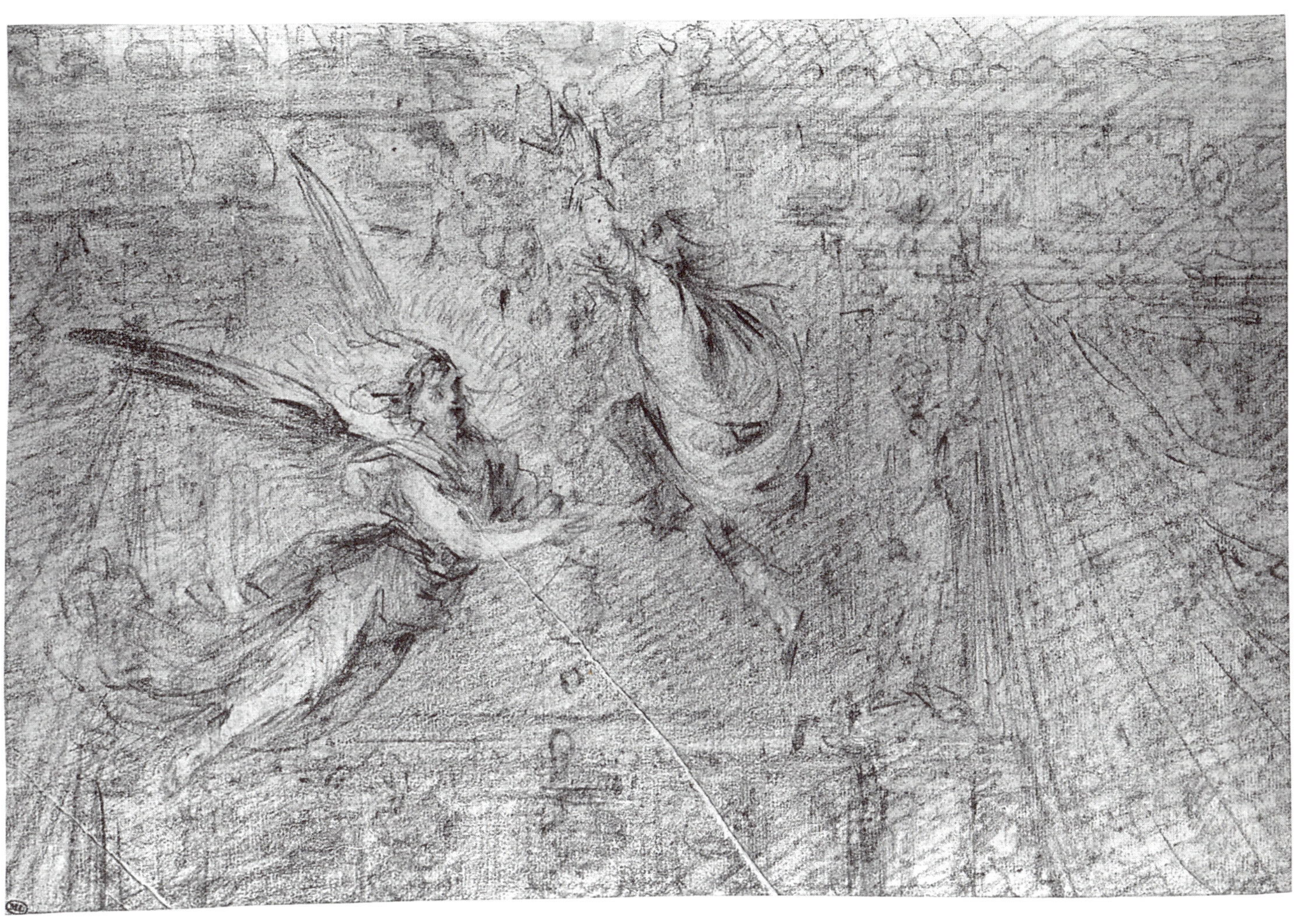

48

49
Giulio ROMANO
Three angels bearing the Virgin's crown

We have found an outlet to the sky and three angels wait there, hovering, holding the crown of the Virgin. Is it a large crown or are they small angels? Or is the crown a symbolic apparatus to be simply held over the Virgin's head and not touch her hair? The angels twist in the updraught of warm air from the heated rooms below, and the open ceiling is a welcome bolt hole to the upper sky. The angels must maneuver with accuracy lest their wings beat on the balconies. The angle of vision on them is sharp. When in life can we see such foreshortening of the human body? It is so rare an occurrence, and in such special circumstances. Witnessing performers on a trampoline? On a trapeze? Do we have to resort to the circus and all its connotations to experience such a viewpoint? Or can it be experienced with figures cumberously descending a staircase, or leaning over balconies? Such approximations are a very limited foretaste of the possibilities. Only when we all learn to fly will such images as this one be truly assimilated. Till then so much of this foreshortening is conjectural. How did the artist pose a figure for such a drawing? Did Romano hang assistants, or children on ropes, from the roof of his studio? Maybe in such a future flying world, the orthodoxy of our consideration for the body may be troubled. Where, in everyday events, can we expend so much attention on feet and legs and thighs, when conventionally, most of our concern for social communication is expended and focused above the navel? We are looking upwards, which not only cranes and strains the neck, but focuses attention on the lower body, the buttocks, the body's seat, the bifurcation of the limbs, the groin, the genitals. In seeing the human body from this attitude and angle, the selective perspective and artistic license cheats, and we have little familiarity and knowledge with which to point a correction. The upper body is invariably proposed as being larger than it could be in such foreshortening circumstances. Impro-

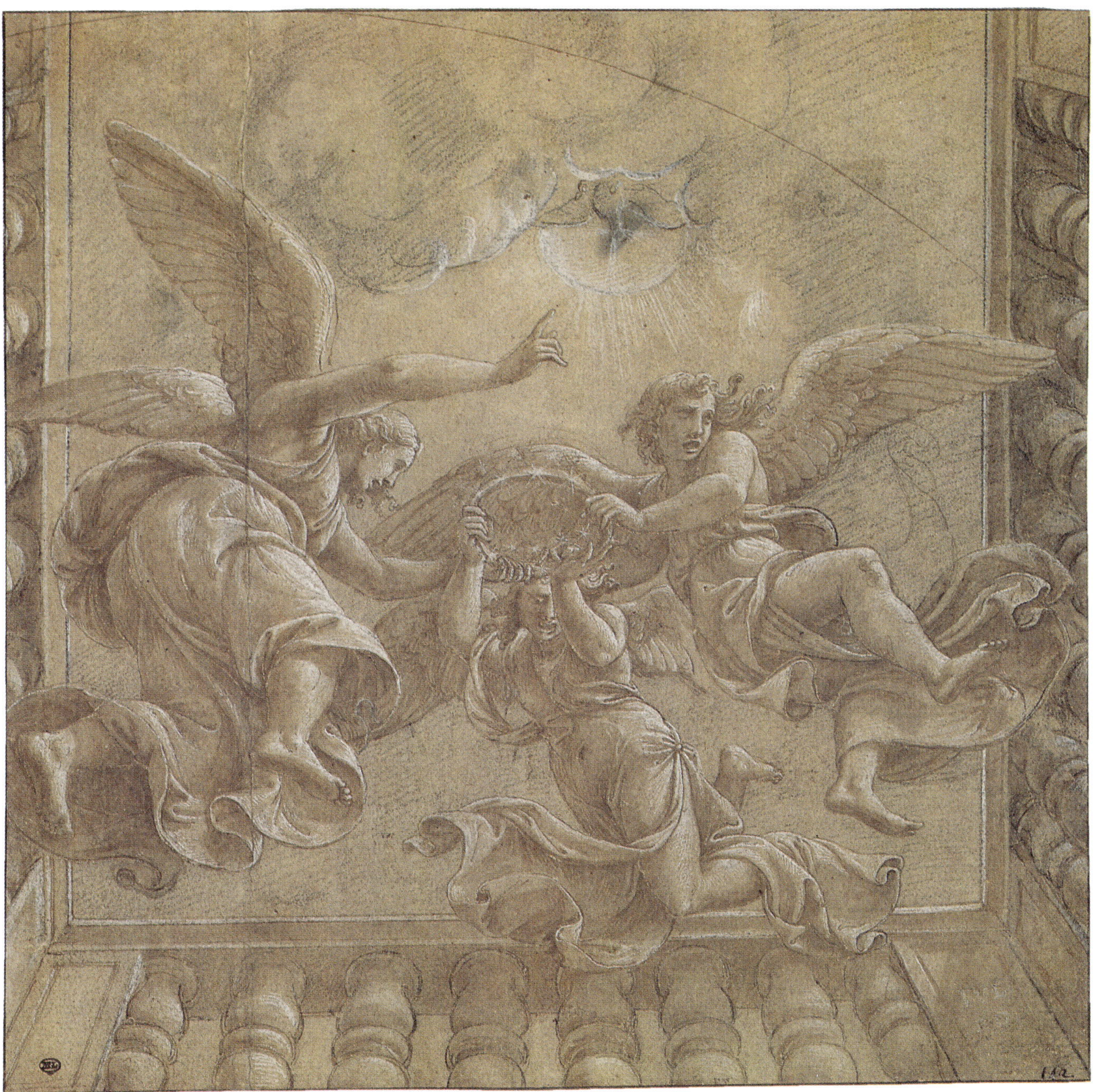

49

priety is adjudicated carefully. Yet erotic effect cannot be denied by the artist, or by us.

High up in the sky, accompanied by the conventional lines of a draughtsman's attempt to express the force of light, is the Holy Dove. The familiarity of ceilings open to the sky, and the unfamiliarity of angels occupying the architectural space above our heads, give us good example to walk with trust on the waters of air. We can follow them up and become airborne.

50
BIANCONI
The Abduction of Ganymede

51
School of LEONARDO DE VINCI
The Abduction of Ganymede

52
After MICHELANGELO
The Abduction of Ganymede

Here are three Ganymedes. Bird-abduction. If you cannot fly yourself, get kidnapped by a bird of provable strength and endurance. "And then flew down a monstrous bird as big as a tar-barrel." Ganymede, son of a shepherd, might know about eagles stealing young lambs. Could they steal away a child? "He was taken by a bird that settled on his shoulders and whisked him away." Maybe a very small child. A baby. Something like the Rembrandt version, the child clutching cherries, bawling and screaming his way up into the mountains with a mole on his buttocks and, in fright, watering the earth with his urine—offered in irony for the wine he might soon be holding as cup-bearer for the Gods on Olympus? Catamitus is the Latin transliteration from Gamumedes in the Greek, and attempts to turn physical into platonic love is endearing but censorious. More cross-purposefully, if Ovid, mediaevally moralised, made Ganymede a prefiguration of John the Baptist, with the eagle as Christ, the Rembrandt infant Ganymede is baptising the earth with Jordan water.

These three drawings show Ganymede, not as a child but as an adult or adolescent male, six foot and 120 pounds: a considerably heavier load. Still, Jupiter is not so much an eagle as a Jovean bird of special identification. Bianconi gives his regal eagle a large, flat-topped head, a ferocious

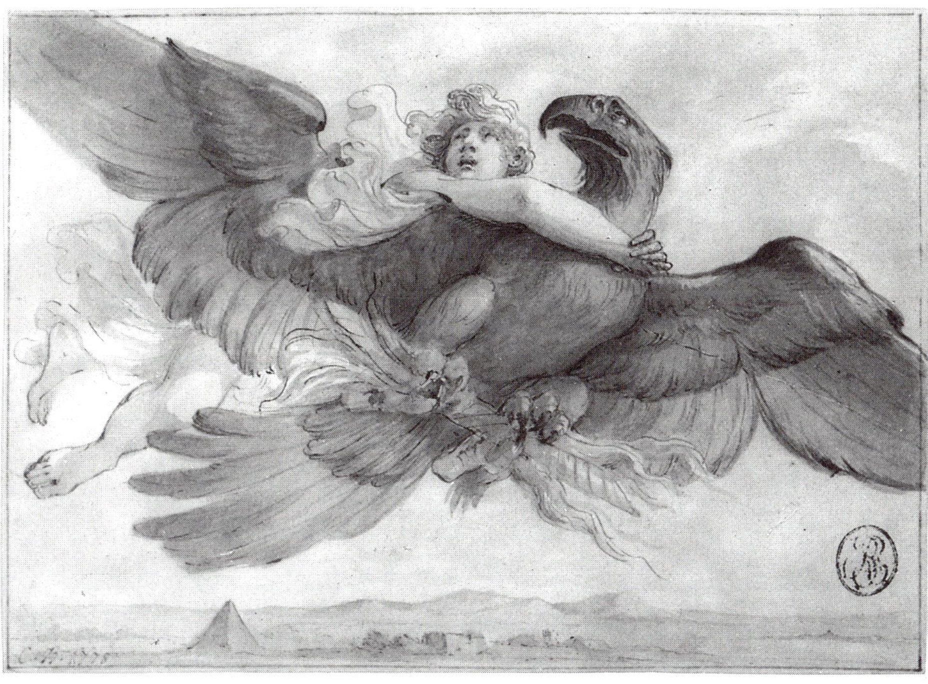

50

beak, and insisted that he should carry his thunderbolt attribute as well as the boy, in case we might mistake his meaning. Both eagle and boy look skywards, ignoring the sights. They are flying over Egypt, over sparse plains dominated by an isolated pyramid, the boy clasping the bird's neck in a wrist-lock. Each and every mighty wing-flap must shake the passenger into tumultous air-sickness.

Better to ride beneath the beating wings as in the apocryphal Leonardo drawing, though here the ambiguity of the flight details confuse an accurate description. The boy is so comfortably seated, is this bird-and-human tableau actually at rest on some rocky outcrop, waiting for a change in the wind? Or are they indeed flying? The boy, it is true, is perhaps lighter here, and maybe younger, but his twisting pose does not seem to augur for comfort on his flight to the mountains.

This eagle's head and curving neck owe more to the yet undiscovered pterodactyl than to recognisable birds of prey, but Jupiter can choose or invent his species without contradiction.

No sensible strategy of comfortable flight is at all envisaged in the Michelangelo copy. In a frankly homoerotic drawing, where airborne sodomy is intimated, the huge eagle-claw grip on the boy's lower calves is

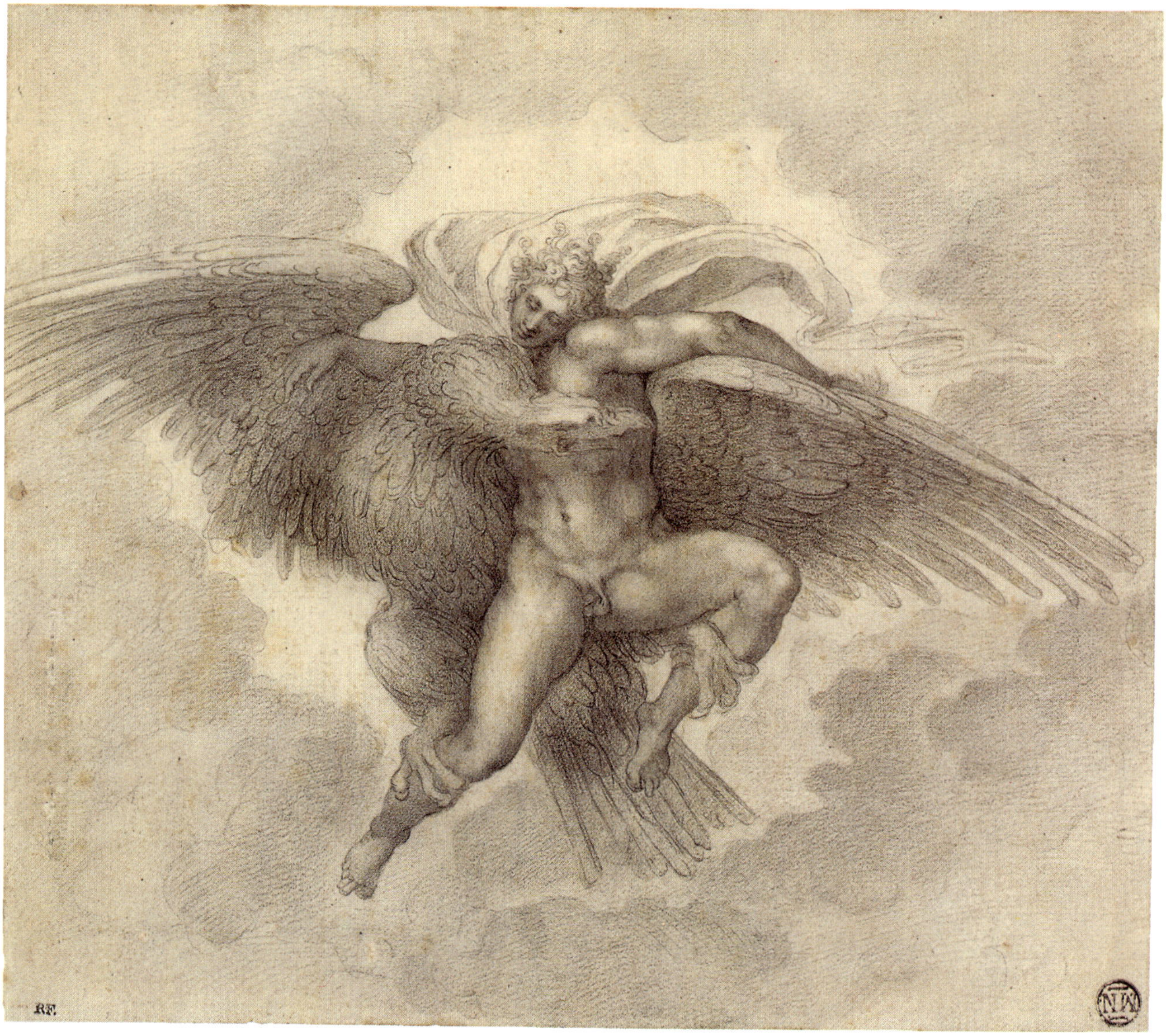

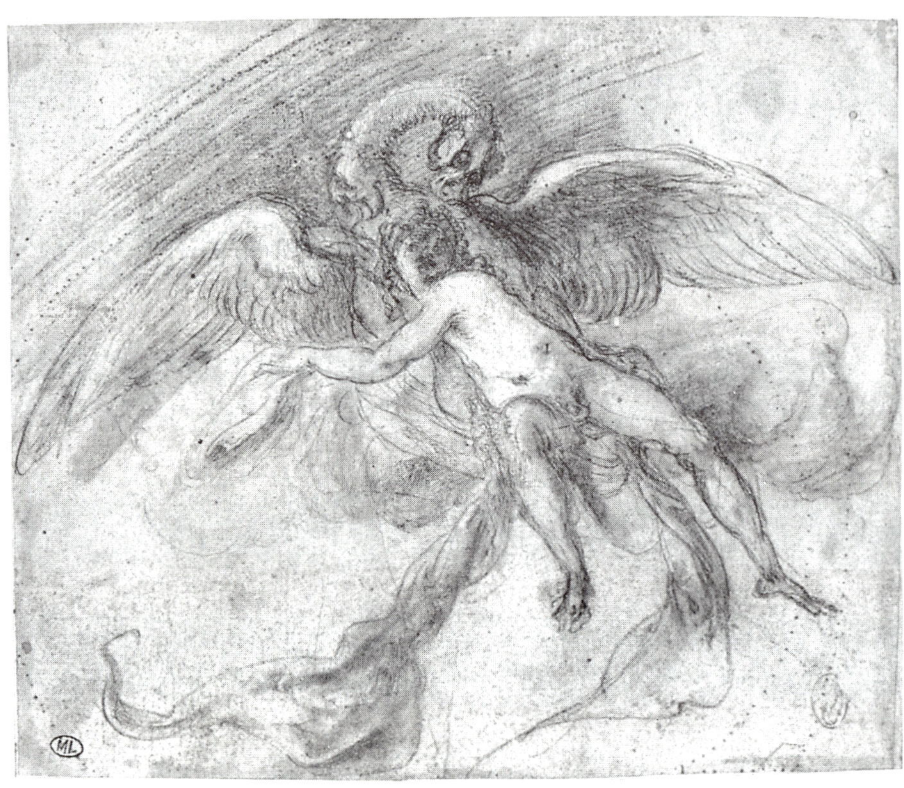

52

51

unshakeable, and Ganymede's languorous hold is negligible. Easy comparison couples this drawing with the Michelangelo Tityus of the same period, and Panofsky would have them counted as a pair. Both these drawings are eagle heavy. The Tityus may well show the selfsame bird torturing the selfsame man, save stories of Tityus talk of two birds picking out the ever-renewable liver and stress the bird is a vulture, not an eagle. The liver, and not the heart, was a viable seat of passion, and Tityus is being punished for sensual passion. He tried to rape the mother of Apollo and Diana, and was felled by their arrows, doubtless feather-flighted and a foretaste of the bird to come.

Both Tityus and Ganymede are victims of bird harassment. Does Michelangelo identify himself with the bird or the prey? With Jupiter or Ganymede? If Michelangelo is the abducting bird then his victim by repute may be Tommaso de Cavalieri, a famously handsome nobleman, who Vasari says owned these two drawings and was encouraged to consider them as models to copy to improve his draughtsmanship. Michelangelo, with a self-revealing pun, wrote, "I am held prisoner by an armed cavalier." Bird and victim, prisoner and jailer, fact and fiction, requited and unrequited, master and slave, kidnapped and kidnapper, sacred and profane; all these states of body and mind jostle for interpretation according to your subjectivity and a reading of the conventions of careful Renaissance rhetoric. But why should we need to seek clarification, when a plethora of meaning is desirable. What is undeniable is a beautiful youth is flying to the mountains without regret, and making no attempt to help his abductor against the lure of gravity that might finally claim them both. If Ganymede's lanquid back-handed grip should not suffice, he'll topple forward and hang upside down facing backwards, dangling, to hit his head on passing rocks, much like that lamb Ganymede might have seen dangling from an eagle's talons over his father's Trojan pastures.

53
PRUD'HON
The Assumption
54
Antoine COYPEL
Minerva
55
VOUET
Force
56
Niccolò DELL'ABBATE
Fortune
57
CANDIDO
Angel
58
Antoine COYPEL
Zephyr

By example, we are airborne. How do you detect movement in a flying figure when evidence of the earth is absent? Up, down, right, left? Do you take your direction from a glance of an eye, from an eye-line, by the position of the figure in the drawing space, flying into and out of the empty page-surface? How high is a flying figure if you cannot see the ground? The need to ask such questions is because all our distances were first measured by our feet walking on the ground. The impossibility, with these next six drawings, of answering the question, is evidence that we have truly left the earth behind. Our feet have now lost much of their importance.

First, the assumption of the Virgin. We, like the Virgin herself, are looking upwards, lips parted, waiting to be received. Wingless herself, this youthful version of Christ's mother whose true age, calculated by the age of Christ, would exceed fifty, is ascending in a symmetrical flight supported by two winged angels. We are rising with her, assisted by a

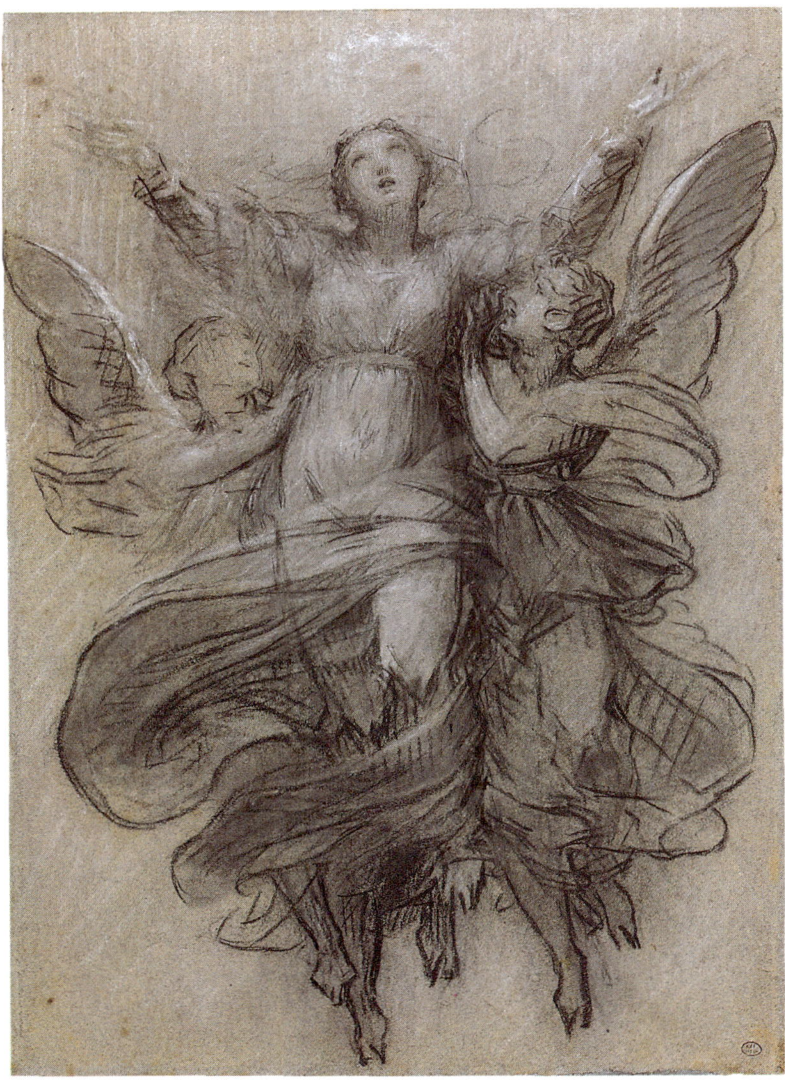

53

light wind from the right. Although her spirit is ethereal enough, Mary's body does not lack female corporeality. Belly, navel, and breasts are scarcely concealed in the first gown to be worn in Heaven with an Empire-line-high waist. Is this Virgin too profane? Is it disingenuous of us to ask that question?

The substance of this Prudhon stratosphere is thick with cloud. It clusters close to the bodies, yet there is nothing to cast a shadow on, for surely the Virgin would not rise to Heaven on a cloudy day?

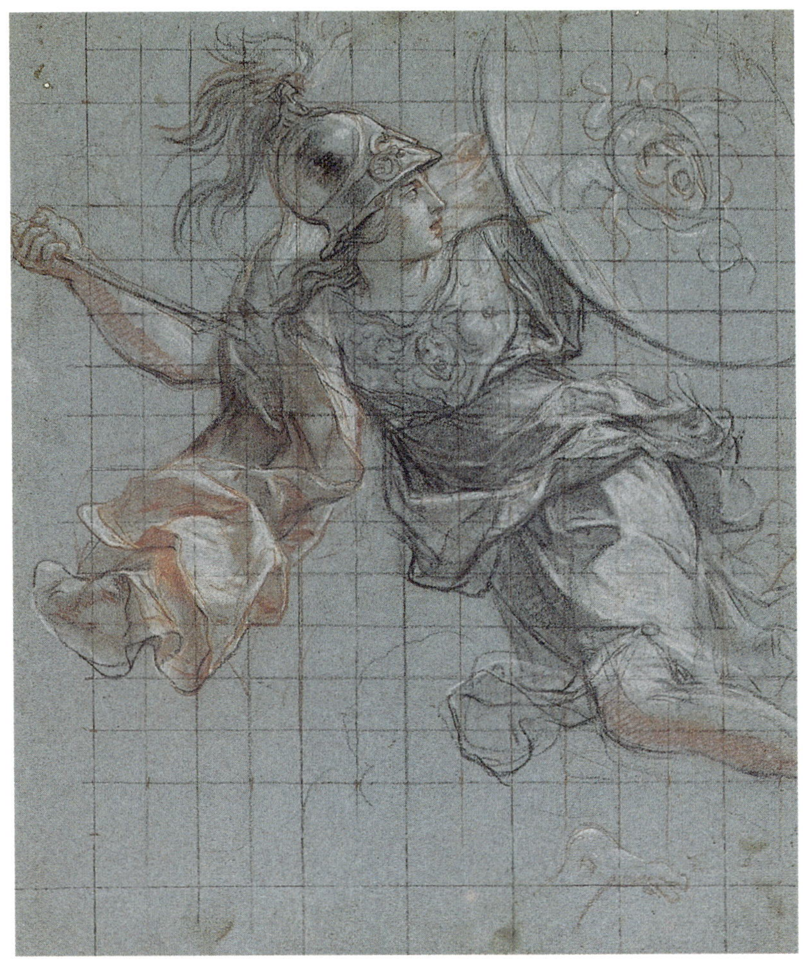

54

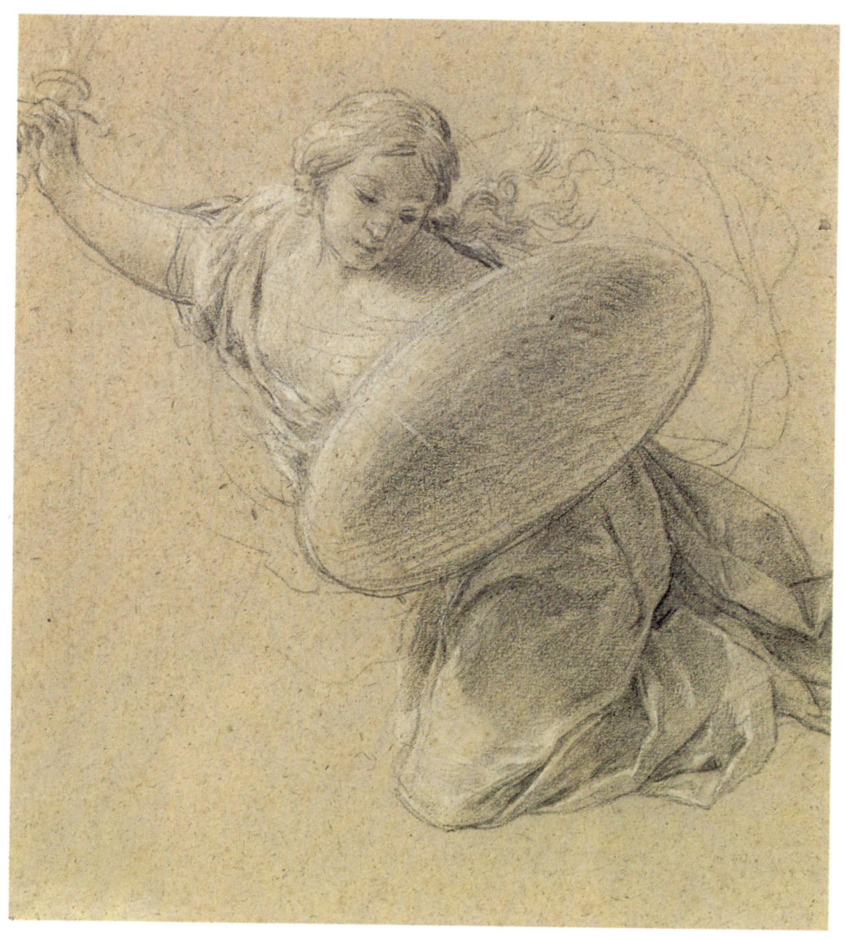

55

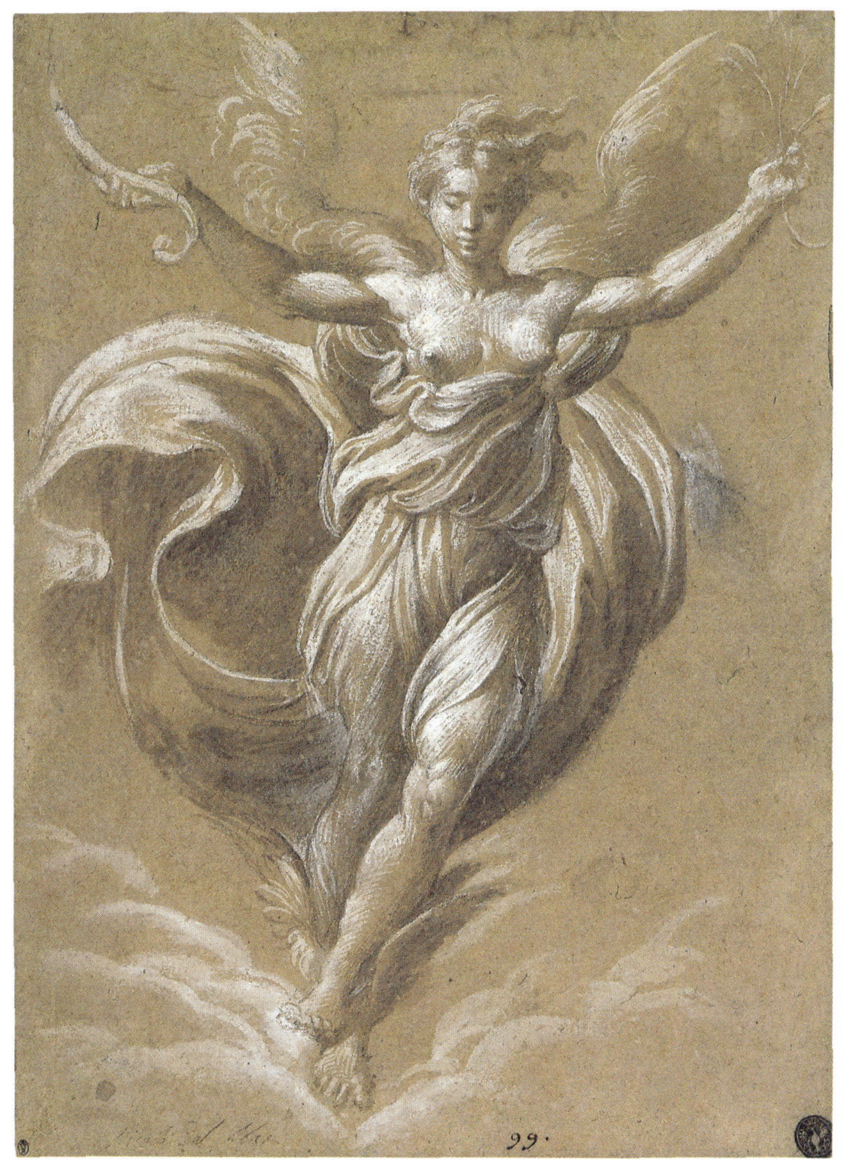

56

By a trick and a deception, for we must not think it meant, the feet of all three participants look cloven-hoofed.

The Coypel Minerva is flying not upwards like the Virgin, but to the left. Like the Virgin, she is a virgin. Like the Virgin, Minerva intercedes for just causes, bearing arms to do so. Like the Virgin, she has no wings, but is upheld undoubtedly by the levitating power of her allegorical significance. She is looking back, and flying backwards, weapon raised, her serpent-headed Medusa-shield catching the light. She has a second medusa-medalion-head of tragedy on her breast-plate in case the first one does not successfully change her enemies to stone, rock-crystal, or salt. Like Eve, virginal until chased from the gates of Paradise, Minerva, Goddess of Wisdom, is serpent-associated, but with the ever-ready equivocation that conveniently makes the Evil Pagan and the Good Christian implacable rivals and good friends, Matthew said "Be ye therefore wise as serpents." Are these equivocations—the martial arts for peace, the serpents for wisdom—relevant to Minerva's present flight through the air? She is wrapped and surfeited by drapery that might, we feel, with our modern knowledge, cause her flying to be impeded by air-friction. As it is, with all her authority depicted here, she still makes flight an act of two dimensions.

Another martial female, the Vouet flying figure, may make us feel that flight could be a more three-dimensional occupation. She is a creature who wears her mythological significance more lightly. She does not so much identify Minerva, but signify Force. She too carries a shield and a weapon, yet her comfortable body, her loose hair, and her gentle face deny the aggression expected of her allegorical function. She seems no Warrior, more a protective guide.

Two further females accompany our upward flight, each balancing on a single foot. Eschewing martial arms, they nonetheless fly the air with hands full of attributes. The dell'Abbate Fortune, bare breasted, rides on four wings, two at her shoulders and two at her ankles, a well-empowered flyer. Fortune is often blind, distributing her favours without favour. Blindness is not a useful attribute for flying. High clouds are indicated, and the sway of the body balanced on a delicate diagonal, makes the flight seem speedy. Often Fortune trembles one-footed on a slippery sphere, a globe of instability which the practical imagination of the Renaissance turned into the globe of the Earth. Here, her toes do not touch or balance on any platonic solid, metaphorical or geo-physical. Her body is wreathed around with drapery. It wraps around her thighs and billows with a sound like flapping sheets, lifting her lithe body effortlessly into the air.

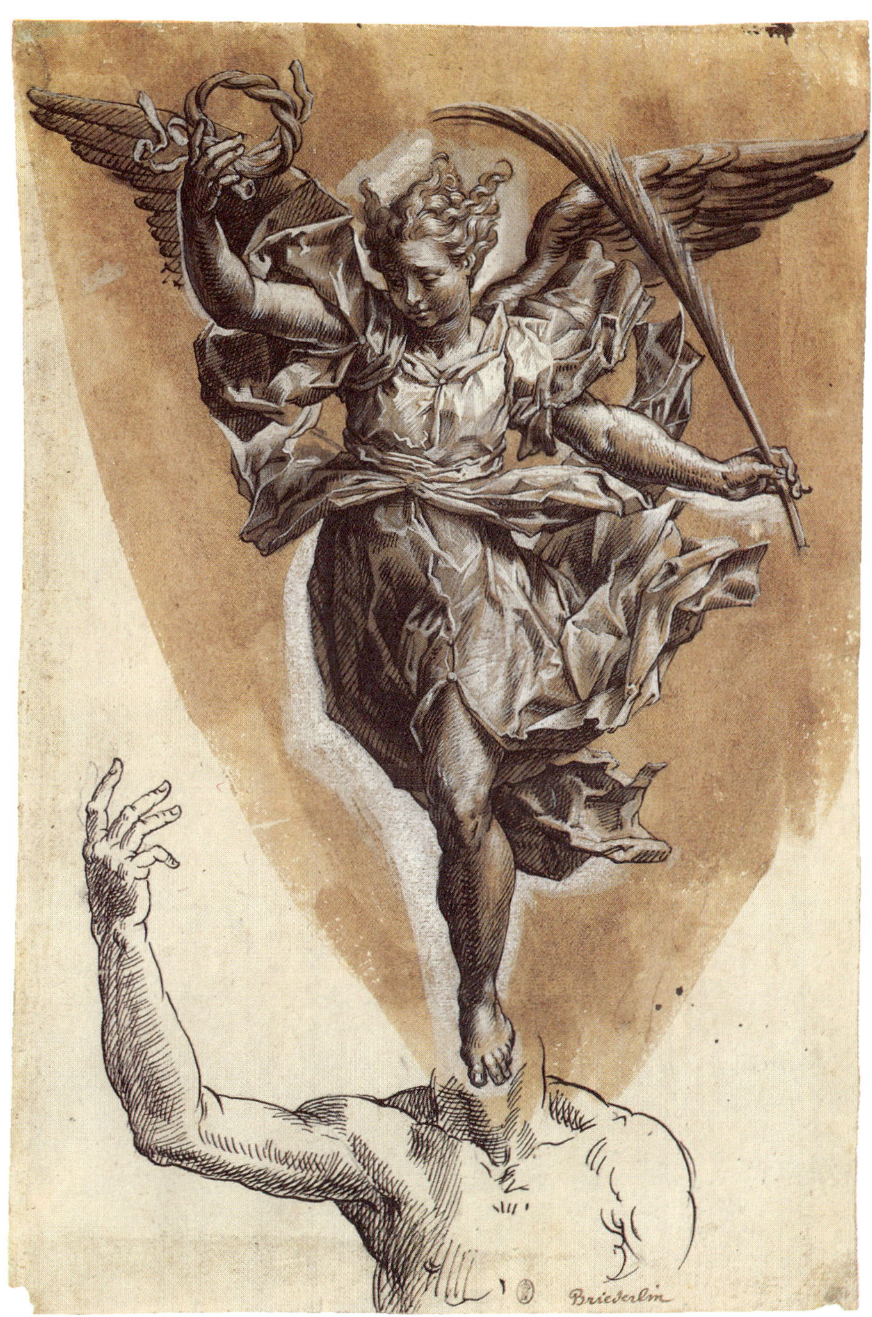

57

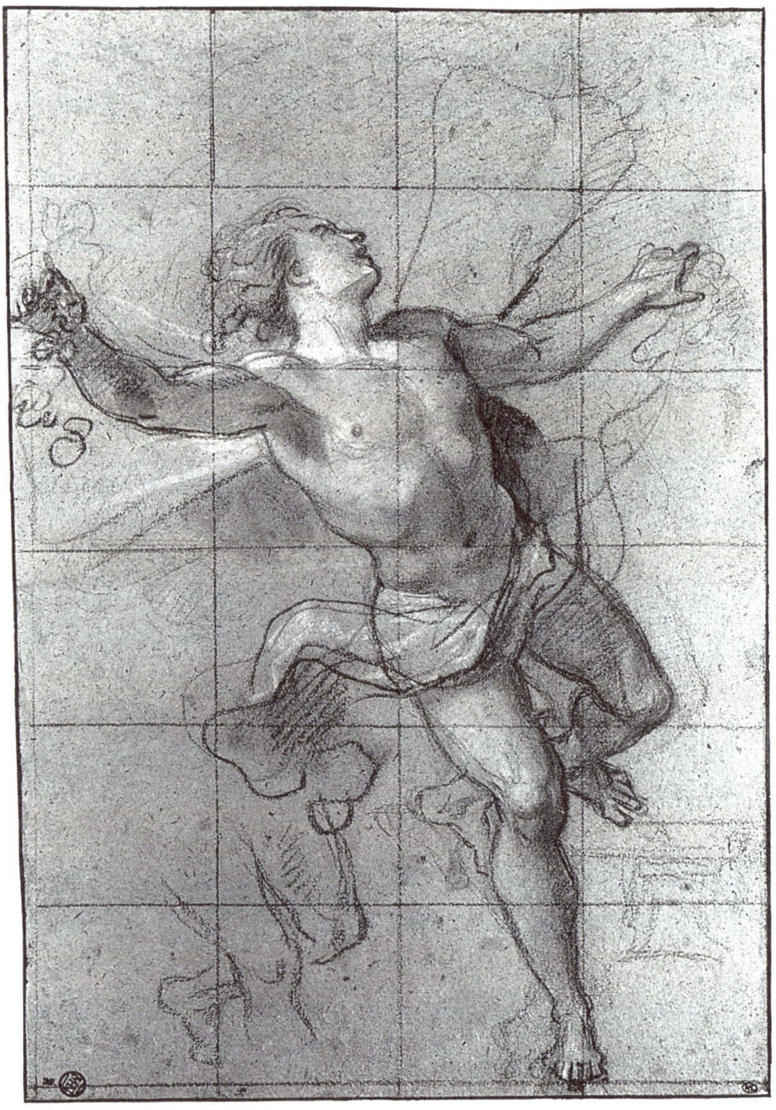

58

The Candido Angel would weigh a little heavier on the ethereal scales, but the vigorous short-folded draperies maker her flight a more energetic proposition in three dimensions, and our viewing position makes us feel she will swiftly pass below us on the left-hand side. We will be brushed by her palm, though the wreath is not for us. Her hair is arranged like twisted horns of hair and the slightest of frowns make us feel she is in doubt of the propriety—by fortuitous mischance—of balancing her weight on the neck muscles of an errant, gesturing male who is a stranger in the sky, and belongs in another element.

The Coypel Zephyr, sustaining the three-dimensional satisfactions of his name and title, is the only male in the fly-past. His limbs vigorously space out the void, left and right, up and down. Perhaps the conventional legitimacies have been upheld. The female is not supposed to entertain such space, her characteristics are to fly with demurer grace. This Zephyr has wings, not of feathers, but of some lepidopterous insect, we could not say a conventional butterfly, more like some bespoken moth. But his body is real and physical enough. Too physical perhaps for the artist to have confidence in those wings that remain, as a consequence, sketched in ambiguity. Such is our notion of insect wings, we feel that the sustaining body must be necessarily small. But smallness or not, this Zephyr is a good example for our purpose, for it has such a positive delight in flying.

A TWELVE-HOUR DANCE

59
After PRIMATICCIO
The Dance of the Hours

A dance up to infinity. And beyond. Twelve heavy females stumping the hours of the day. You can choose yourself who is at twelve o'clock in this uneven hexagonal. It depends on the way you hold the image, for it's designed for a ceiling and any viewpoint from the ground is valid. Which, in itself, is a good omen in the gravity-free, directionless world we are seeking. And if there is no gravity, who needs hours? Isn't time a close relation of gravity? Who is it in Heaven that needs a twelve-hour watch? This group of females needs a watcher, a voyeur. By my account, the six o'clock hour says as much. She is looking straight down at us from her elevated height beyond small breasts, wide hips, and massive thighs, her feet dwindling to insignificance. If you do not lift your feet high in this roundel, they do not exist. All this dancing and cavorting is candidly sexual. Maybe their exhibitionist confidence is bolstered by the fact that they all hold hands without a single breakage in the chain. Despite the mature bodies, they are like small girls making a ring of interlinked hands. Only these children will not fall down. They are supported up there by the vortex of our glance.

They are certainly above us, ringed against the light around the the lip of a volcano whose central fumes have taken some of them away. The thermal risings have wafted their plump, bottom-heavy bodies, against expectations, to higher dance-floors. However, such is the shape and the lay-out of bodies we could be looking at a spinning-top. Spin the top to make the bodies simulate the dance of the hours. Spin them in an empyreal praxinoscope and they will dance. And the cinematograph praxinoscope has been described as both a philosophical toy and a peepshow. The peepshow characteristic will win in this disordered and disorderly can-can of legs to an unheard music. More evidence that, if we cannot fly, if we cannot take flight, we reserve its unexperienced delights for metaphors of sexual desire.

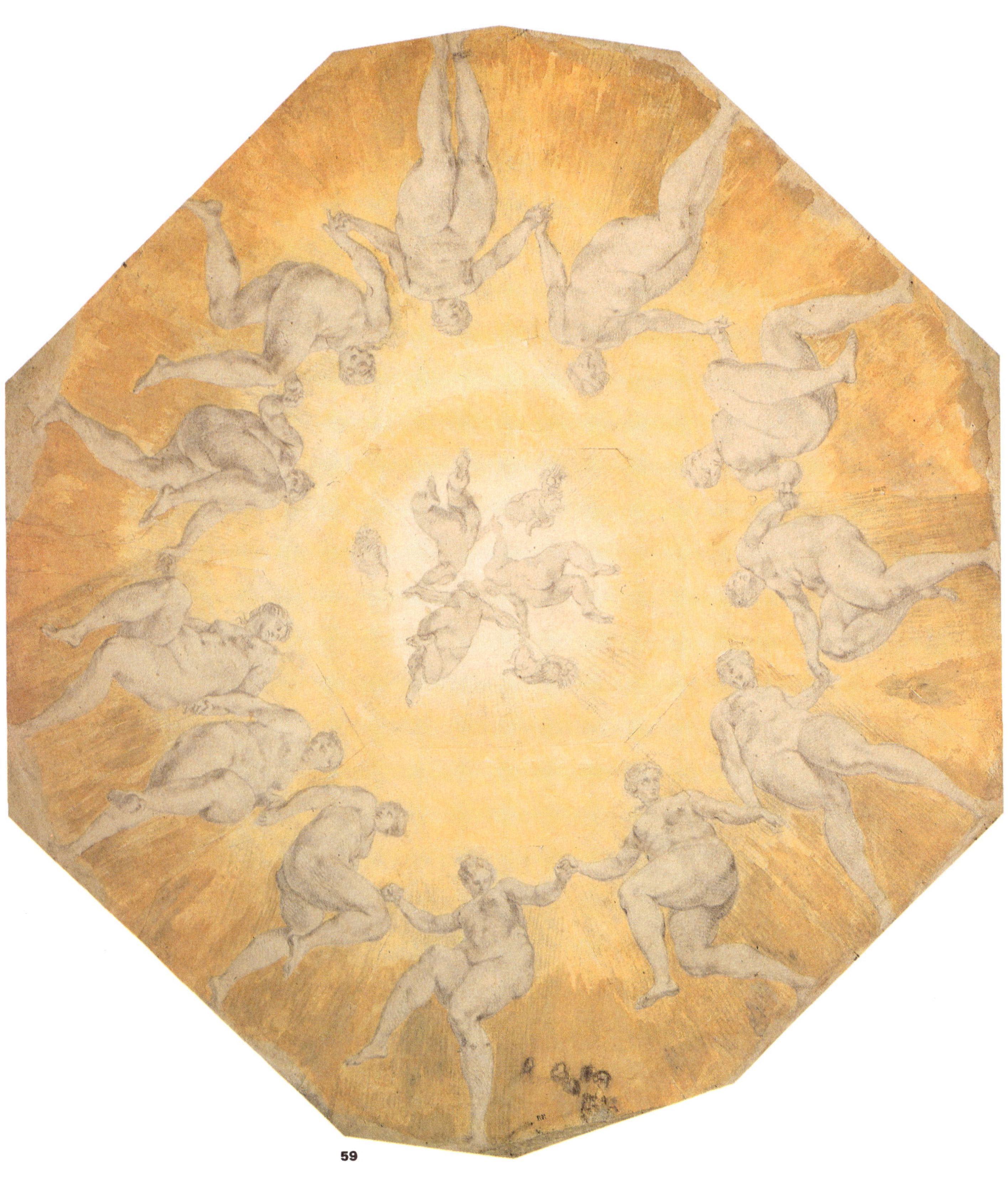

59

The Stratosphere

With God and Apollo in their rightful place in the Heavens, Flight is assured. We have flown out of this world.

60

Antoine COYPEL

God the Father

Have we arrived? Is this the destination of our flight? It might well have been until the twentieth century, when Heaven and Hell have been cosmographically well and truly displaced. Let us ignore mere geography. Let us agree that we have arrived.

God is in his Heaven. A little wild-haired according to Coypel, but glowing. This is a squared-up-for-enlargement drawing. How big does God need to be? At God's feet are the barest suggestion of an accompaniment of putti. They aid the clouds to support God's naked feet. All the rest in invisible support. God's left foot is thrust forward from a strong and agile knee. His one-piece sheet garment, without seams or clasps, stretches across his body and his body's clouds. He is enthroned on cumulus and the aurora of his glory reaches far. On his right-hand side, it reaches out to his outstretched hand. He is a God that directs and upholds, a wild and white-haired Brahmin with a widely expansive gesture to embrace us all. All his visitors. And mostly those who come to stay.

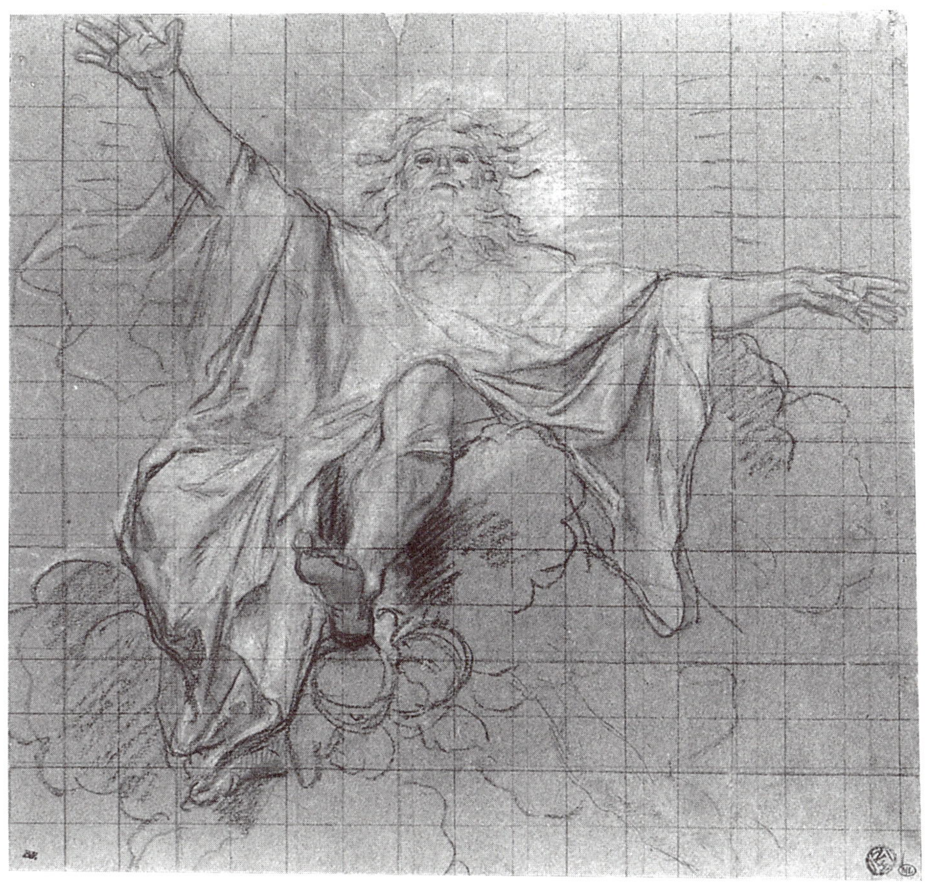

60

61
Camillo BOCCACCINO
The Ascension

The Boccaccino *Christ* is also seen in a foreshortening, making the magestic knee the most cogent physicality. His holy head is a mystery pushed back in the clouds. He is broad-chested, barrel-bodied in fact, a figure held in a cross-wind, broad and heavy with a gesture of some complexity, some part text-book canon-posture of compliance, some part even a suggestion of knowing compromise—"These things are so because they are so." Certainly he offers a statuesque welcome without frightening us.

Thanks to the white highlights, his right hand seems skinned, and the whole is again squared up for translation to a larger and more developed version. His feet are buried in the cloud layer. He is like a figure in dark water. Swirled around by an incompleted oval of which the outstretched fingers of his left hand may be the creator. The placement of navel and nipples are proof enough that man was made in this image. For all the success of a flighted arrival, he has the man-of-sorrows countenance.

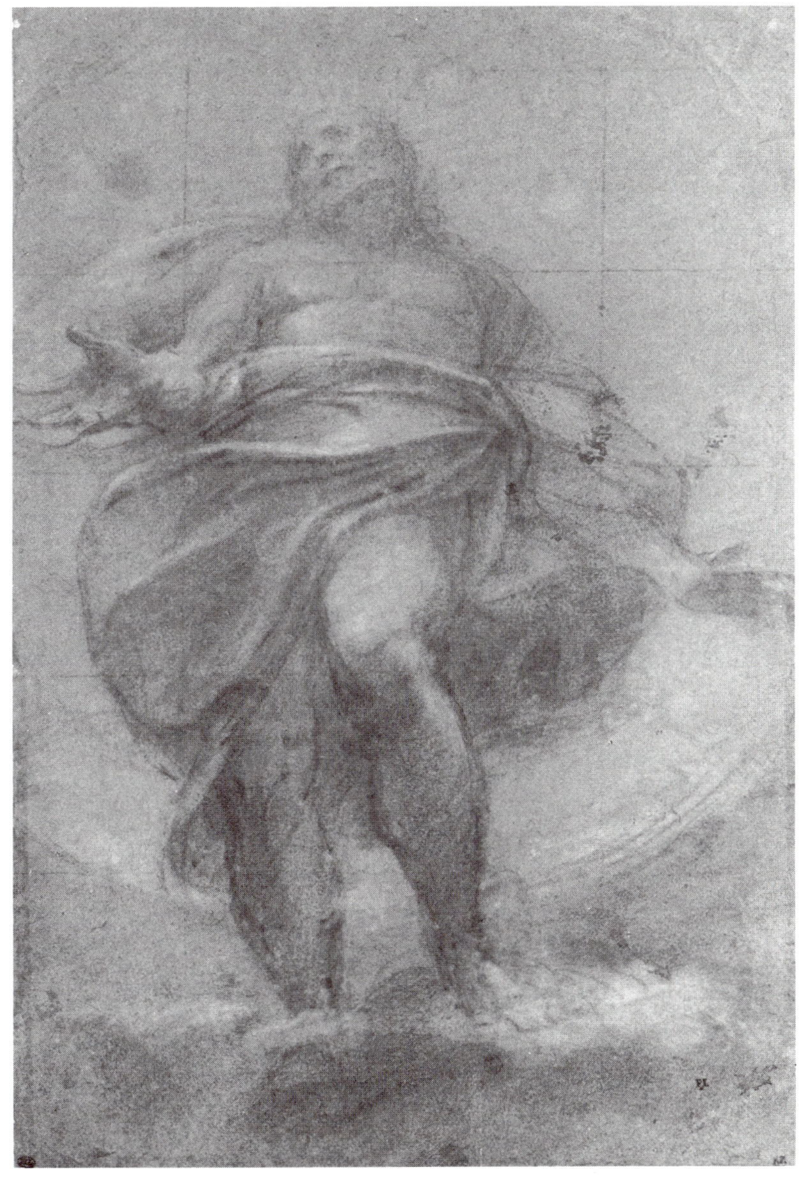

61

62

PRIMATICCIO
God the Father

In the Primiticcio, God is a patriarchal organiser directing the motorways of Heaven in a tumultuous crowd of stuffs and peoples. He makes a rectangular breach in the vapour of the firmament, master of a theatrical space for a rippling blazon of angels whose bodies flee from the centre like planets at the first explosion of the universe.

Above him, Holy Twins, in deep foreshortened perspective, head towards us in identical slanting poses. Viewed from where we fly, they appear as a single double embryonic form. To their right, and westwards from their north (it's important to talk cardinal directions), a slanting flying figure, moving speedily down, complements his opposite diagonal creature, moving rapidly upwards. On God's left, away from his gaze, a company of angels kicking out the length of long bodies, speed away like swimmers making for a distant shore. There is a passage of some earthy immodesty beneath God's feet, where a figure departing straight into the cloud-base, head and upper body already subsumed in cloud, is appreciated only as writhing legs with a cloth for propriety between his legs. On God's right-hand side, is a further androgyne, thighs whipped to nakedness by the flurry of the winds.

Zeus-like, with a Greek straight-nosed face, a right hand held out in benediction, God does not look at us, but at some distant arrivals.

The Christian God was put in his sky-heaven before man knew how cold and barren are the upper skies, before man knew that the air is rarified above two miles high. These men who wanted God above them, willed him to the tops of the mountains they knew of in the Mediterranean. But even those mountains were not the Alps but the Jordan Heights, tempered with earlier mythological mountains of a Greek origin that doubtless lost their snows in summer. And now we know of mountains as lonely, isolated, freezing deserts far from any comforts. Not the place

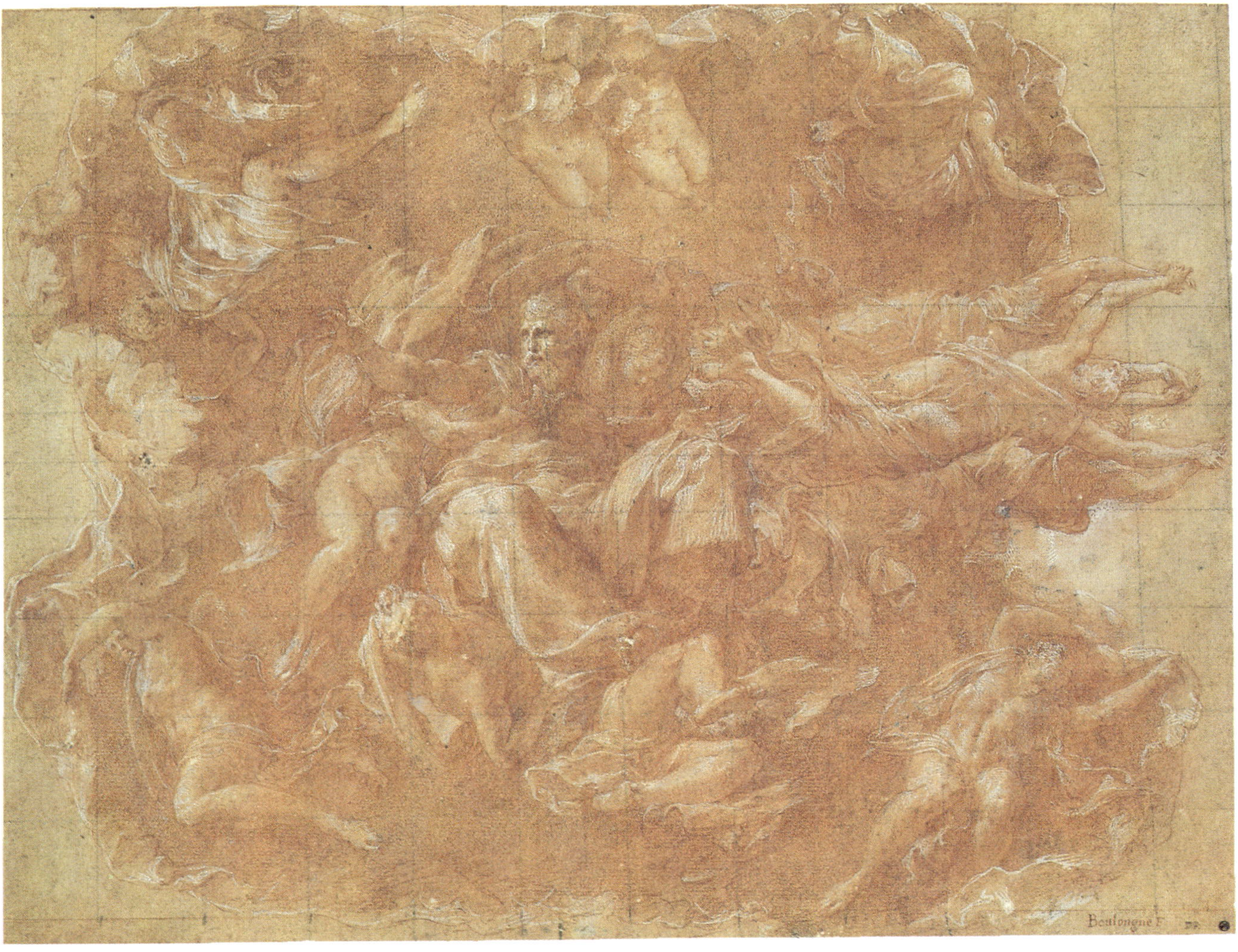

62

for Gods modeled on their makers, man. We have now discovered, too late, that we have relegated the Gods, sacred and profane, to icy realms of tedium.

Clouds seen from earth, or close to the earth, can be glorious. Clouds from high heaven are not so warming in spirit or in temperature. What is God doing up above the clouds far from the earth? Three miles high is too high. The glory of the land retreats to a blur of insubstantiality. Its characteristics are too small at that height to register any value. The excitement of the cloud blanket, however heaped and scooped like an eiderdown viewed in close-up, quickly evaporates. It is cold up here. Is God warm enough?

63
ITALIAN SCHOOL ca. 1600
The Trinity

A relaxed trinity, God the Father, God the Son, and God the Holy Ghost, travelling in casual state in the Heavens, not especially dressed for professional business, and surrounded by a frolicking band of winged putti who fly and dart among the billowing folds of cloth and cloud like butterflies in bushes. The putti are more going than coming, and faces are rarer than buttocks. Two putti, nearly identical in expression, and mirroring one another almost exactly, fly forward enough to greet us with a certain shy precocity.

I make no apology for a delight in describing the little-known drawing. It is pitched in that rare and acute angle of iconographic orthodoxy and familiarity that has due respect for the subject but is not bombastic, not didactic, not awesome, not exhibitionist. In this symmetrical U-shaped composition, God and his son have equal status, and Time, or the artist (or both in concert) have reduced the presence of the Holy Dove truly to a position of Holy Ghost. If we did have problems of identification, the symbolic language is strong. God, bearded and patriarchal, carries a sceptre, and is haloed by the holy triangle, his hand on a transparent terrestrial globe. Sceptre and orb, regal attributes, are offered without forceful demonstration of kingship, God rather proffers them with light apology, most suitable to the role of a travelling grand conductor of affairs. Christ, in his orthodox position at God's right side, raises his hand in conventional blessing, though it could also be the most friendly of casual greetings. Naked to the waist to demonstrate his human corporeality, he lightly carries a banner whose mast is as vertical as the squares on the paper drawn to assist transference to a wall or large canvas. His figure is serene but benign. He is familiar, we saw him last week in the street, his long curly hair caught in the slightest breeze of the travelling slipstream. He is

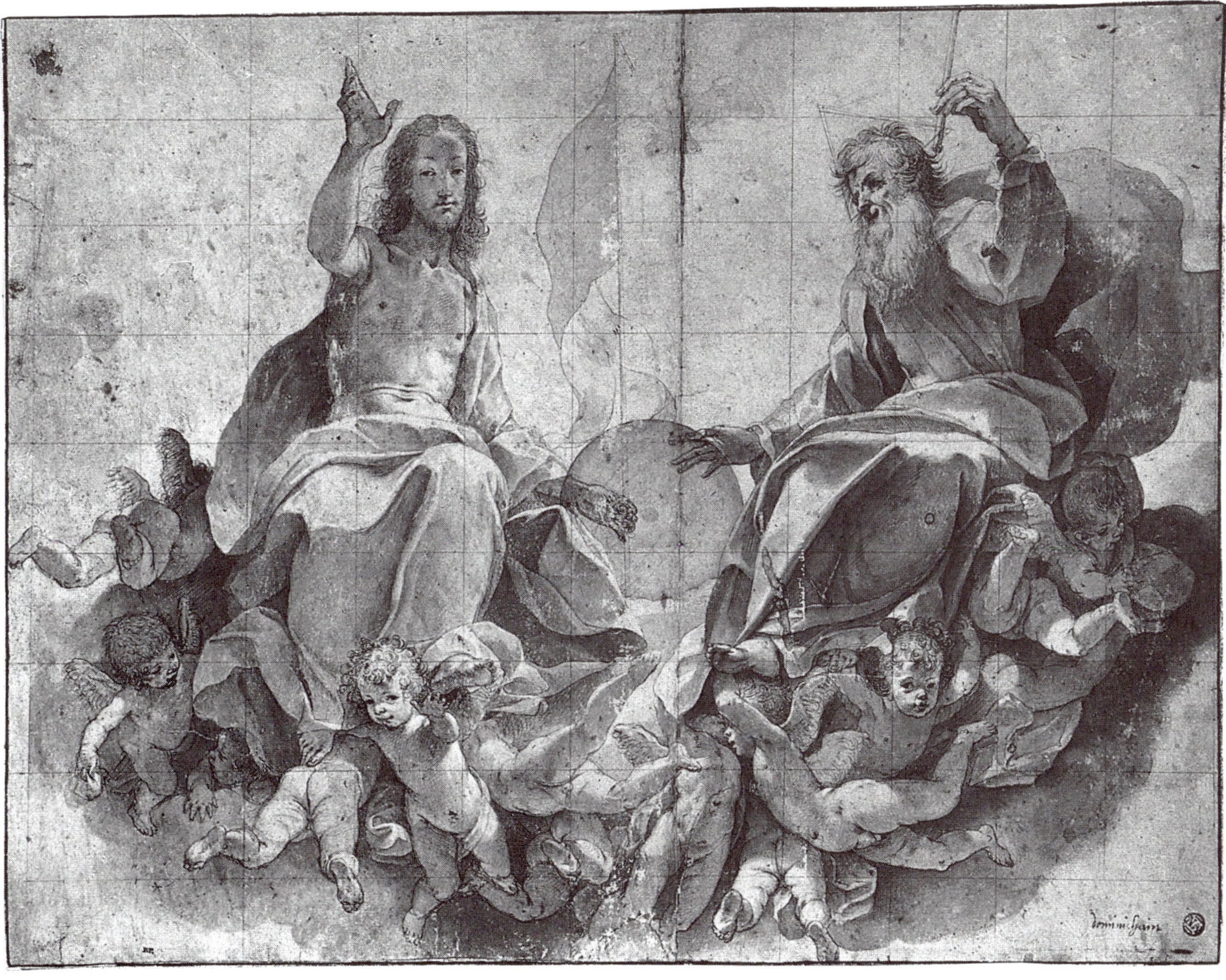

63

lit from below with a light that makes his belly whiter and lighter than his face and his wide forehead very dark.

God is wholly cloaked down to the long wide sleeves with the neat turned-back cuffs, an artist's garment, and one right foot takes the air from among the folds of his voluminous robes. This is a most relaxed depiction of that complex concept of the Trinity, and a vision of most effortless flying that satisfies an expectation as we make a flight out of this world.

64
CALVAERT
The Coronation of the Virgin

God the Father, God the Son, God the Holy Ghost. And the Virgin Mary. And an assemblage of putti, seraphim, cherubim. All in states of grace. And flying. A plethora of flying. We have met the Virgin on her journey to Heaven before, but then she was flying in the lower reaches, here she has arrived in triumph.

Heavenly flight has no age barriers. Flying is unreservedly unprejudiced towards age. Christ has aged no further than his experiences on the cross. God is a traditional septuagenarian. Only Mary, presumably the only natural female in this presently rendered area of sky, is aged beyond the times of her greatest Earthly glory. She has to be older than her son by at least 33 years, by at least 48 years to observe due matrimonial propriety. She is a potential grandmother and all the Marion apotheoic apparatus is here. Crown, aurora, clasped hands, even, perhaps, an emphasis on the Holy Womb, suggestively preconditioned by a navel, the womb's enveloping concavities suggested by the peeled-back hem of the gown making a dark space for nourishment. This might be no superficial surmise when compared with Christ's necessary appearance of corporality revealed by a gown pulled back by a diminuative angel-escort to show the extent of his masculinity.

What other clues are offered that we might seek flying advice? Mary's investiture-crown is shining with the bright graphic-lines, and is softer in outline than the sharp-spiked version worn by God. Is a crown a repository of magnetic power that might draw flying strength? The Dove is an unremarkable ornithological specimen, its wings more heraldic than pragmatic. God has his hand placed on the top of a globe, that globe or sphere which has borne witness as a gravity-symbol in so many of these images. This globe however is no mere passing semblance of a sphere of

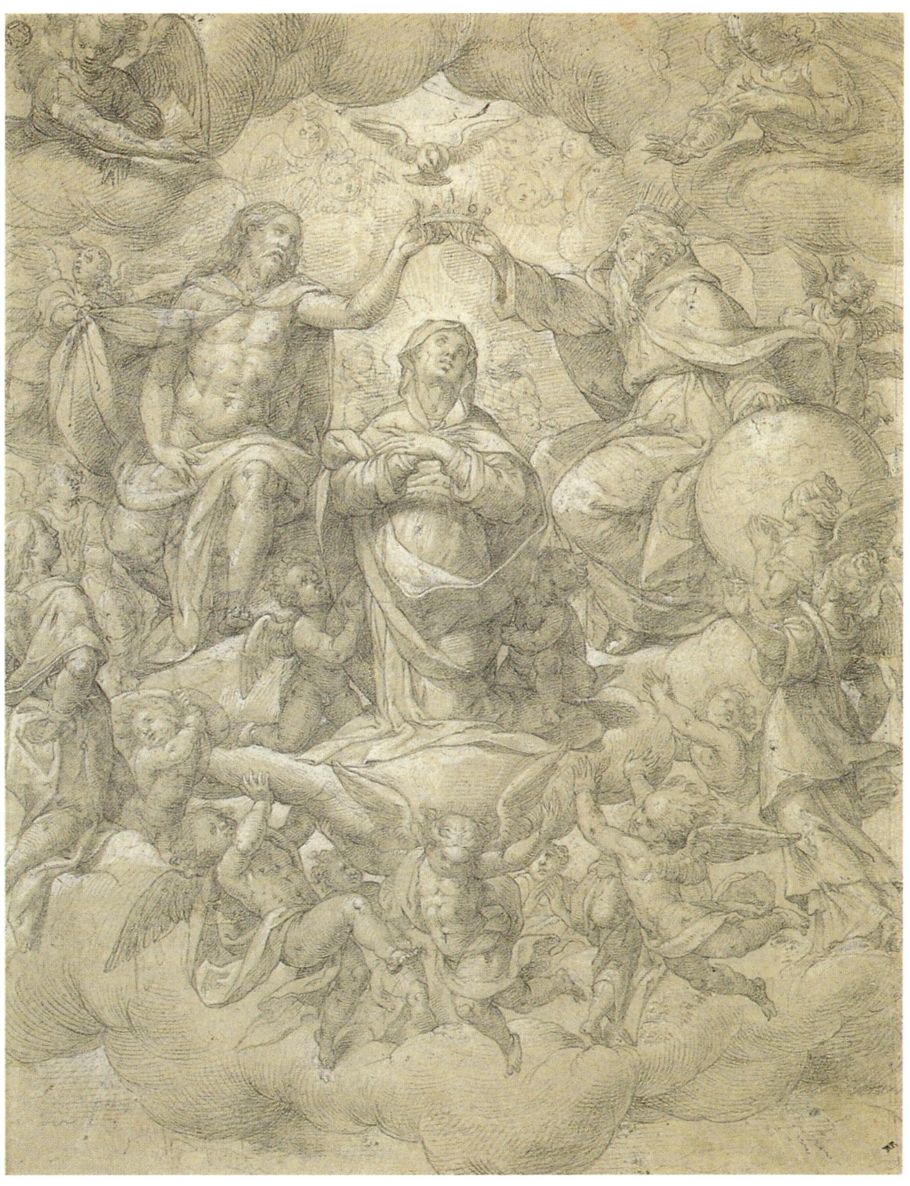

64

Earth for it seems to bear the outline of continents and oceans. And the Virgin rides upon a cloud-platform that seems to take the form of a bivalve shell, a scallop, a cockle, and the angels support the mass as though indeed the cloud was formed in some material way of hardened vapour stiffened in a mould.

Have we now arrived where we wanted to go? Or is the state of flight for itself enough?

65
Antoine COYPEL
Apotheosis of Psyche

66
School of GAULLI
Glory of the Name of Jesus

These are the images of architecture into painting, designs for illusionism, ideal amalgams of insubstantiality to depict the upper reaches of the sky in the tumult of their makers, whether sacred or profane. Such drawings presuppose pierced ceilings, like the oculi in the roof of the Pantheon, but no building could countenance such gaping holes to the sky.

The subjects to be accommodated, worthy of such tumult between substance and vapour, need to be grandiose. In the Coypel, the event is a breathing space in the long-running saga of Psyche's love-lorn search for Cupid. Finally pitied by Jupiter, Psyche is carried up to Mount Olympus by Mercury to be reunited in marriage with her lover, an excuse for an Olympian celebration to which all the many Gods of the Greek pantheon are invited with their respective entourages. Psyche herself is emerging from a cloud cover whose darkness spills into the ceiling space that insists that we are indeed below, and all this desired spectacle is well above our reach, unattainable. So small a drawing for so large a ceiling.

The Gaulli scheme is intended for a greater and more auspicious ceremonial still, a celebration of the name of Christ. An abstracted concept taken from St. Paul's *Epistle to the Philippians* which calls for representatives of all the continents of the earth to assemble. In the completed ceiling painting on the nave vault of Il Gesù, the continental ambassadors are relegated to the niches around the windows where they deport, modelled in white stucco. This central ceiling space, a mighty swoop of vertigo in

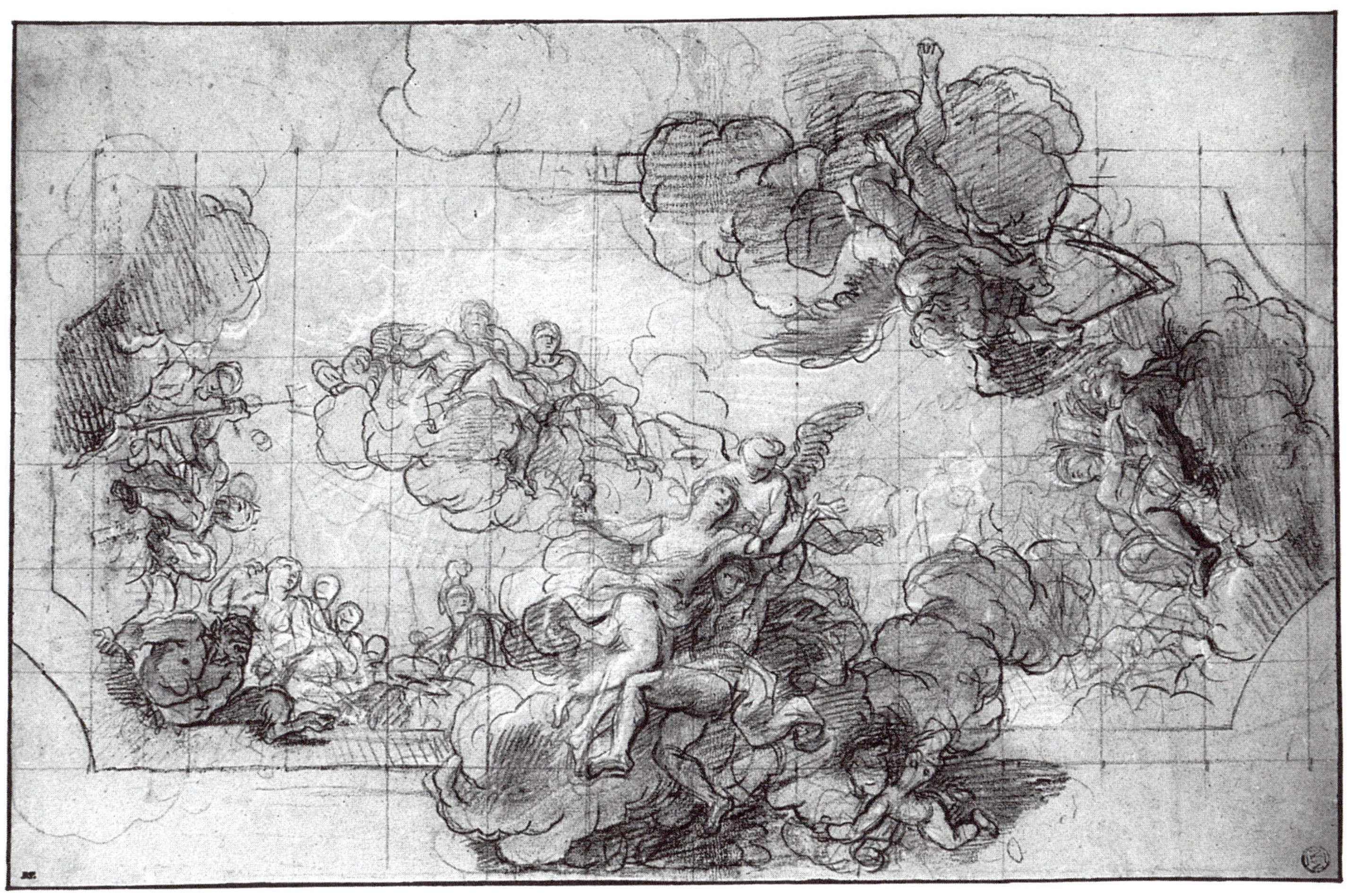

65

reverse, sucks the viewer up from the already high ceiling to the far end of Eternity. Clouds again are the conveyancing vehicles for hosts of angels, their undersides diagonally hatched in this drawing to effect a surprising flatness at cloud bottom. Cloud shadow spills over the repetitive architectural decoration of the ceiling, and this drawing is curious in its necessary plan-flatness, giving little indication that this ceiling will eventually not be flat at all, but a huge curving barrel that will emphasise the distance of the illusionistic painted centre from where we stand on the church floor. Some say the painted ceiling that ensued from this drawing represents the height of the baroque ideal. Afterwards theoretical discourse began to talk of single viewable positions, and illusion restricted to laws of perspective. The drawing hints at a concerted plan, comprehensible in groupings and curves of activity, and easily understood by a rapid glance of the eye. The ceiling painting, by no means showing any increase in compositional complexity, is a different matter, for the scale and the depth of aerial perspectives and the flush and draw of the light, push and pull the viewer into dizzying distances and spaces. If we fly here, we fly in a crowd.

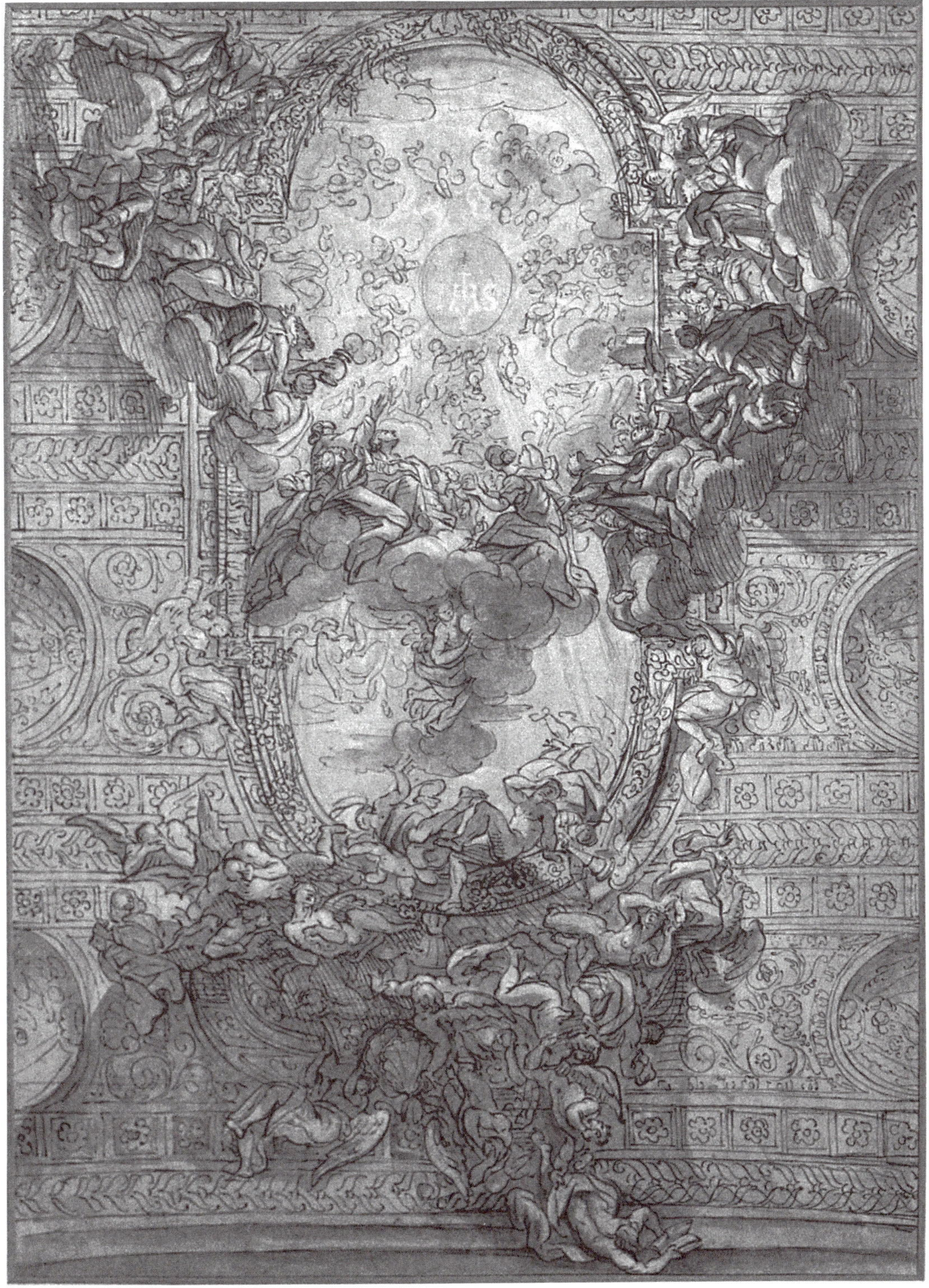

66

67
PRIMATICCIO
The Antipodes

Primaticcio was a lover of flying horses. Thundering across the sky without ground for hooves to beat against. The most curious, exciting, and insubstantial of visions. Horses are heavy, chariots are heavy. There are no circumstances on the ground where such a phenomenon would be realised. Especially in the 1590s. You could stand under a bridge and imagine this full-flighted event rushing over your head, but you could not see it. With painstaking elaboration perhaps you could have stood a horse and a chariot on plinths, piles, and pedestals but what you saw was static, and I doubt whether you could have persuaded the most patient of horses to be so sympathetic to your intent; in all events it would be such a dubious caricature of its orthodox behaviour. Could you have stood under ice and driven a cart across? Impossible. You can't draw under water. I doubt such elaborations. You could have laid under a cart to draw a cart's undercarriage, but that's no inspiration. You could have rolled a horse over, strapped a horse up in the air with a sling around its belly—all difficult and wastefully extravagant gestures which would not have given you the acute observation points you needed. So all, in the end, must spring flying from the imagination. Primaticcio's imagination. It's a good lesson. If horses can fly, then it must be easier for men. Unless there is a correlation here about speed. If a horse runs fast enough, will it take off? Could the same be said about man?

Along with the horse, the flying forces are out. Putti and maidens. Big bottomed, big footed. Grappling with the insubstantiality of the vision is making our senses uncritical, but the scale and proportions of men, women, babies, and horses are constantly changing, and do not stand examination by common sense. Who is interested in common sense, when this vision rushes by? And such is its speed, you can only experience it

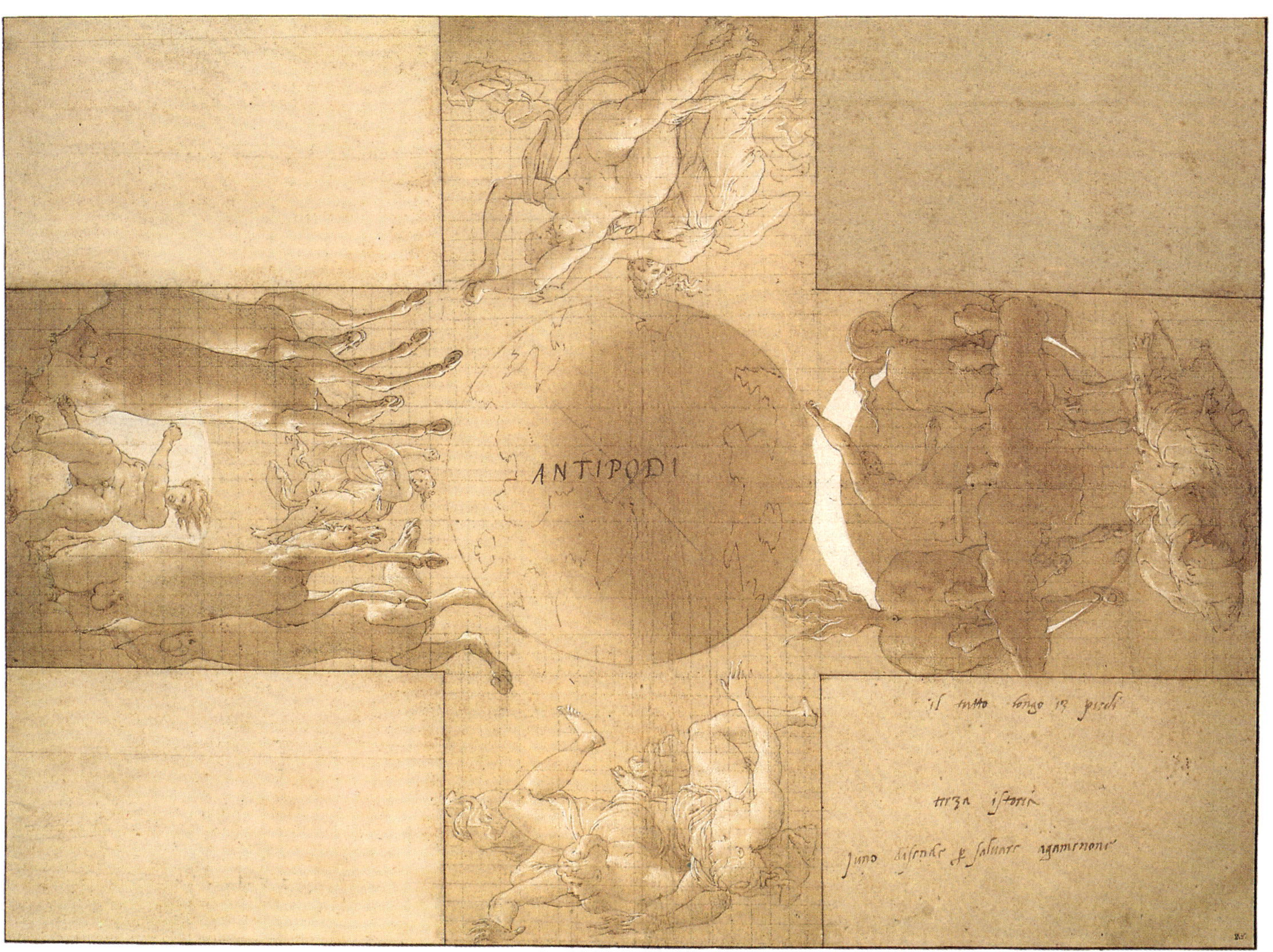

67

for two seconds, three seconds, and must rely on your memory for ever-more. Such a vision of flying exuberance is scarcely ever repeated, and if it should be, with all the sky as a highway, what is the chance it will fly so directly over your head again so that you can identify the horse's sex, and be winked at by a chariot maiden?

68

PRIMATICCIO
The Chariot of Apollo

A schedule, strategy, and scheme for Time and the Sky. From varying viewpoints and with a nice disregard for familiar unities, this panorama at speed unfolds five images in one. The images are relayed in a representation suitable for a ceiling textbook that is to be cosmological, theological, geographical, didactic, and sensuous entertainment. From the left and from the right. From below. From behind. Racing over. Running away. Standing stock still. Allegory, graphic symbol, map, mimetic gesture, idealised heroics, hedonist display. All naturally accommodating to a problem of how to view a ceiling, but, when constructed on paper, in its multi-viewpoint bravura, capable, unlike a ceiling-painting, of being taken in by the eye at a single glance.

Mixed viewpoints are familiar enough now. Unfamiliar then? We can imagine the complaints of dashed unities. The Earth, the Sun, and the Moon are graphisms, splendidly unassociable in scale. Day is Apollo from below, driving no chariot but four sleek-bellied horses lined up for anatomical comparison in chest, belly, thigh, and genitals. These animals, with distant dinosaurian heads and bodies stretched like skinned reptiles, seem a better bet for the amalgamation of the genes of horse and man than the orthodox pattern of podgy centaur. Were Apollo's horses shod? They leap off clouds, but onto what? One out-stretched hoof has disappeared behind the world. Maybe it is their kicking that spins the globe? Are they therefore work-horses on a treadmill?

Across the world, on the other side, Night races from us in an entirely different direction. Away from our faces and into the dark shadow under the smooth bright arc of the moon that is the brightest light in the drawing, brighter even than the sun. Night rides a racing chariot hell-bent over the shrouded body of Morpheus who grips a head with a hand to avoid the

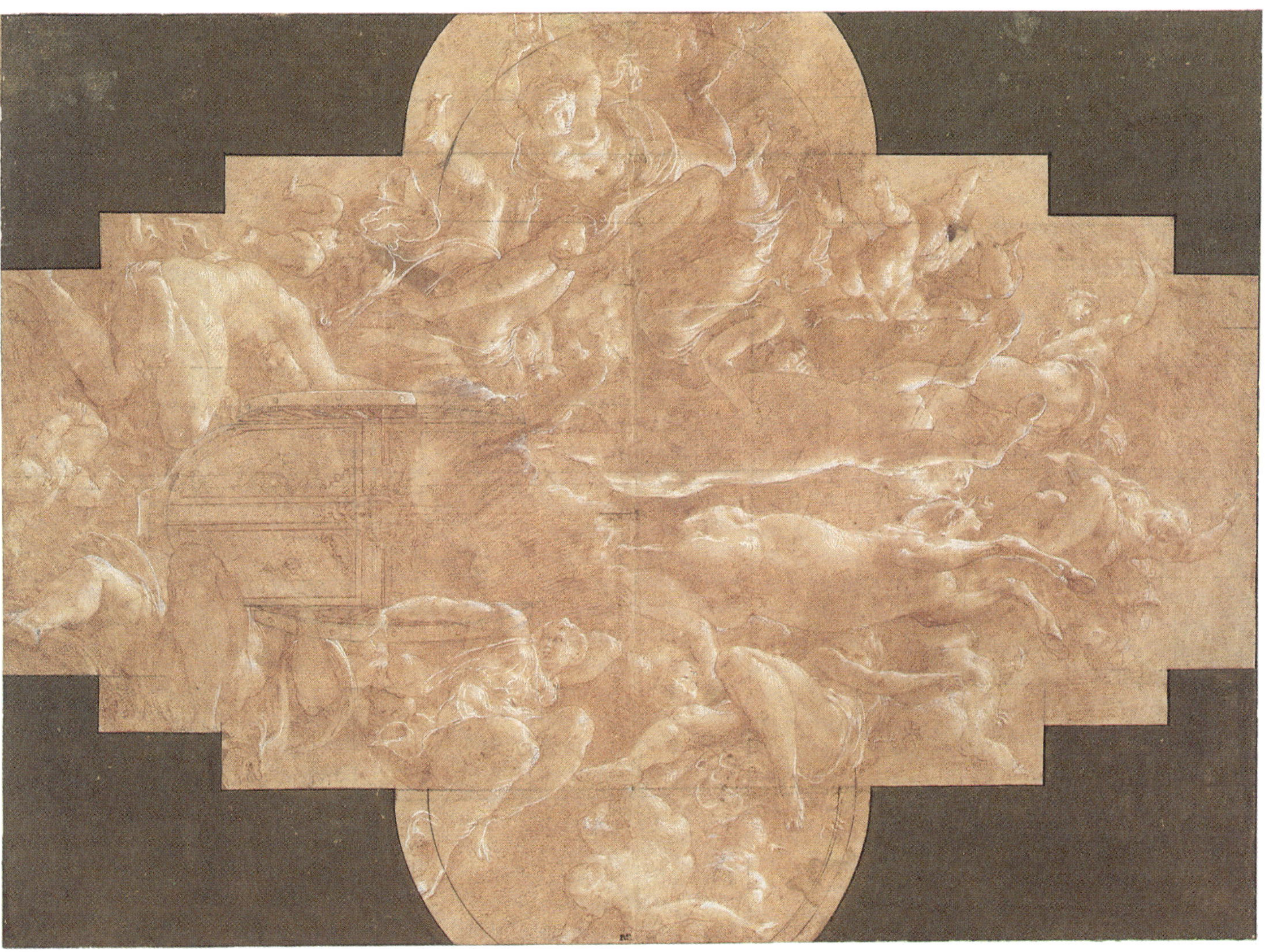

68

flying hooves. No wheels, just a neat seat on clouds. The uplifted hand is
a familiar gesture from a thousand horse dramas, ancient and modern.
No whip. No discernible reins. The figure is surely female; the persistent
bias of the iconography of Night suggests it. So does a suggestion of
breasts. And probably too those neatly-seated buttocks. The example of
the comparative belly anatomy of Apollo and his horses might lead us to
compare anatomy here with three buttocks in a row under the moon.

The other figures are out of stock. Draped and drape-revealed females, reacting with understandable gesture to all this flurried flying, all this lengthening and shortening of shadows, this astronomically central revolving world. Impersonating Dusk and Twilight. Sun-up. Sun-down. Dawn. Evening. Such women keeping their places to the North and South of the globe are reminders of who we might meet, their hip-heavy bodies laughing at gravity. Choosing one reading of this graphic-literal manifestation, may we safely say these women are antipodeans of a new world. Alaskans to the North. Australasians to the South. A wider world. The classical heritage came from a parochial, coastal strip, around the perimeter of the inland Mediterranean sea, alongside the world's smallest continent.

And what of that great globe itself? According to its shadow, it is a globe and not a disc. It is the sphere again that persists in finding a space in so many of these drawings, the ghost of Gravity that haunts this exhibition. But this globe is not exact projection. Possibly we can see an outline of France and Spain stretching up to the Baltic? Or is that wishful thinking in a Greenwich-meridian prejudiced world? For by rights Africa should be an anvil and seems instead to be an archipelago of uncertain land and sea on some private tectonic plate of its own wandering, a Gondwanaland relevant to some mythic past when Atlas was still straining with his problem before moving on to lift other loads.

The Great Fall Begins

Hubris. Over-reached, the aspirations of those who wanted to fly are dashed. The Great Fall out of the sky begins.

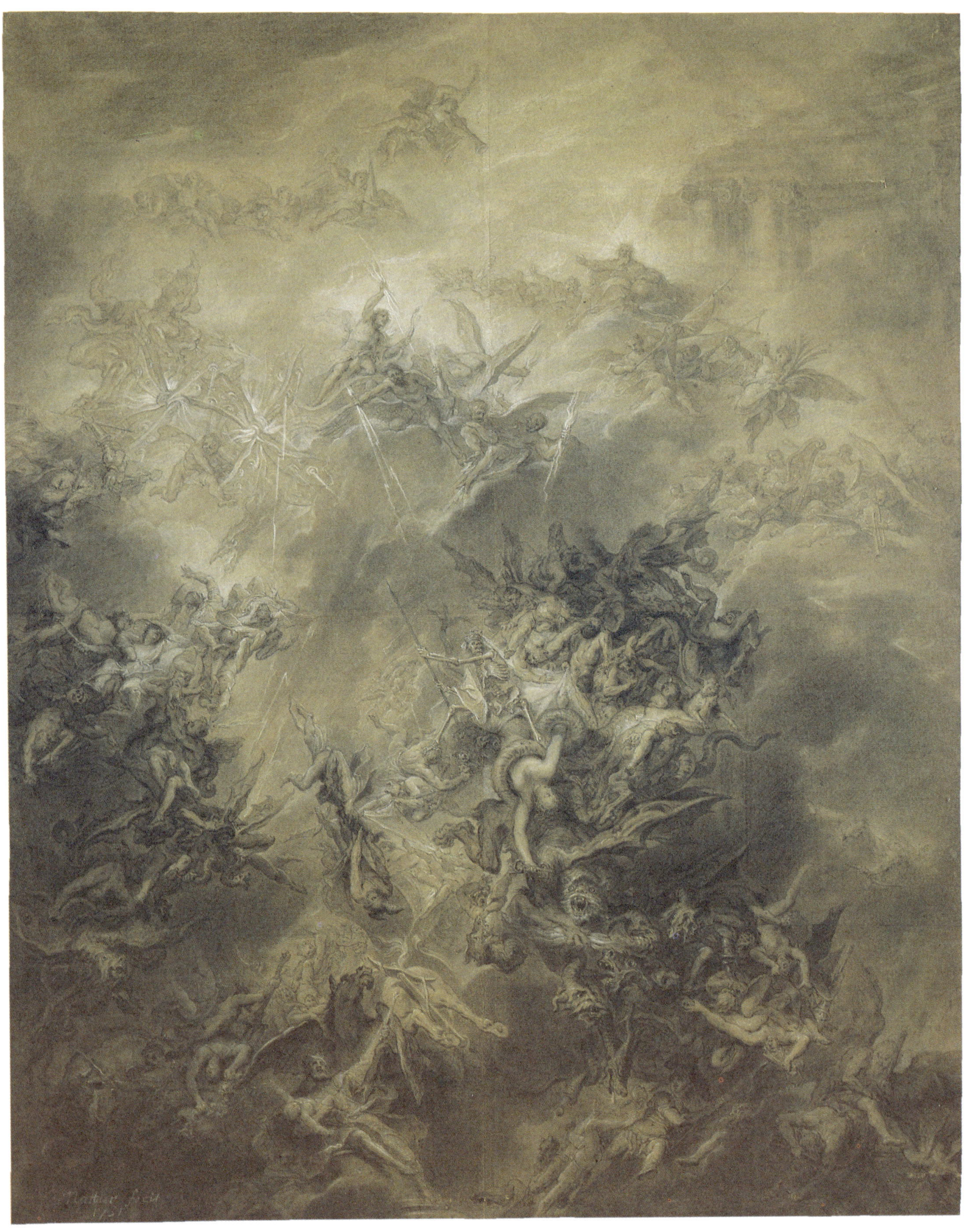

69

And so the Great Fall begins. Spilling out of the sky. Gravity as the Great Leveller. Newton has offered us a greater metaphor than he knew was possible when he sat under his apple-tree and watched the fruit fall. Is it more than a coincidence that he was sitting under an apple-tree? Think how the imagery would wither if he had witnessed, not the portentous fall of an apple, but the insignificant fall of a plum or a pear?

What can be done to alter gravity's insistence? The slope and angle of Fall can perhaps be engineered. Perhaps the pace of the Fall can be very temporarily ameliorated, and thus Death just a little postponed, disintegration just a little temporarily checked. Or only as much as a sky-diver can check or alter it. A sky-diver can steer just a little, slow his speed just a little, by spreading the greatest area of his body out against the uprush of frictional air. But he cannot rise one iota, and he knows that if all goes as he planned it, then he can finally float to the earth's surface on a parachute. It was not the prospect of ever-increasing speed that made man rush headlong to test the speed of sound itself and maybe to equal the speed of light. It was his ability to stop at will. A powerful brake is the greatest encouragement to fly faster. All of which is far beyond the conscience of these poor biblical devils cast from heaven into the great eternal abyss.

Having succeeded briefly in flight, they now tumble out and tumble down. Such an event should not be a surprise.

Finally, too, the bluff is called about this suspension of disbelief about the clouds. Finally, as we knew it would be, the insubstantiality of the clouds is recognised. The clouds finally break and foment and crack. But they break and crumble where God wants them to.

It is an awesome sight, repeatedly drawn and painted. How long did it last, this Fall of Angels? Was it all over in an hour? Or did it take days, weeks, years? Is it still going on?

Upwardness and downwardness have no correctives. So universal is the reality and the metaphor that they meet uncontested. No artist has contradicted the direction signs. Even in a negative world, even among outsiders, even among antiheroes, even in Australia, up and down are wedded irrefutably to plus and minus, gain and loss, flying and falling.

The palaces of Heaven, according to Nattier, have Ionic columns. They stand firm, whilst yards from their base, the clouds dissolve. God has only to stretch out a hand, and inches from his throne, the clouds become insubstantial and the downward journey begins. Then God can sit back, issuing corollary directives, as the screaming disappointed host slip by to the bottom-most pit. Is the Great Fall the beginning of Hell? Did Hell exist before this event? If it did not, then the Great Fall is the combined big bang theory of theology and cosmography together. Nattier would argue with this, for in his drawing of the Rebel Angels, the Fall does not seem so much of a beginning of Hell, for there are devils abroad already. And with them Death. Serpents and skeletons are present to assist the downward path of the disgraced angelic host. As if gravity was not enough, the evil have to be pulled. To show them, and us, what they are to leave behind, the accoutrements of heaven are there. There are bows and arrows, trumpets, a harp. God lives like some baroque potentate, for with their fall, the angels take their furniture (his furniture?), shod horses, flags, and halberds into the abyss. The mould of the sexless angel is disregarded, women stretch without ambiguity to make sexual suggestion stronger than fear, and they scream like they practised how to scream in the seraglio.

In La Fage, there are no accoutrements, just naked bodies and just masculine ones; the strict laws of a masculine heaven are obeyed. One mass of the damned cluster together as though tied to a meteor. Are we to think that as they fall, they transmogrify? The angel wings of Heaven transform into butterfly wings that transform again into the wings of a bat, because daytime butterflies are beautiful and nocturnal bats are not. But God made bats and butterflies. A spinal column, overcome by the

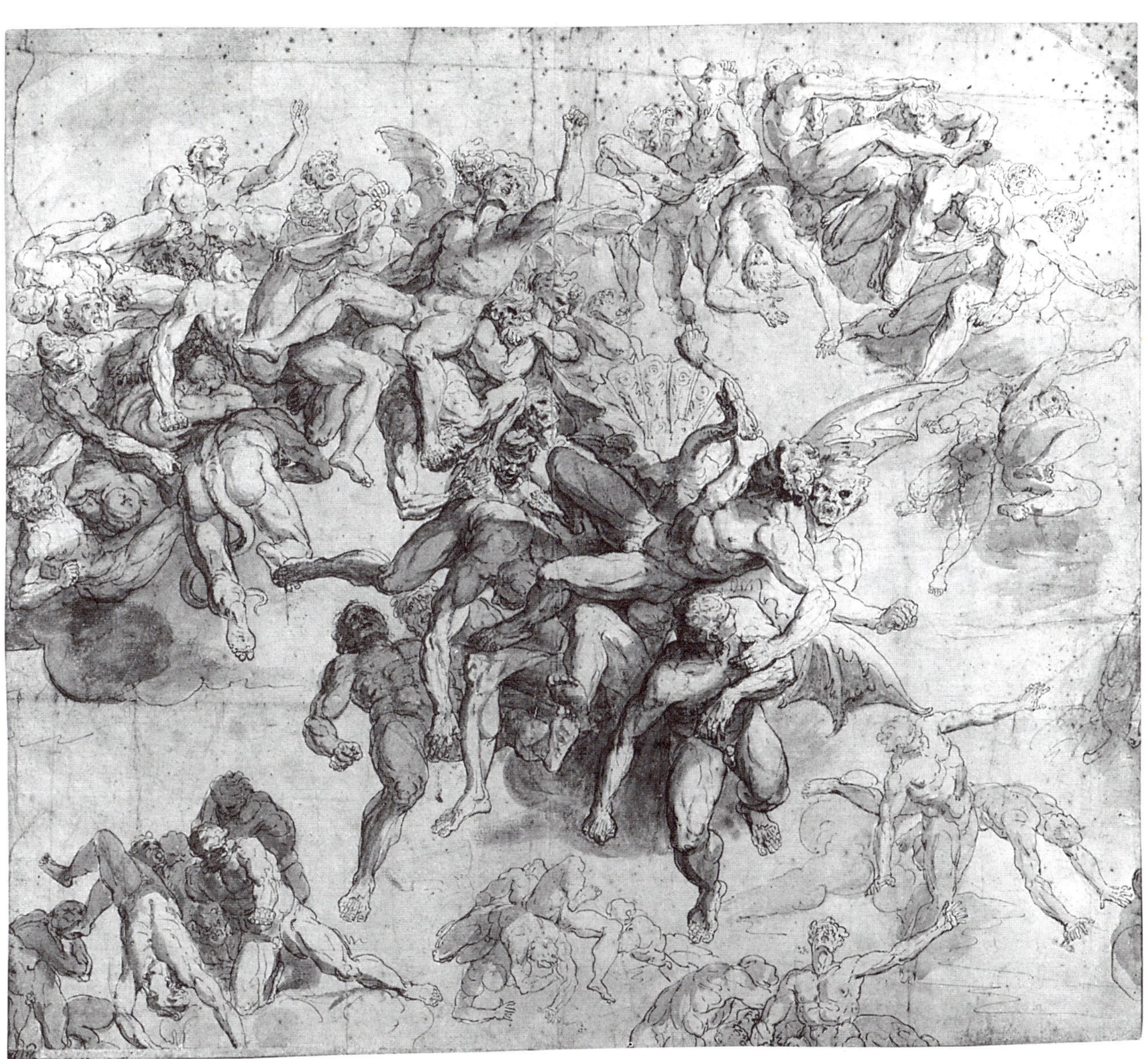

70

disgrace of the Fall, lengthens and grows a tail. Soon it will be wholly serpent. Heads sprout horns; soon they will be horn-headed monstrosities. Head holding, hand biting, the first time such gestures of the melodrama of grief are to be experienced is on this savage trip down to the abyss. Even whilst falling, there is time to consider the future, because the transformation of your body gives you enough material to suggest the nature

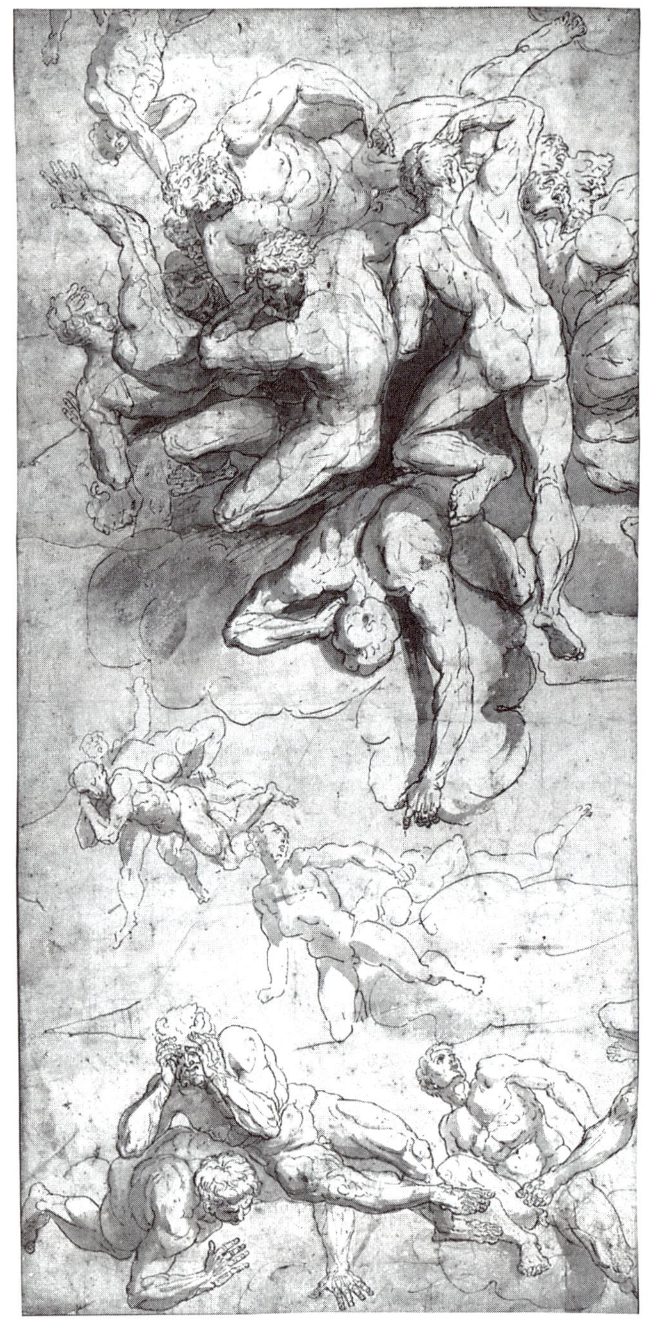

71

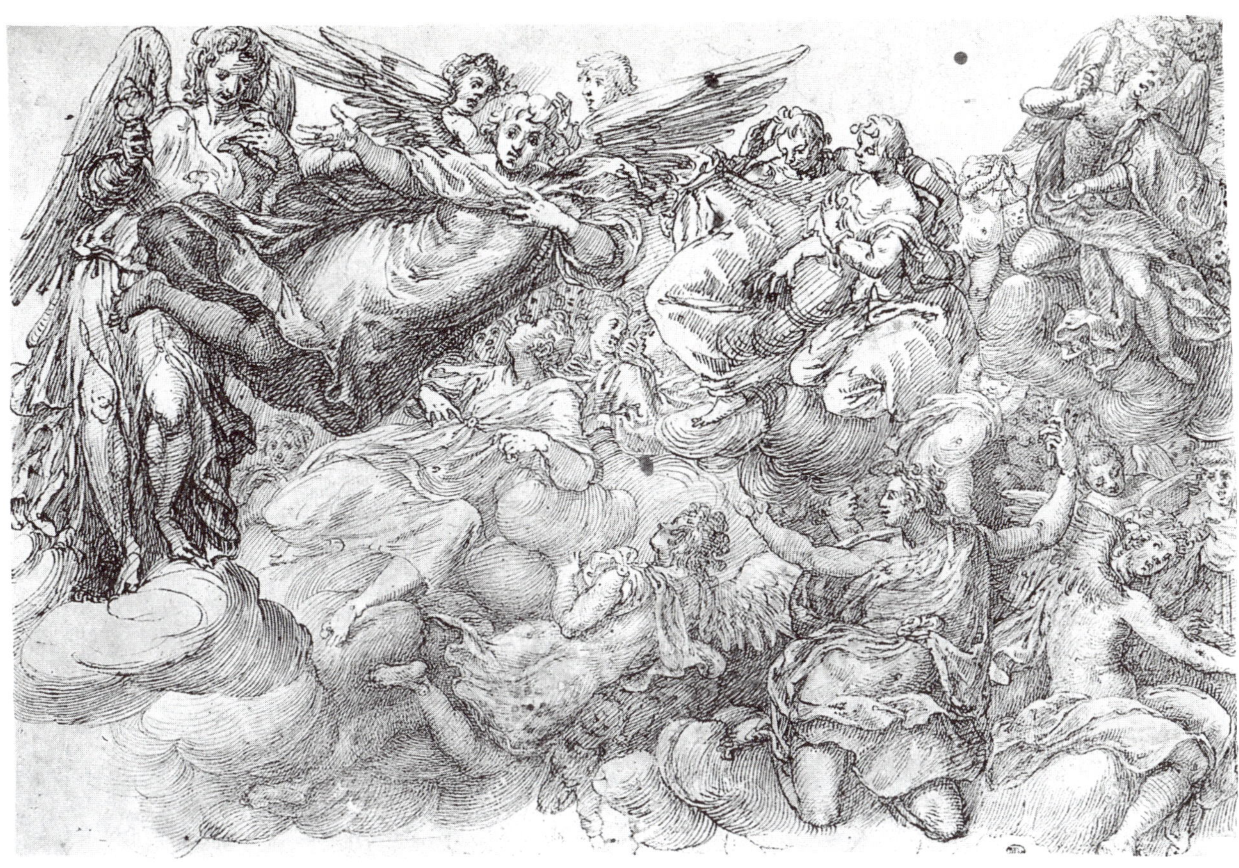

72

of the place you are falling to. They are certainly not falling to a better place. Falling is indubitably a punishment.

Commodi's *The Fall of the Damned* seems a milder activity. The renegade angels here are distributed on a stepped landscape of comfortable cloud. Many of them still sit as though at picnic, their bottoms on the cloud base. Their resistance to the avenging angels is no more effective than much exhibitionist snarling and angry fist-waving and the two-fingered salutation which they must have just this minute learned, for who would have taught it to them when all was peaceful in Heaven? Surely the avenging angels are not going to be intimidated by such resistance? The malingering devils seem an ineffectual bunch, bruisers of little danger value. It is God's angels who are the true aggressors. With thunderbolts and flame-swords, they are like gauleiters in angel uniform sent to dispel rowdy drunks. The winged avenging angel is a borrowing from the figure of Roman Victory by the Christians adopting and adapting the imagery of their persecutors. There is no Old Testament reference that is keen, eager, and emphatic to stress wings. If the Tobias angel had been equipped with wings, Tobias would have recognised his wrestling companion for what he was, and as a consequence, changed theological history.

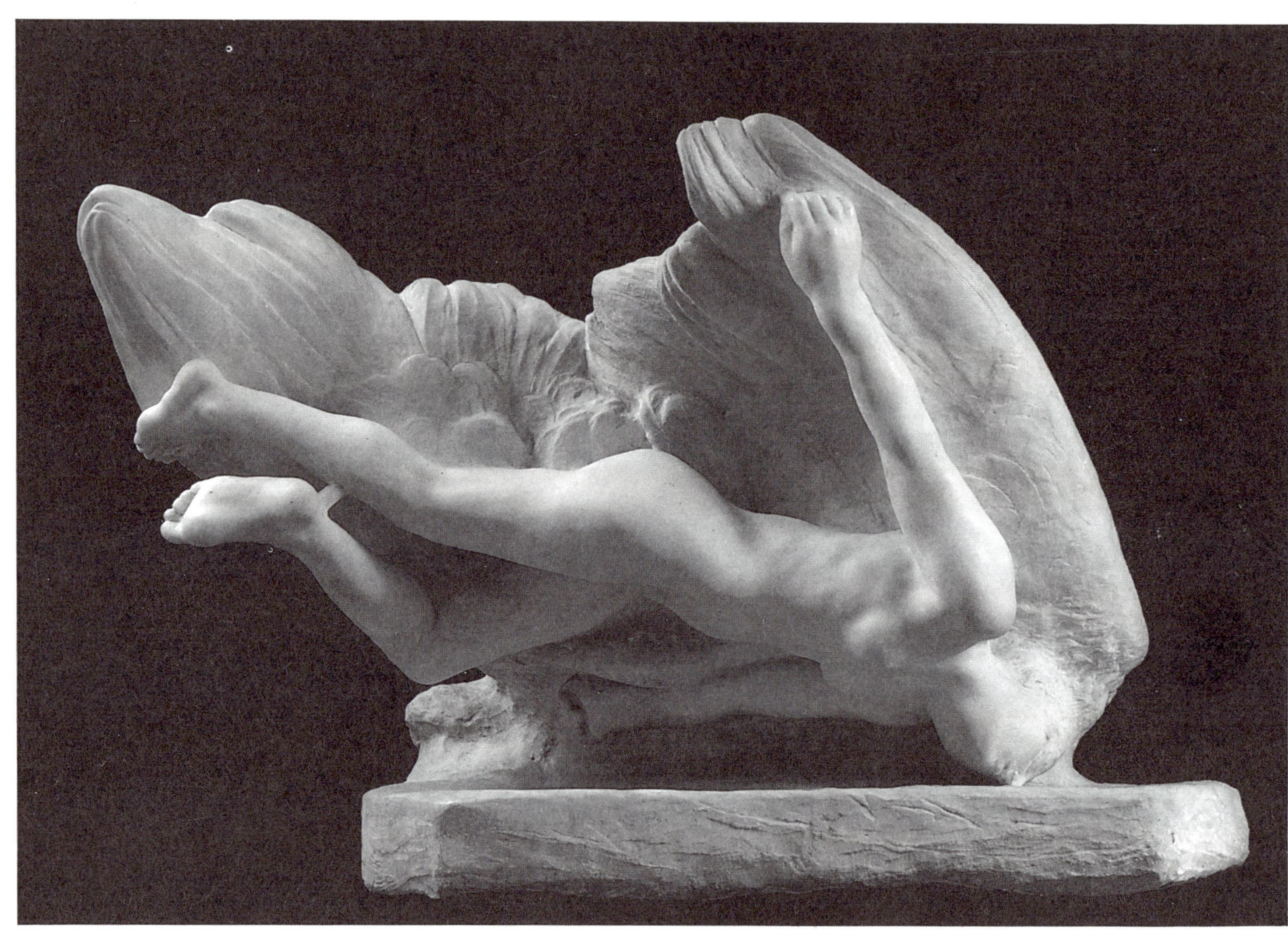

73 RODIN, *Illusion, sister of Icarus*

The Disgraced

*To take the Great Fall as material for personal example of hubris is not so easy.
But there is no shortage of examples that make the identification simpler.*

74
Gustave MOREAU
The Fall of Phaethon

75
SUBLEYRAS
The Fall of Phaethon

76
FLORIS
The Fall of Phaethon

In any pantheon of flyers, you would have to include Phaethon, closely associated in a mechanical eighteenth-century age with his own namesake cart, the phaethon; not so much a cart, more a carriage, a lightly-sprung open two-wheeler used by young bloods to travel fast on the newly tar-macadamed roads.

After Leda the bird-lover, and before Icarus the bird-lover, came Phaethon, the most arrogant of the aeronautical triumvirate; he sought to attempt flight without eggs or wings or feathers, or copulation with a chicken, or any reliance on mortal contrivance, brace, crane, harness, inflated pillow, or enlarged sunshade. And certainly without an ornithological treatise in his hand or in his head. He sought to fly by thievery. Phaethon sought to fly by stealing the chariot of the Sun with its fiery wheels and sun-bred stallions that leapt around the world bringing dawn and taking sunset.

Phaethon kept looking up at the sky. He was a meterological novice. The sky was empty and uniformly blue. Except in the early mornings before the sun rose, when a pale grey mist lifted off the beaches and settled over the sand-bars out at sea, and then evaporated inside ten

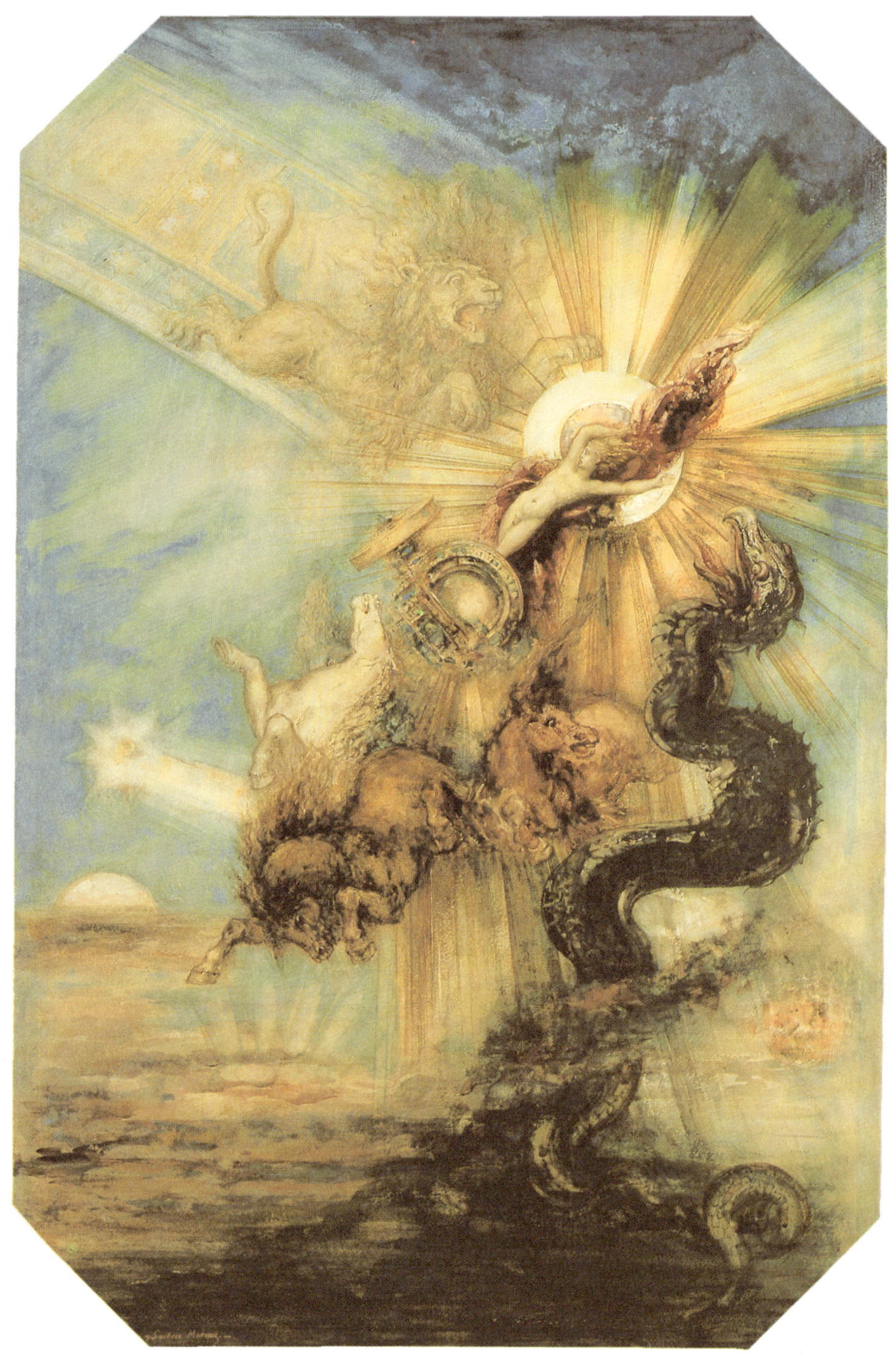

74

minutes. High up, a mile high, perhaps two miles high, hundreds, maybe thousands of pale grey birds flew south, like pages of flickering paper let loose from a small book caught up in a wind above a bonfire. But birds were not weather.

Phaethon waited impatiently all night on the highest mountain and when twilight showed the imminent arrival of day, he leapt to seize the trailing reins. Here was excessive arrogance to be punished with due rewards. For Phaethon could not control the flying horses, could not brake the fiery wheels, could not even hold the lashing reins. Encountering the scorpion of the zodiac, the horses panicked, and the chariot was out of control, scorching the earth, set fair to embroil the planet in flame. Jupiter applied the brake—a thunderbolt—at Phaethon's heart. It entered his chest, searing the flesh, blackening the nipples till it charred them blue-grey and then a powdery white as though they were natural metal conductors, the button terminals fashioned deliberately to carry a legitimate electric current. Phaethon's shiny teeth clamped over his tongue and he fell. A fine hubristic downfall, steeper than ever plummet sounded, steeper than Icarus's gliding collapse in a pillowfull of feathers. No smooth declining trajectory, much more than a gravitational disaster, for Jupiter's thunderbolt forced Phaethon at the greatest imaginable speed to smash the earth. Who could find his body cratered in blood, charred with fire, blasted to the bone? Some said he splash-dived into the River Po. Don't believe it. Water is exclusively reserved for Icarus's gravity-driven corpse.

Here is a melodrama. An example to all would-be flyers, pilots, aviators, and aviatrix, an excessive example of over-reaching. This man should be made an example of. He is the archetype who thinks speed to be an aphrodisiac and wants to drag all with him to certain crumpled doom against a rock or tree or signpost. This sort of young man is always in a hurry, a wild chaser, nervy, dashing, elegant with long ringlets, thin fingers, bad teeth, gum disease, who would never eat a regular meal, so determined was he on quick rushes to be on the move, damaging the paths on Mount Olympus with sudden skids and turns of speed, scaring sheep and old men walking the foothills. This phaethon creature ran forwards and sideways, and backwards if necessary, his long legs fitted into bony ankles and bonier feet. Boniest of all were his toes.

If you had to allegorise this creature, not finding his charred body, but needing a personification, find some half-way handsome lad, give him a garland of two wooden spoked wheels and a wreath of flame-coloured rowan-leaves as attributes, and scratch him from front to back with a

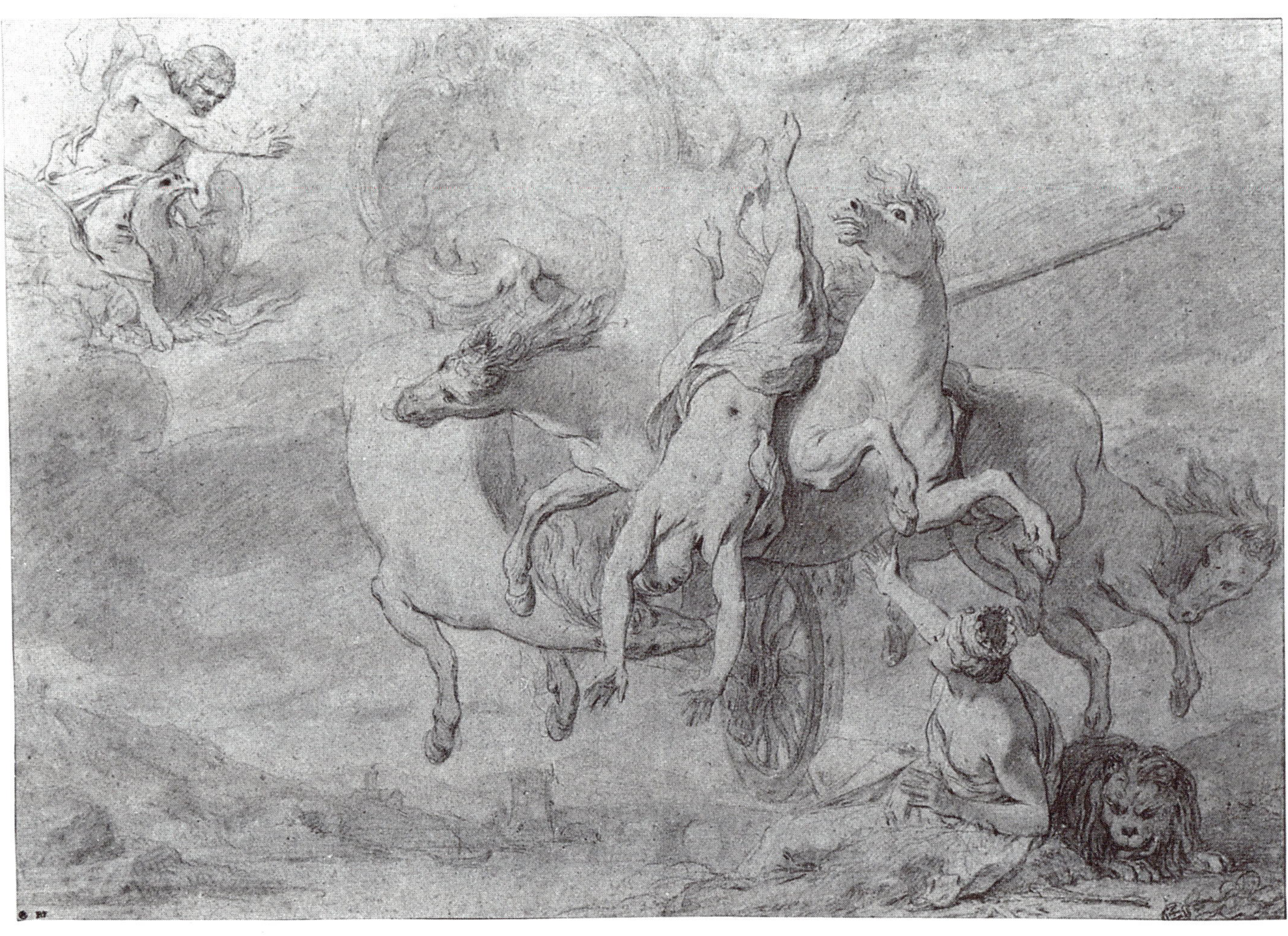

75

thornbush to indicate the speed he had travelled such that the invisible gritty atoms of air had marked him like glacier-held pebbles scratch a softer rock. And flash him all over with a large smokey lamp till his skin bubbled and blistered, to simulate his brush with the forces of a fast earth re-entry. Stand him on a cross-roads, patron of crashes and speeding, his license forever endorsed.

Moreau plunges Phaethon out of the sky at the confluence of serpent and lion, and illuminates him in a blaze of straight-lined dazzles. They contrast violently with the serpent's curves and the lion's roar. They could be made of wire lengths, organised like short straws. Phaethon was the victim of a straw-poll. A conspiracy of those who dared to challenge Apollo chose him as their champion. Many have challenged Apollo. Marsyas was another unworthy candidate. What was it about Apollo that they took him on, at such risky odds to themselves? Marsyas was skinned alive and now Phaethon drops to earth like a scorched stone. Moreau's chariot is a tangible vehicle, unlike others in Apollo's stable and garage. Perhaps its design is useful for us. We could perhaps construct this one from the correct materials. However, with Moreau, it looks as though, not just the experimenting Phaethon comes to grief, but also the four horses and the thick-wheeled chariot.

Floris is keen not to accentuate the mighty drop from heaven to earth. He makes the distance some few yards but nonetheless fearful and damaging—what difference if we fall fifty feet or five miles, since the body has no resistance to the drama of hitting the ground at either height? A man falling over in his own height can damage his skull. What curious creatures we are that gravity has crept up on us so forcefully. When it is time, in the near Future, for schoolchildren to compare planet gravities as though they were comparing atomic weights or the efficacy of their footwear, what differences of the state of life on each planet will each comparison make. If we were freed a mere three percent less of gravity, the shape of our heads, the structure of our bones, the speed of the fluids that shift through the body, would all be so different. At ten percent less of insistent gravity, we might not recognise ourselves. When the serpent was originally created on this particular planet, was gravity a lesser thing? Floris's Apollonian chariot has a shell structure and rimless wheels whose spokes go thudding on the empyrean clouds, getting sensible purchase on that intractable material. And a proportion of the world is there to witness the hubris, including a river god with a startled reed crown and maidens who hurry fearfully aside. The horses are already disassociated from the cart. Here at least is evidence of the thunderbolt-bearing Jupiter riding on his eagle, the eagle of Ganymede's abduction, the eagle of Prometheus's torment.

Subleyras has a Phaethon swoon-diving amongst horses in a space that ambiguously denies much danger since there seems to be such little room between sky and earth. Phaethon's head sees death approaching and his arms and hands are stretched down already to welcome and anticipate it. But so ambiguous is the space of falling and the depth from cart to land, perhaps he hopes to land on his hands, turn a quick somersault, and

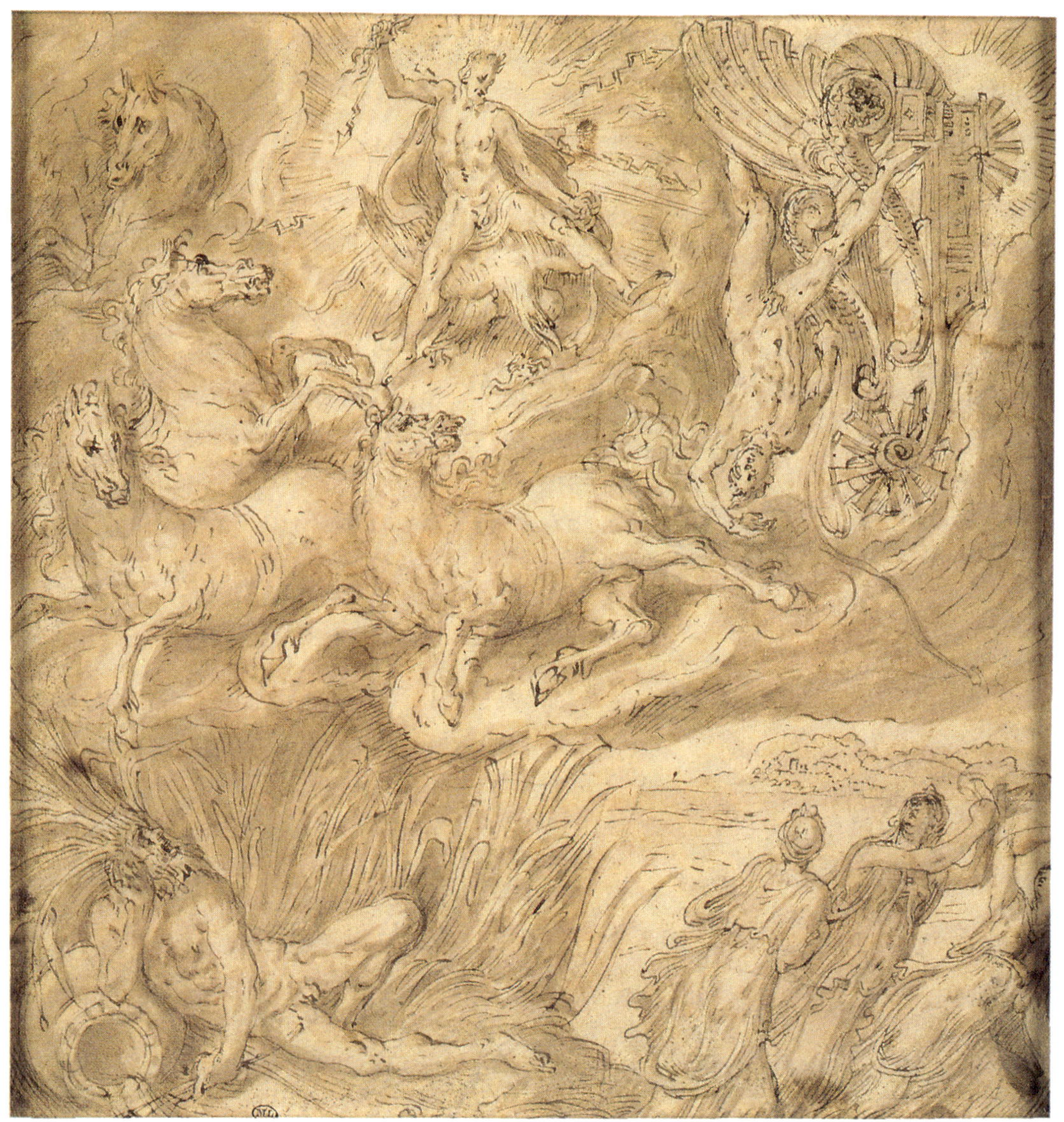

76

saunter off to breakfast in the town by the lake, saying nothing to the townspeople for fear of ridicule. Despite the drama in the sky, the lion sleeps. And what of the crowned matron? Is she opportuning, begging alms, or merely dramatically outlining the path of the fall? Can she really demonstrate shock and surprise from such a comfortable sitting position?

77

Giulio ROMANO
The Fall of Icarus

78

BLONDEL
The Fall of Icarus

Icarus is the most popularly over-mighty. A man with wings made of feathers stuck together with wax, obviously the product of much ornithological examination. What birds did Icarus choose to examine? Straightaway, we ought to say the albatross. Ever since Coleridge, the albatross is a bird of some omen, a bird of some hubris. However, it is unlikely that Icarus ever saw an albatross. He would certainly have chosen a bird with a large wingspan. Probably a high-flying bird seen through his father's optical glass, because Daedalus, his father, is bound to have invented an optical glass; some bird of prey circling on the thermal up-currents, riding down from the Urals and Siberia into Africa by way of the land isthmus of Macedonia. Or, by land and sea, hopping across the Greek islands and Crete, to Egypt. Maybe Icarus was familiar with vultures. He no doubt was familiar with storks, carrying, or not carrying, babies like stuck frogs on their impaling breaks.

Looking for sympathic magic, bees fly. Maybe their honey gives them lift-off. And bees make wax. So, with wax, Daedalus stuck feathers to the chest and backbone of his young, seventeen-year old son. How old was Icarus? We cannot tell from his bones because they have never been found. You can tell the age of a skeleton by its teeth or its height. But there are no bones. Maybe one day we will find them, identified like that celebrated Haberlein discovery in the limestone—the archaeopteryx—a reptile half way to being a bird. Icarus, a man, was half way to becoming a bird. Maybe seventeen is too young; Romano's Icarus looks seventeen.

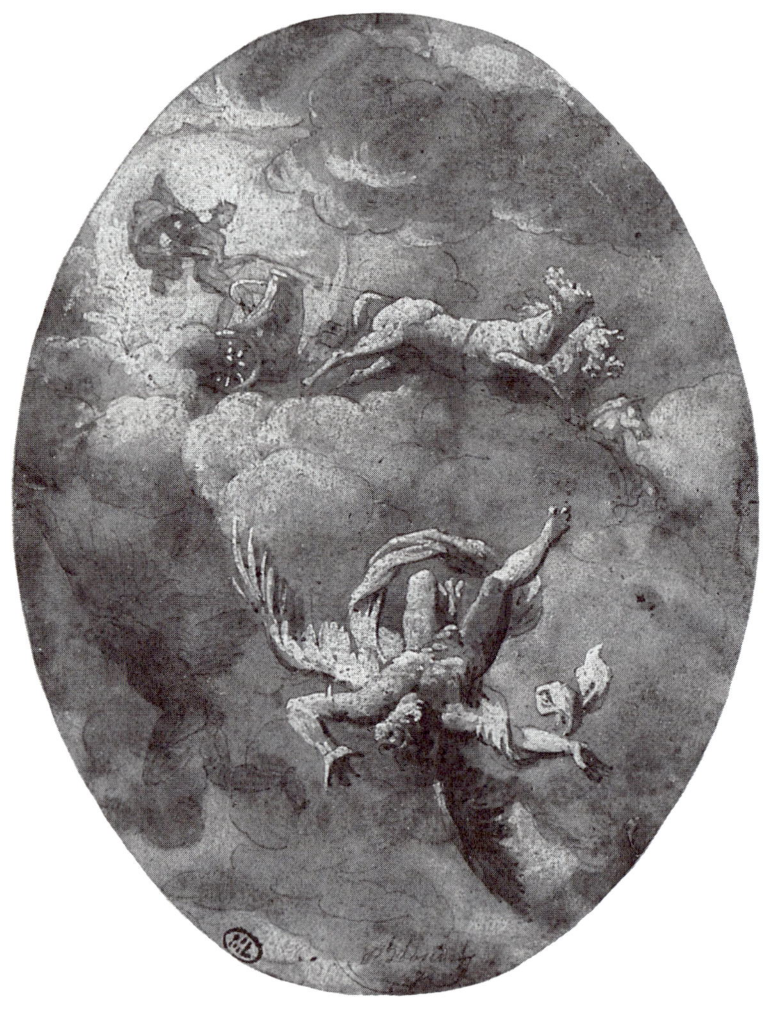

78

And Daedalus trained him to jump from the cliff-top. First from a height of a few meters just to get the feel of the wings. Even the shadow of those wings could have been intimidating; he would have felt himself umbrella-ed in a rustling cave, hidden, even against his will, from his future enemy the sun. Eventually he grew bolder. And bolder enough to take instruction when his father could tell him to aim his first flight down a slanting cliff-face to land in a shallow sea. Just for practice.

There is another possibility. Icarus is a hybrid, a product of bestiality, a product of bird and man, and all the stories of aeronautical mechanics are just ingenious censorship. The death of the offspring from the illicit union is planned as an elaborate euthanasia, a scheme to destroy, without

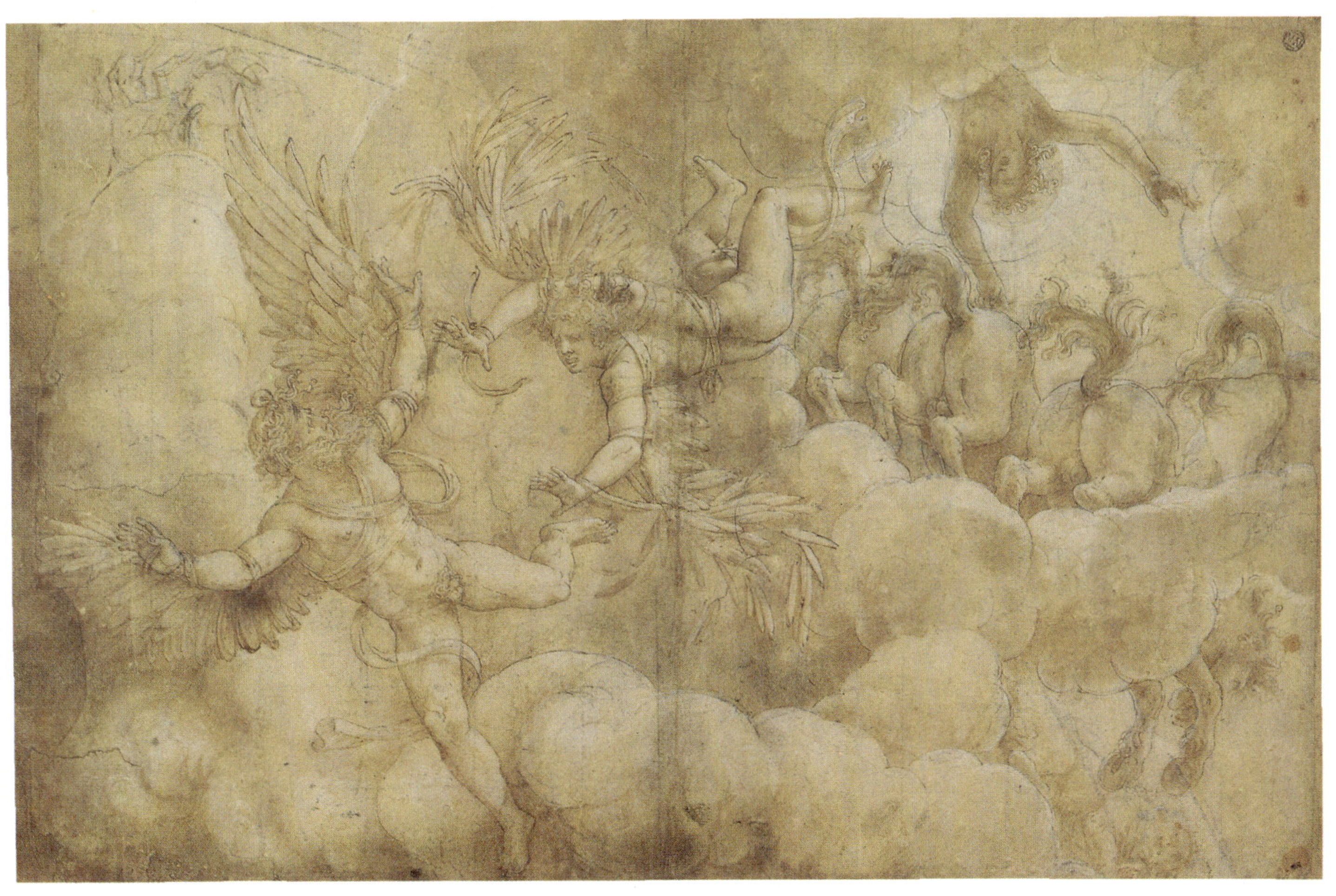

77

evidence, an exceptional freak. After all, where does the the evidence come from? Why, from the example of that other Cretan marvel, the Minotaur. That progeny had to be killed by elaborate mythological causes; why not this bird-monster?

From Daedalus's point of view, what sort of a bird was it? For Daedalus was a practical scientist, aware of limited resources. Was it—paradoxically—a bird that had already relinquished the splendour of flight? A turkey, a chicken, an ostrich? Conceivably, it had to be a bird of a certain size. Daedalus knew there was an ostrich in the royal Cretan menagerie.

"An ostrich is a bird who refuses to face unpleasant truths, like the fact it cannot fly."

Would Daedalus have crept into the Cretan zoo to realise flying dreams carnally with an ostrich?

What do we think Icarus looked like? A restless lad, forever flapping his arms? A scrawny young male, eagled-eyed, with thin and meager white feathered wings that had been salvaged from the backs of underfed and ill-treated geese that his father had stolen from the kitchen-garden? With three peacock-feathers for decoration? A svelte, down-covered anorexic youth who wore his wings like a new coat, or a plump, dove-shaped pouter pigeon narcissus who preened two hours before takeoff?

For the maiden flight, Daedalus, like Abraham about to make a sacrifice to his flying God, took his son to the very edge of the maritime grasses and told him to grip the crumbling rock with curled toes. He showed him how to swing his arms, to imitate a gull. Then he changed his mind and thought a swallow was a better example. In the end, the many possibilities of bird-example postponed the flight. But the young man was determined to jump. Daedalus in the end was hesitant. Couldn't he find a more suitable candidate? Sacrifice a slave? A criminal? A prisoner? Out of the question. And the rest is history. Off they went in the morning light on copious updraughts. And Apollo, stretching, yawning, unconcerned, parted the morning clouds and lifted the local mists to let a hot sun through, and Icarus, shivering a little in the slip-streams of his own making, flew higher, and of course, the bees took their revenge and the wax dribbled down the young man's pigeon-chest. The wings fell apart.

Who saw Icarus fall in such an under-populated place, to watch whether he died of drowning, or of the impact with the water? In any event he must have been a minor splash in a tepid sea.

Giulio Romano has Icarus in recognisable distress, the feathers are scattering, the binding is coming loose, the realisation of disaster is on Icarus's face, any special pleading glance towards Daedalus is lost. Daedalus flies below him, but not that further from the sun that makes a difference to wax, melting or not melting. Icarus's body twists, and here is evidence of what true three-dimensional flight might be. In what other medium, in what other circumstance, could a body cavort so three-dimensionally, feet walking in the sky one way, head and shoulders going another? But too late to seek correct direction, the walking feet and the turning shoulders are pointlessly directed. All is destined for the earth straight down below. Apollo watches and the four horses are already over the hill and fast into the next valley of cloud.

For Blondel, as Icarus comes to hopeless grief, Daedalus is a dark winged silhouette making off into the cloud shadow, surely off to report the accident to the sky police, or else quick to escape the details of hubris. Perhaps he is simply unaware of what is happening behind him. Daedalus will disappear into the clouds like a ship into fog, Apollo is again secure in his chariot, and the four horses are back in the sky under firm control.

79
Federico ZUCCARO
The Fall of Simon Magus

Simon, one-time sorcerer, magus, wizard, quack, does not fall in some distant uncharted region of the sea, or onto barren rocks, or into bushes, or far away from witnesses in the desert, but into the familiar squares and alley-ways of a crowded city. He must know this city's streets and open spaces, its taverns and where best to practise his chicanery before gullible citizens . . . before he was baptised a Christian, and doubtless promised to put his trickery behind him. And then he offered money for a piece of the Christian miracle and was sharply rebuked by Peter. The power to heal by the laying on of hands was not to be bought. The apocryphal acts of Saint Peter tell of Simon's subsequent challenge to the Christians in the superiority of magic, but Simon, in front of the Emperor Nero and his assembly, failed to bring the dead alive. He climbed to the top of a tall building to summon demons to make him fly. Peter and Paul prayed that the power of these pilot-demons should be cancelled, and Simon fell. How often could the citizens of Samaria witness such a fall from a high building, a crash down from a balustraded parapet, a slip on a high roof where the breezes are cooler at siesta time? Bodies raining in the streets was not a familiar phenomenon in the two-storeyed cities of Samaria, but in the high towered towns of Zuccaro's Tuscany such events may be more predictable.

Simon's bulky body fills the sky. It blocks out the sun. It fits in between the neat spaces of cupola and pediment. His hands, by a deceit of draughtsmanship, could be balanced on the rim of the distant terrace. But this is not to be. Simon is about to involuntarily, and very swiftly, squeeze his body-mass into a prepared drawing space, an alley-way of right-angled kerbs and pedestals, and hard and flat flag-stones. He will crash into the space that seems neatly prepared for his body. Beyond the

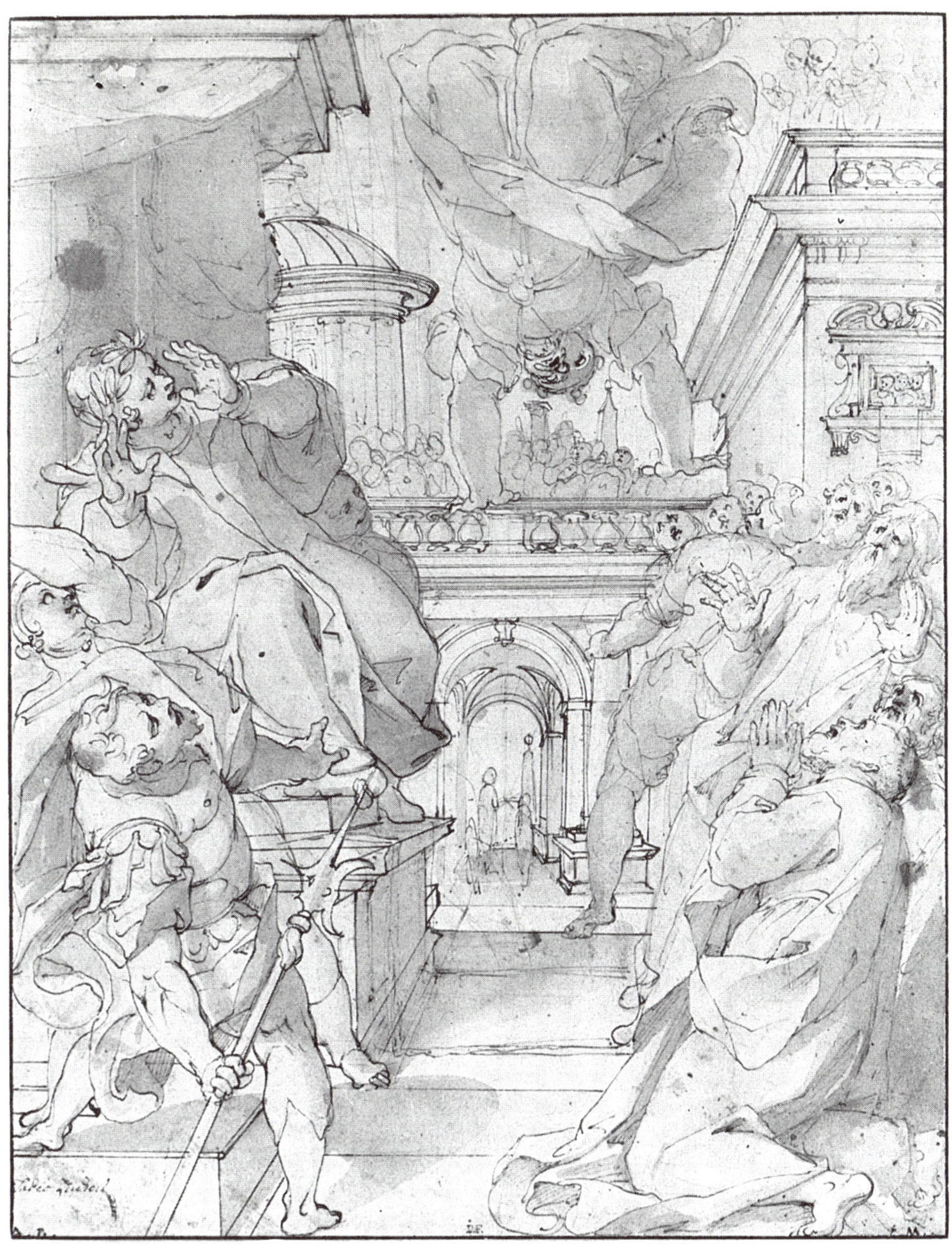

draughtsman's evacuated open tomb is a barrel-vaulted passage-way, a pleasant walking-space, a perspective with an obelisk. Sauntering pedestrians walk children slowly home in the afternoon sun. The conventions are curious and nonchalant—a heavy body falls into a tight space heralded by a deep nostalgic perspective. Near and far, intimate and spacious. And all to carry the image of death by falling out of the sky.

The volumes and the plains arranged to couch Simon's death are set correct for this body which, on the page, will never smash the ground and bring all the drawing spaces together like a stopper finally entering its rightful bottle, but in our mind's eye he is going to make a bloody mess upon the municipal pavement.

Now, at this very minute, another thing is happening which we cannot hear because most paintings do not have a sound-track. Peter is inventing the word "simony" to explain ecclesiastical purchase-power, for which, since his Church later exercised it so expertly, Simon Magus ought to be revered as a patron not a rogue.

Was Simon the sort of magus who could have seriously offered flight? Could he have truly offered levitation in a back room, rising high enough so that your nose touched the ceiling? With music and small mirrors, and a sweet smell of incense, could he, without doubt, have offered you the wherewithal to fly above the parapets?

80

CHASSERIAU

The Death of Sappho

81

GIRODET

The Death of Hero

Flight by distraction. Over the cliff edge and into the sea. Or on to the rocks. Born in Lesbos, an island, died in Sicily, an island. Always looking out to sea from a high vantage point, not unaware of the perils of vertigo. Walk to a high place to face the frisson of the deep drop, and sway on the cliff edge, daring your body to take a step to doom.

And then came Phaon, scruffy boatman, sometime fisherman, catcher of sea bass with a hook and a line. A patient fisherman, too patient. He stayed in his boat all day, bouncing on the calm sea against the sparkling bright light. A handsome rough diamond, he didn't see her—ever. She was just the lady on the cliff with the educated voice, carrying her lyre, carrying her skirts, hugging her breasts, a poetess.

For love of this fisherman, Sappho's cliff-top walks become more distracted. One day, seen by Chasseriau, clutching the lyre, she takes a distracted apology for flight. Her lyre comes with her. It smashes on the rocks some instance before she does, turning and bouncing out some accidental tune—her last. Sappho is not thinking of falling, of flight, of vertigo—it's just an accidental gesture of flight. Can we use it? Her feet trick her; they have been coming this way so often, and now they take charge and walk her over the edge. Phaon pulls in his line with only nine silver fish to show for a day's catch, one fish for each string of Sappho's lyre. He looked up at just the right time, for a fall like this is very soon over, and he slowly rows his boat to the ragged rocks and lifts her body

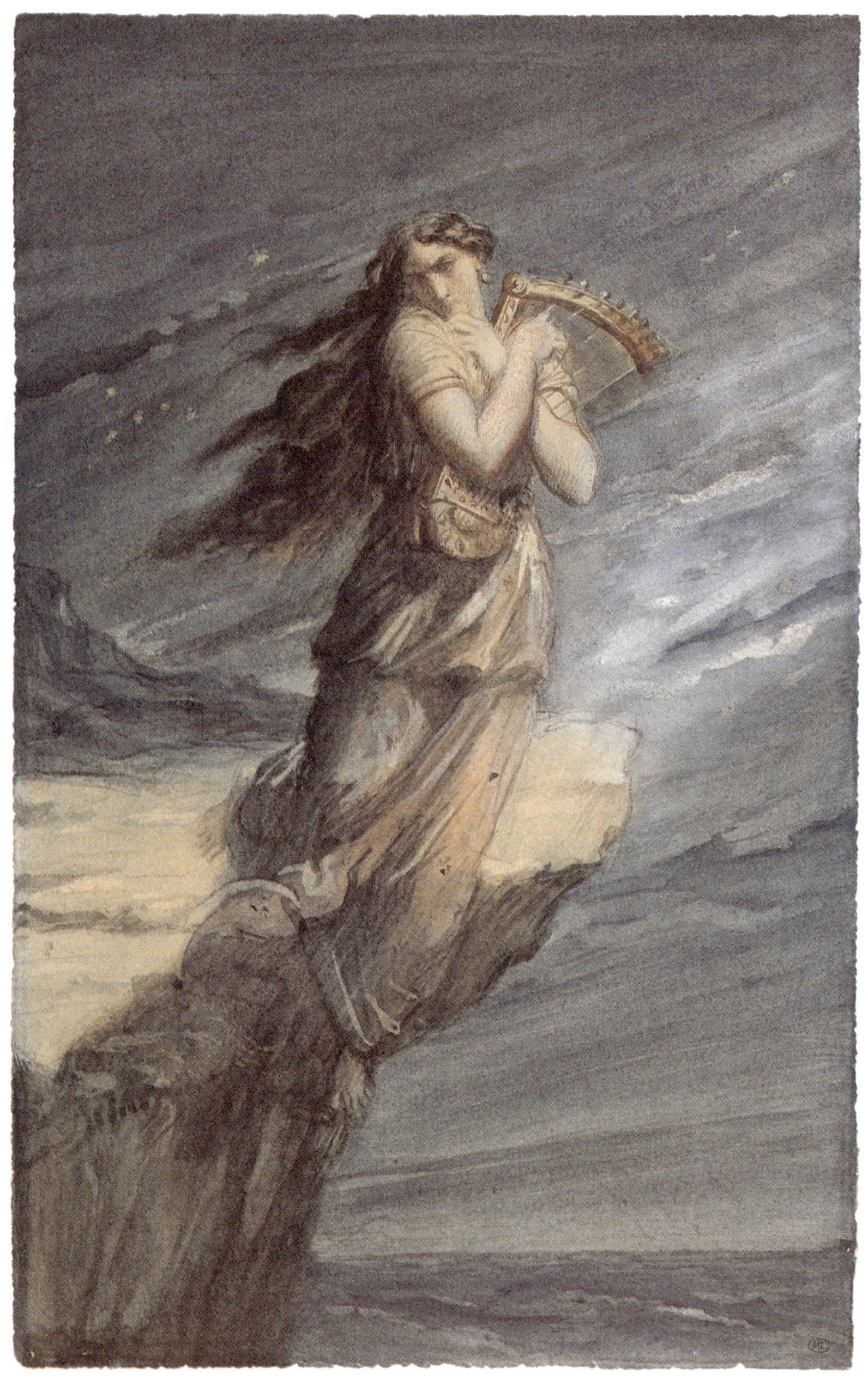

80

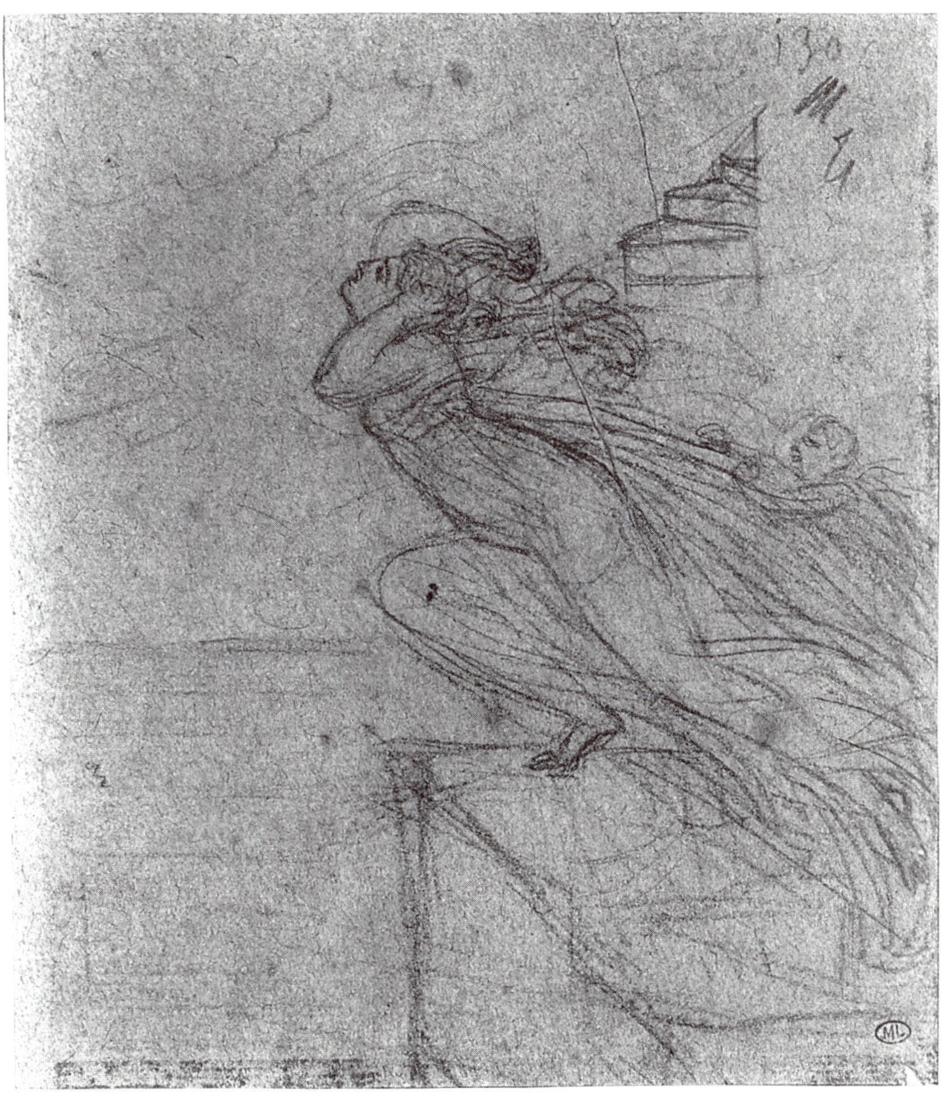

81

out of the water and takes it back for someone to claim and bury. Or
return to Lesbos.

Girodet has given her more ecstatic purpose. She rushes for the edge.
Is she pulled back by a child? Did Sappho have children? Her body is
wrapped in her empire dress, her fists are raised in distress above her
shoulders, her face is turned away from the deep drop, not looking at the
one hundred and twenty-seven meters to the sea's surface. How come the
palace architecture makes it so easy to leap? No balustrades, no protective

barriers. We could see that the child could have fallen down the one hundred and twenty-seven meters at any time.

Sappho has a classical profile and a scream we cannot hear. She certainly has a flurry of speed lines traced backwards, using the folds of her gown as an excuse. Are there stars in the sky? And if there were, in either the Chasseriau or the Girodet drawing, they could be an acknowledgement of one of the very few pieces of her poetry to be discovered, an elegant lyric found on a scrap of stained papyrus tucked up in a dull and turgid work of Renaissance etymology.

> Evening star, bringing back all that the bright dawn scattered.
>
> You bring the sheep,
>
> You bring the goat,
>
> You bring home the child to its mother . . .

No more. A puff of writing long gone. Is this the child pulling on the flying cloth of its mother's last worn dress? Is Phaon, the fisherman, a complete fabrication? Sappho was a worshipper of the Aphrodite cult and on the island of Lesbos there were many cliff-jumpers. They all jumped. Some may say they flew in ecstasy. If only for nine seconds—one second for each string of the lyre.

82
GOYA
Falling man

Over the balcony. There is no telling where this man is falling. And he could well be falling at night. And he could well be falling in an interior. Let us suppose this man is falling in a theatre whilst watching a play. In a moment's ecstatic distraction, or in appreciation or admiration of an actor's gesture, or in awe at a break of pathos in a young voice, he stands up, and falters, and over you go. Clutching the theatre programme. It's a short falling flight to the stalls, down into the expensive seats to be that much closer to the stage where you admire the performance so much. What was the play? Can you feel the dust of the theatre coming out of the velvet plush seats, swept off the balustrades as you swiftly rush by with your clothes acting like a sweeping brush on fifty years of not cleaning in inaccessible places? Hair streaming backwards, lumpy trousers, left hand wide outstretched—to resist the mess of complicated theatre furniture awaiting you below, to smash your neck, crack your arm, bludgeon your face, stave in your rib-cage. You could, of course, have fallen on a fat and comfortable widow.

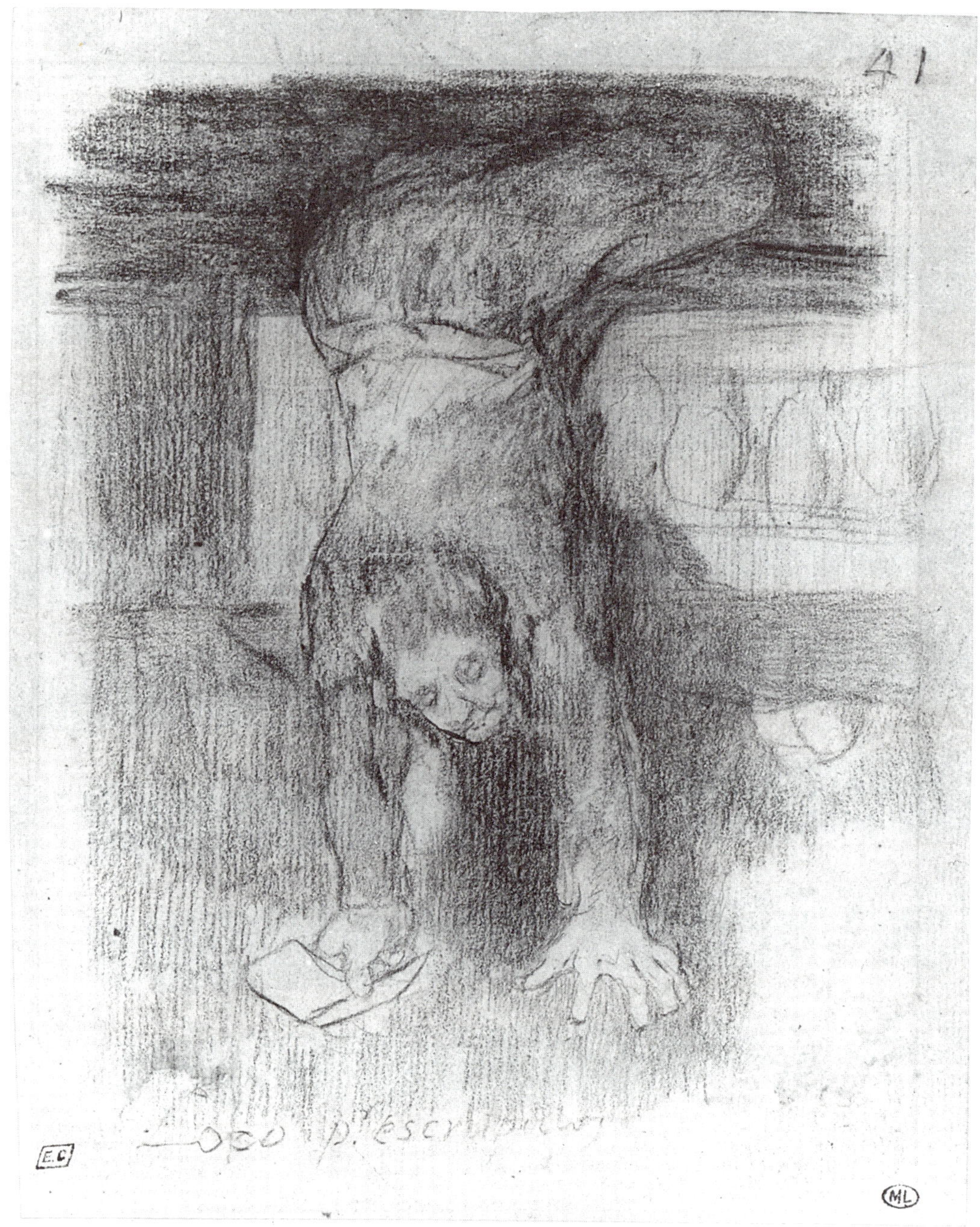

82

83
BANDINELLI
The Deposition of Christ

84
Nicolas MIGNARD
Cyclops struck down

85
CECCO BRAVO
Fallen Angel

These men have landed. They are broken backed on the floor. The breath
has been knocked out of their bodies. So much for flying.

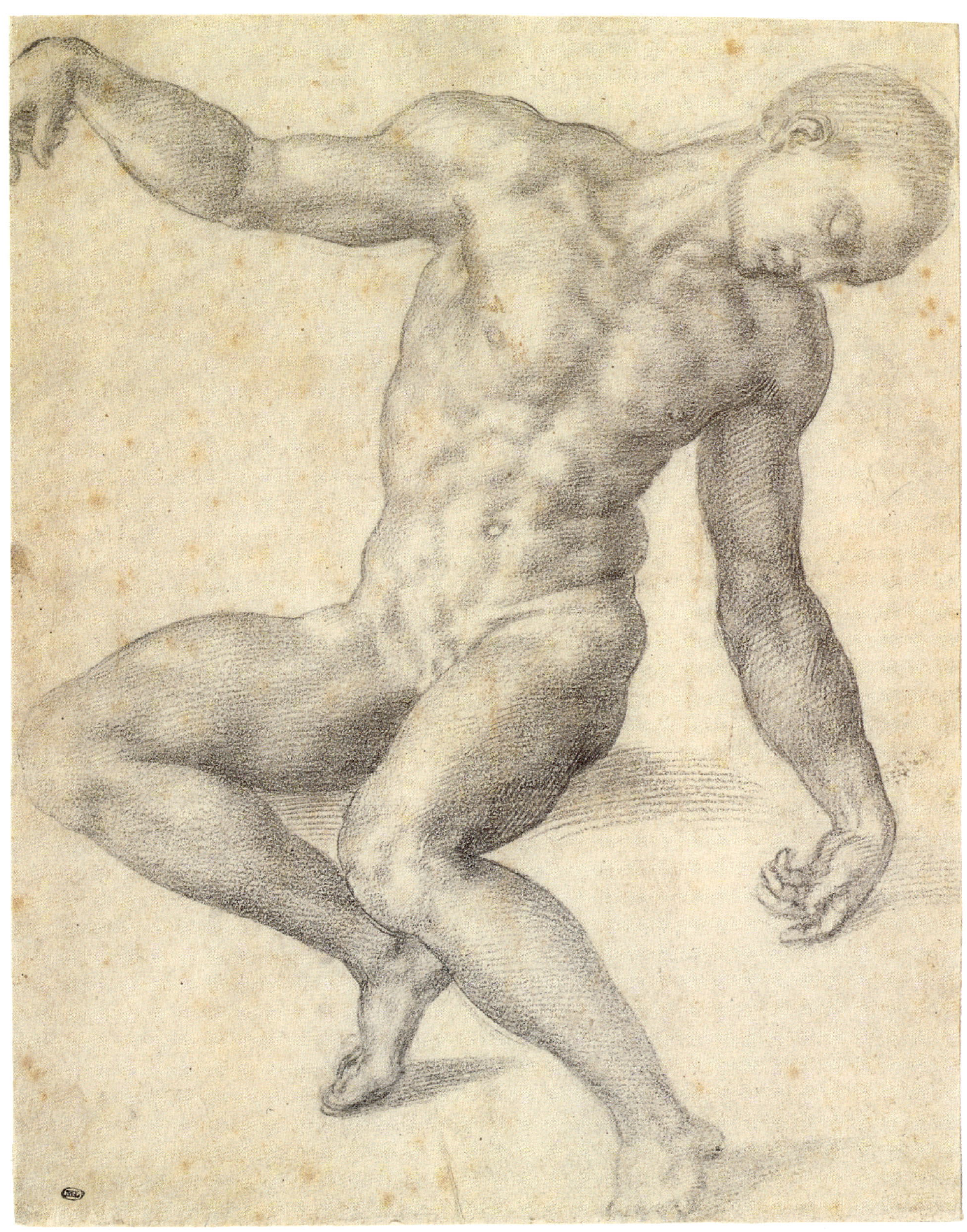

83

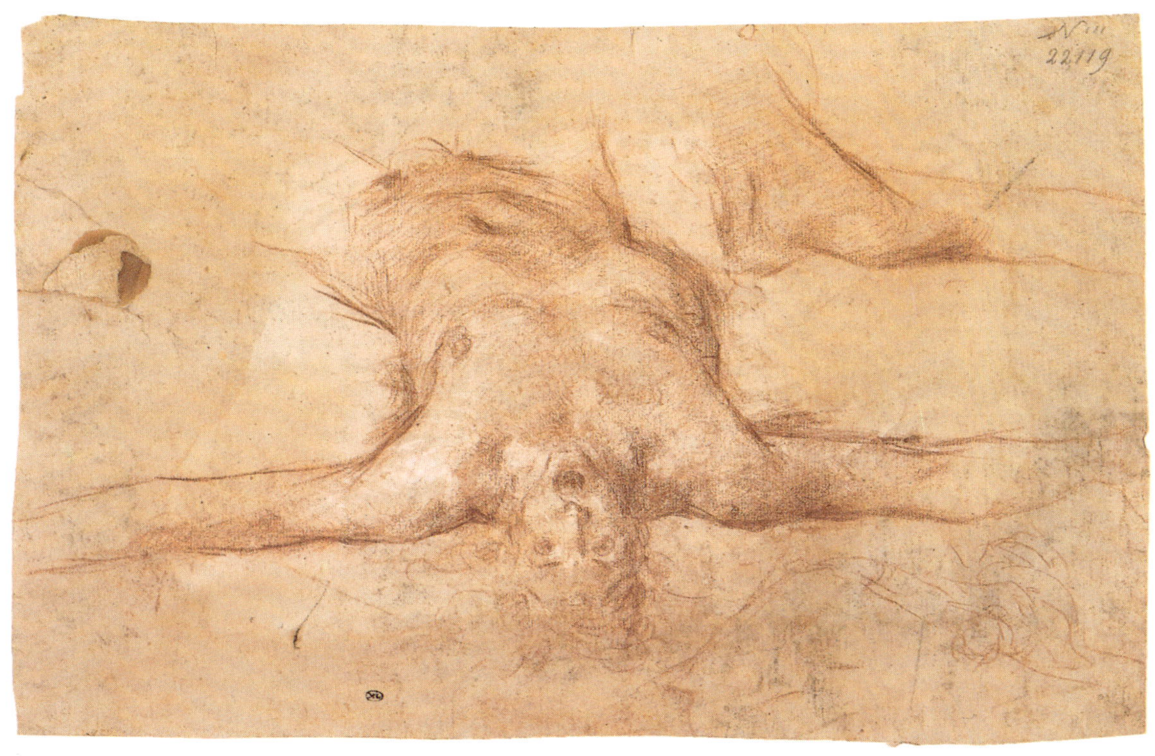

85

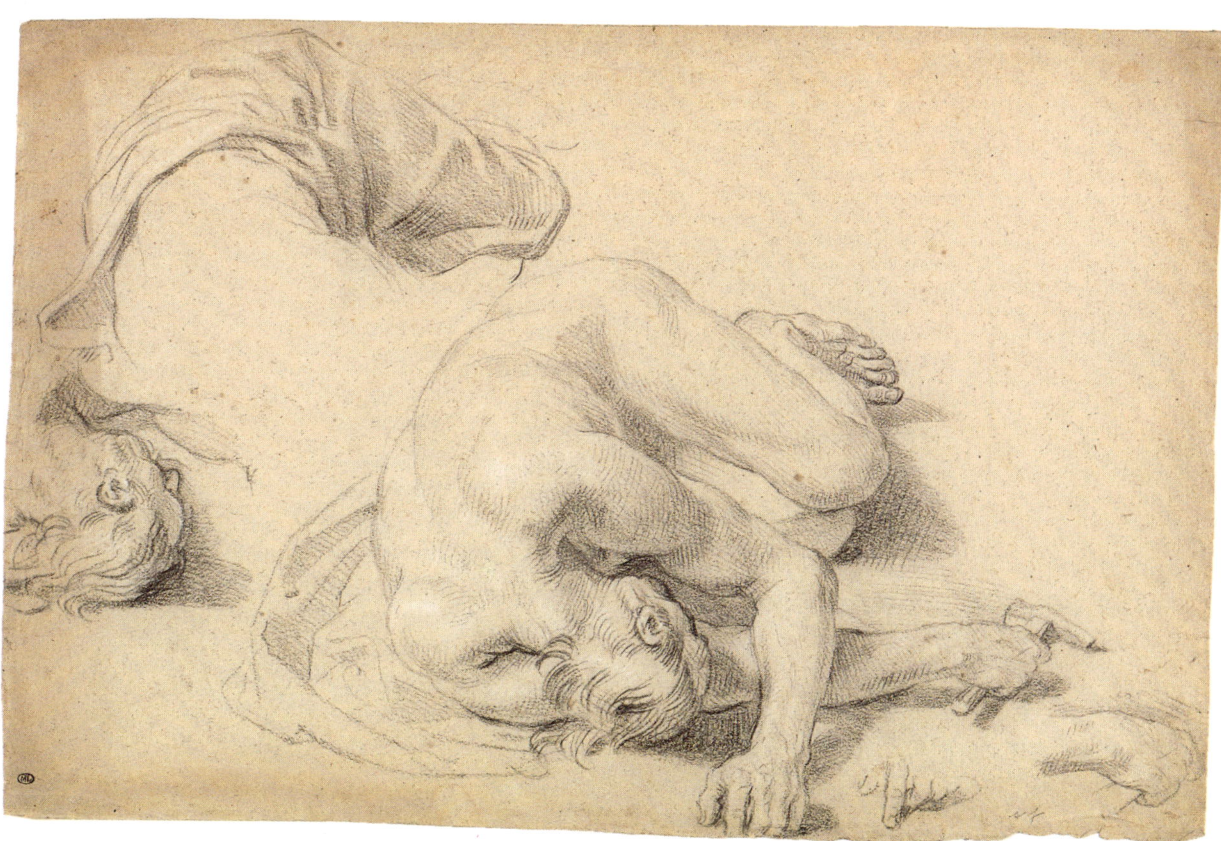

84

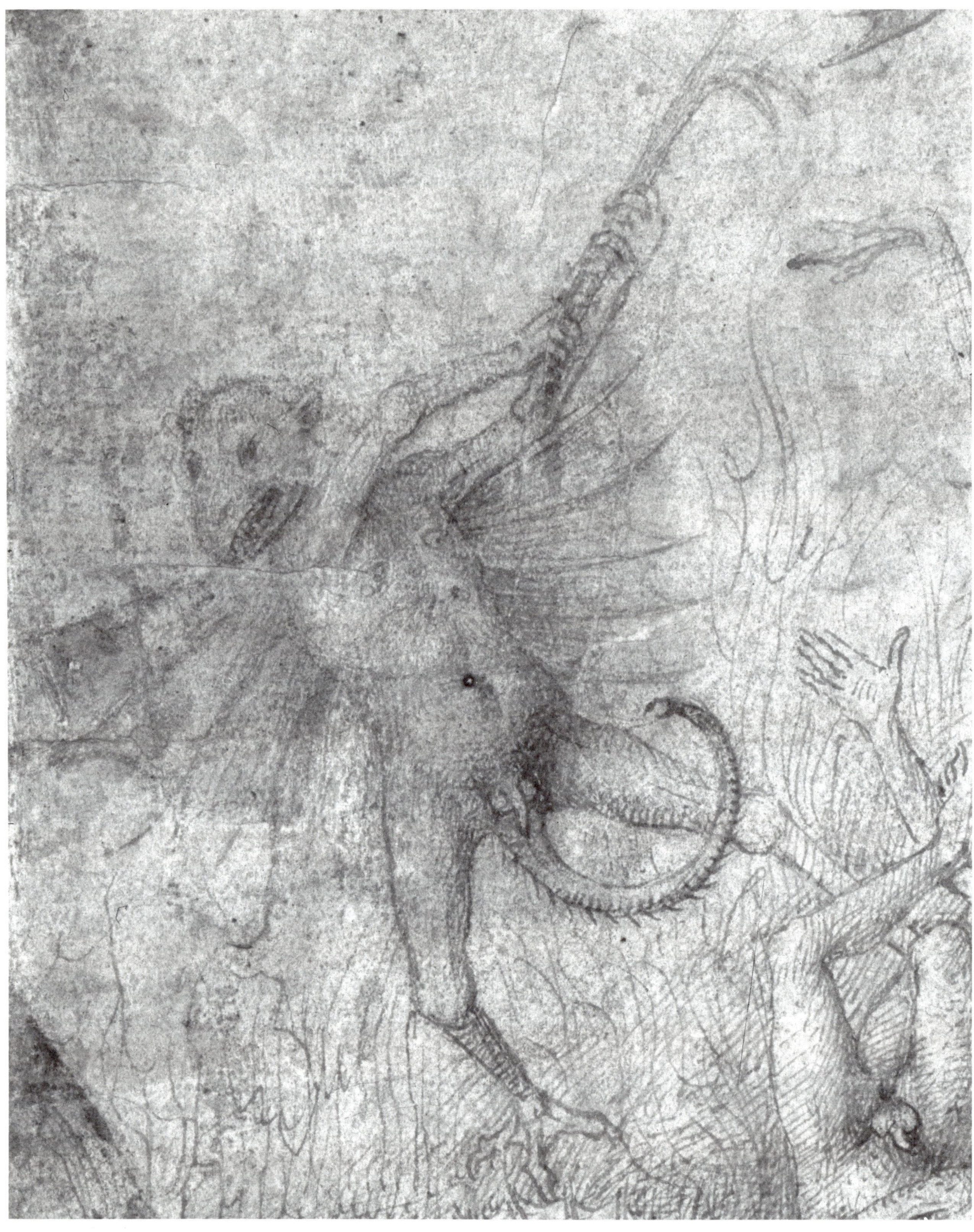

89 (détail)

CHAPTER NINE

Flying in Hell

We are flying in Hell. The Ninth Circle. Not content with merely crashing us on the hard crust, gravity has pulled us through the surface of the earth. And still we are obsessed with flying. We are confronted with its nightmare, until the very weight of our own bodies is the reason for our demise. And then we are back where we started.

86
Taddeo ZUCCARO
Allegory of dreams

Zuccaro places us, appropriately for nightmares of flying, in a dishevelled bed, on a hard-edged podium with only a thin sheet for covering a naked body. We have small feet. And open legs. And are bare-breasted. And suffocating. As in bad dreams we are vulnerable. And this time surrounded by a whirring insectivorous buzz of flying creatures. They flop out of the dark ceiling, screaming, and we do not trust their ability to fly. Some appear to fall, or are so engrossed in copulatory business they forget their responsibilities in the air and may fall on us. They grow branched, arboreal arms that could be the perch for harpies. They batter their inadequate bodies against the rock-chamber doors. One creature is too old to fly; he has wings that scrape and rustle on the rocks, and a torso with an impossible anatomical twist. He has two tails of gross serpentine nature, one for each leg, reducing an old man's buttock to a worm-like root.

At the foot of the bed there is a seated and winged maker of masks. Or is he manufacturing faces, sticking his finger into a decapitated head on a block? Is he a maker or breaker of heads? Certainly he could be a maker of dreams. His wings are posed for imminent flight. They are fine wings, with a shadowed curved structure that gives them thickness and hints at their strong abilities to function. All this nightmare is played out in a roundel, like a view through a peephole, a peephole into a prisoner's cell under the earth.

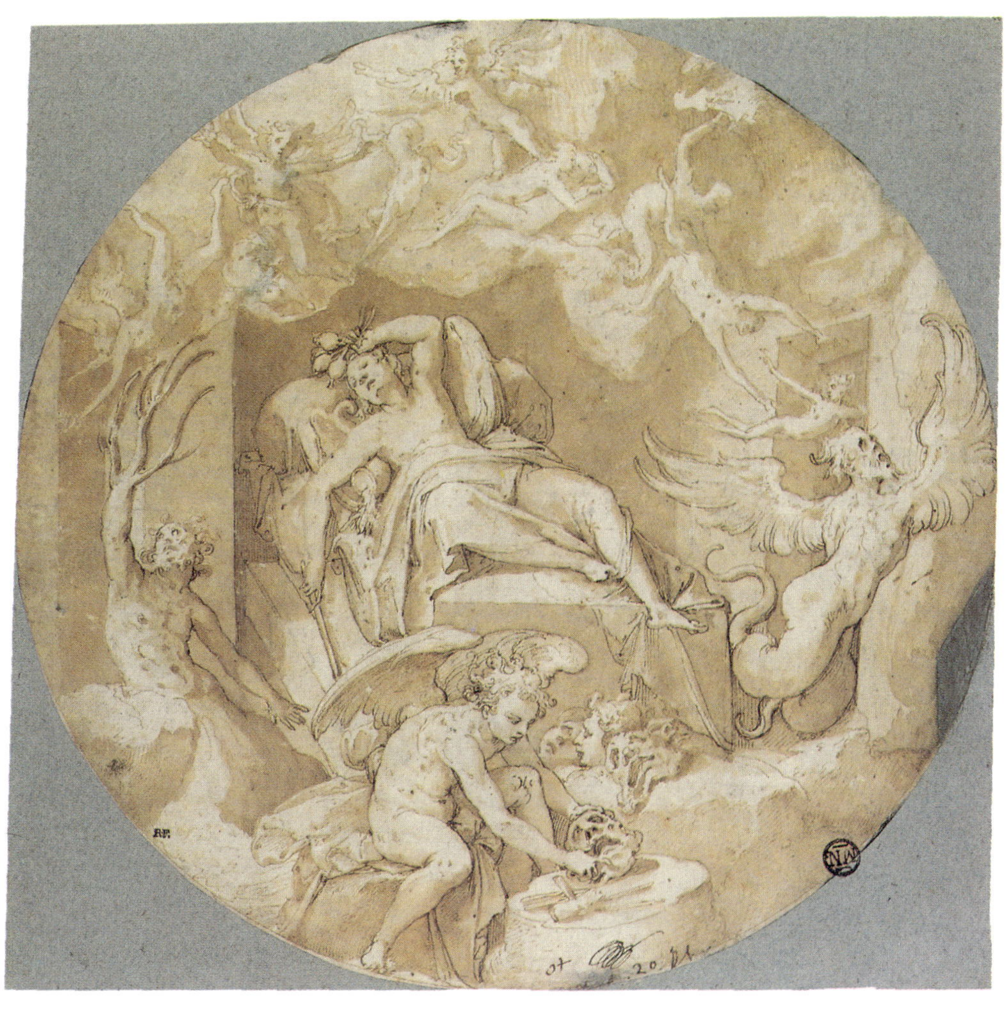

86

87

Giulio ROMANO
Psyche and the water from Styx

Not an illustration to a classical myth, but an image from a late-antique fairy tale. First written by Apuleius, the stories of Psyche, changed to a North European context, are now often more familiar in the mythological tales told in the nursery. After dropping hot wax on Cupid whilst trying to see her lover's body by candle-light, Psyche is set a series of well-nigh impossible tasks to regain his love and forgiveness. She is the female equivalent of Hercules and his Labours, beset with tasks that are designed to be impossible because the perpetrator does not truly want them accomplished. Those impossible tasks like cutting a forest of grass with scissors, emptying a lake with a spoon. Here Psyche is in Hell, with Jupiter's help, fetching forbidden water. The water is guarded, on the lower shelves of this underground cavern, by two winged palaeontological experiments which have never left their bones to fossilise on earth. They are caterpillar-track necked chimera with tendril tails, extravagant taloned feet and low slung bodies that must scrape the earth. Are the wings made of feathers or skin? Their tongues are snailing strips of ribbon. And Jupiter in a familiar sharp-beaked guise of undeniable strength, helps the weary Psyche with the forbidden vase. Whilst her companions in this dark half-circle have wings, she does not. Jupiter can transpose his shape if wings cannot fly him out of this shelf of Hell, but what use are wings for these monsters in an underground cavern without reach of the sky?

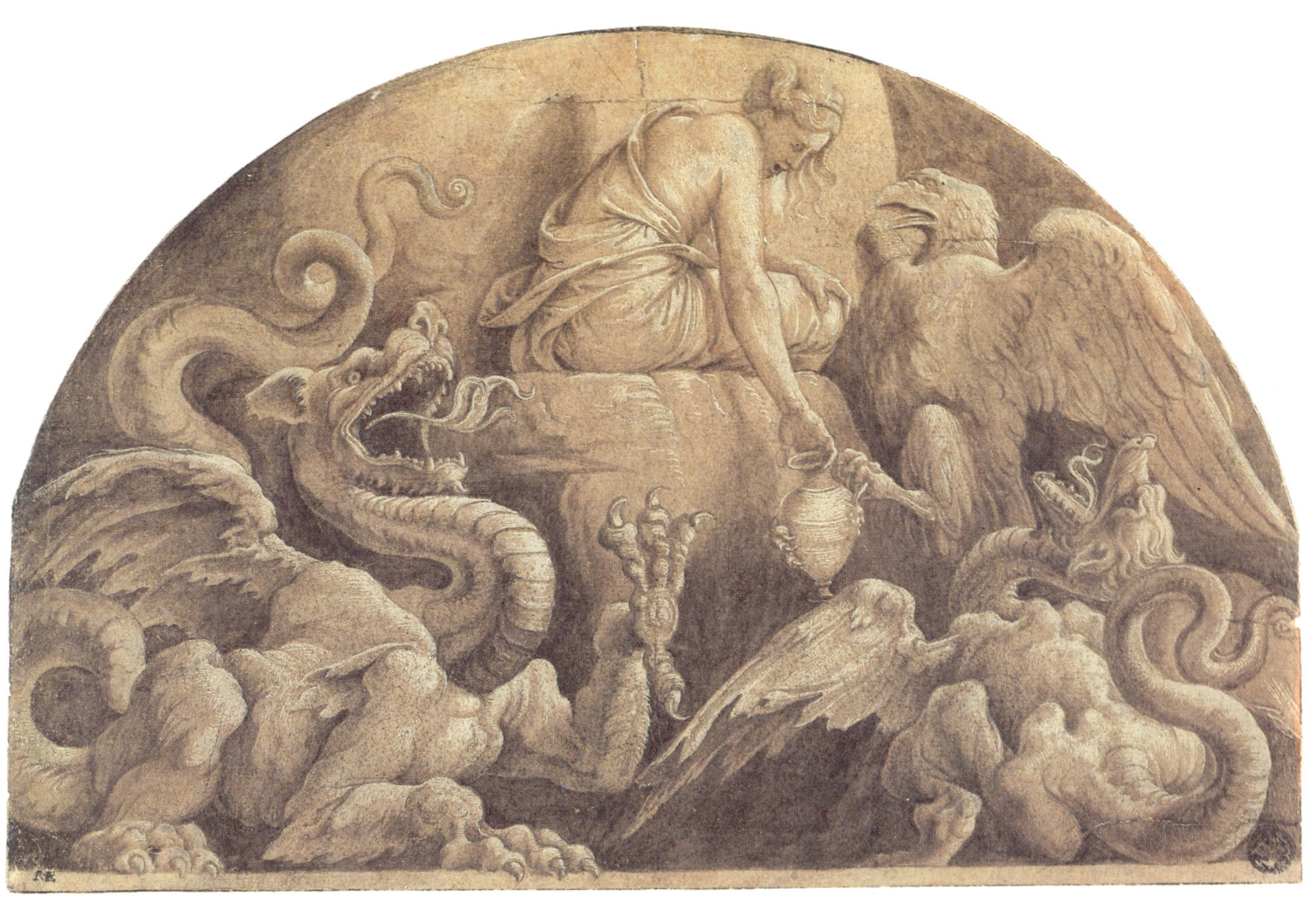

87

88

PRUD'HON
Divine Justice pursuing Crime

A dead, murdered body in this moonlight, metaphorical underworld, and a murderer attempts to escape pursued by two avenging angels, one carrying a light, the other a sword. Does the wretched murderer flee or does he fly? The dead body and the winged avengers are separated by the smallest of physical spaces, but the largest of mortal ones. One so dead and still, the other two, so heavy, but flying. The fleeing murderer seems an extra, running out left, the sinister direction, against the grain of a positive left to right reading. The murdered victim seems glued to the ground, his head so heavy on the earth, his hips must be elevated on a stone or rock or clump of earth. The deadness of the body lies in the head, which is half way now already to making a decomposition contract with the soil. Unutterably dead and never again to rise, this scene could reprise the world's first murder with Cain fleeing and Abel dead on the ground.

This criminal flees with his hair trailing sufficiently in the moonlight to give him a little extra imagined speed, a jagged floss of clothing helping him to move out of the scene of the crime, though his legs are strangely bent and flexed and his feet rooted. He'll not flee far.

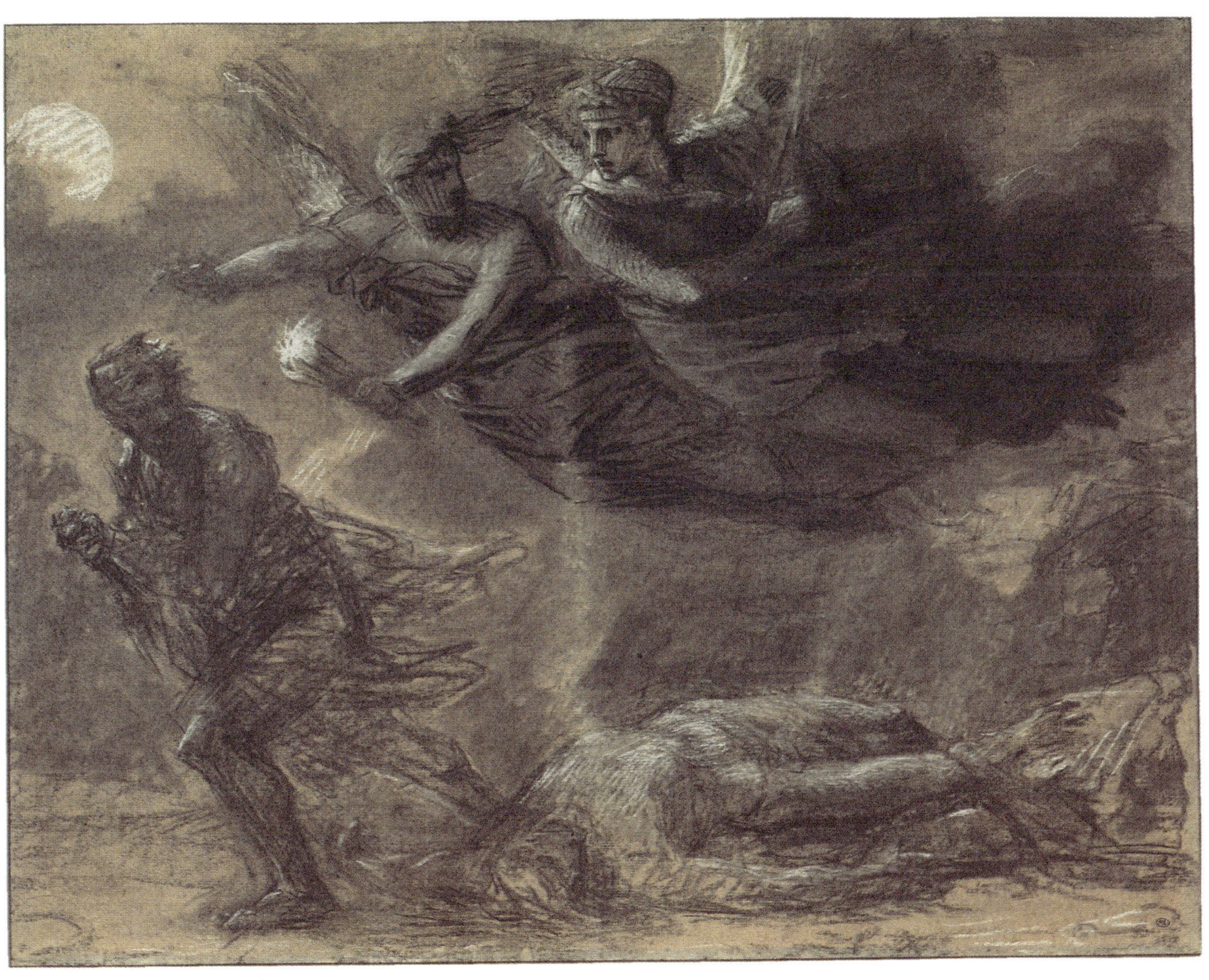

88

89
School of BRUEGHEL
The Fall of the Damned

Here are more impossible specimens of amimal phantasmagoria. A little lizard, a little bat, a little porcupine, a little prophetic dinosaurian beak and claw, all composite reptilian monstrosities that each beg a species name though conceivably all belong to one genre. They have spikes and spines, teeth, claws, and scratching nails. Implied excrement and filth are concomitant horrors to be endured. The centre-piece is a female soul, screaming Eve, bane of all sins, caught by the hair. Is she pushed or pulled by the cat-headed frog with a reverse question mark for a tail? Either way hair-pulling is serious, more than an indignity. Is it more than an accident that three men in agony frame her, and at least two are tonsured priests?

The medieaval mind invented the hippogriff and the manticore. Perhaps they are here, doormen to Hell. Invent a name and then give it legs. All these flying horrors are humanoid, shaped like the human body so that, in the end, we can understand the horror quicker and more effectively. The head, torso, and four limbs are necessary; the wings, breasts, genitals, are optional. They fly like cats might fly, like rats might fly, like prickled hedgehogs might fly. In a flying attack from the air, a naked body with no prospect of cover is a well-nigh indefensible target. And not satisfied with current miseries, there is, in the distance and approaching fast, a flying insectivorous beast, not much more for the moment, than a thread-like silhouette, but soon possibly to be the most dangerous of them all.

We are wholly convinced that there are flying creatures in Hell to plague us, and that all are eager to ram us into a hole like a hard-rimmed cooking pot, to make, as the spaces get smaller and smaller, a remembrance of any prospect of flying inconceivable.

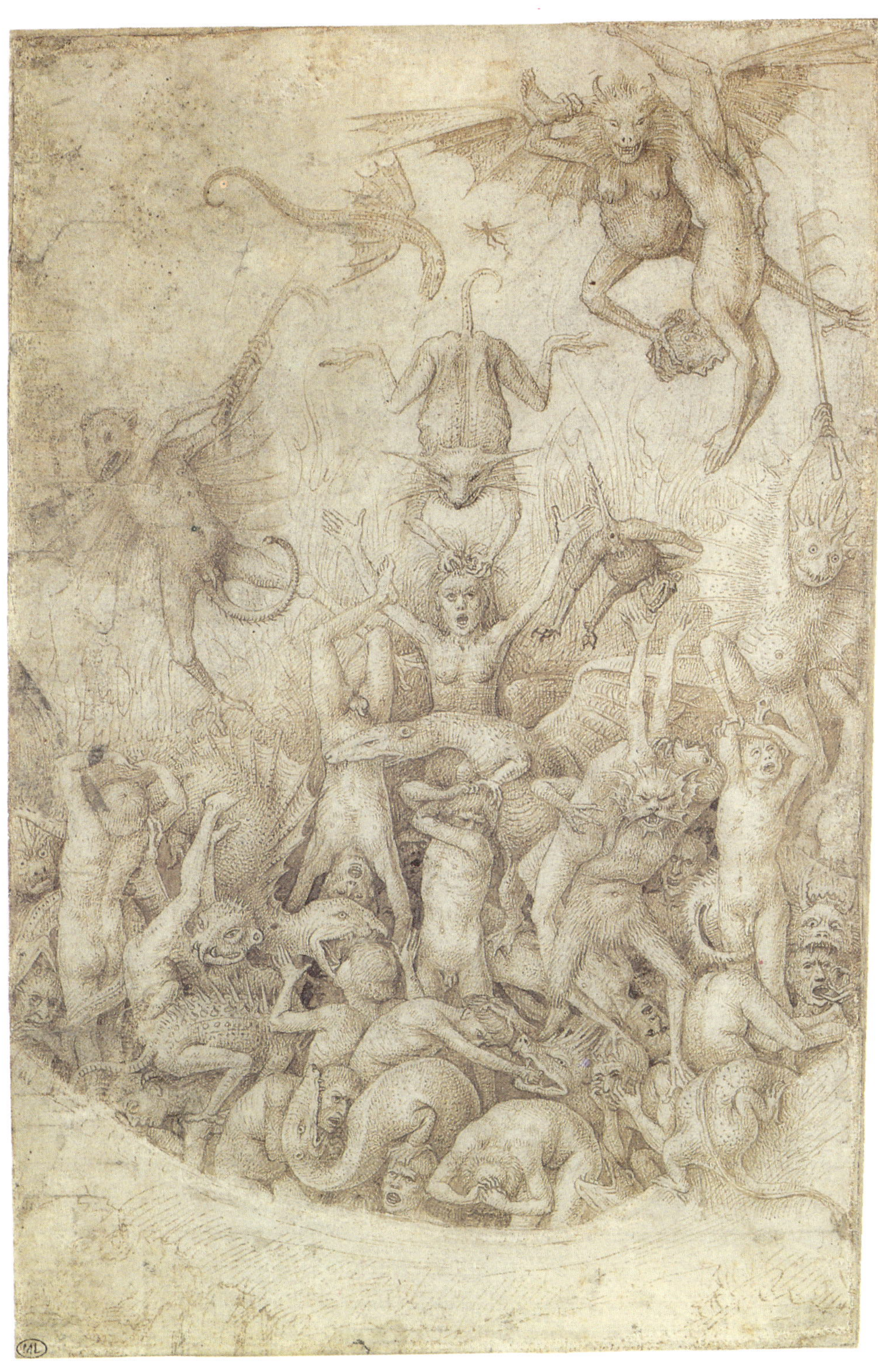

89

90

SCHONGAUER

The assault on Saint Anthony

Saint Anthony, above the emptiness of the Egyptian desert, is beset with flying creatures from an imaginative entomological kingdom rather than from the kingdom of the birds. They are creatures worthy of examination to see what flying things the artist had in mind to scare Saint Anthony and us.

Anthony is patron saint of skin diseases, including leprosy and syphilis, and the mysterious condition of ergotism or Saint Anthony's Fire, caused by fungal diseases on rye-flour baked as bread. Saint Anthony's Fire caused hallucinations, perhaps like these depicted here, a case of the biter bit, turning his visions to the greater good by example.

The ariel space of this image hovering in the sky is indeterminate, but there are rocks below to remind us of Anthony's desert hermitage. And above is an ambiguous distance marked with dotted lines that could be the sea upside down, or the approaching bright light driven by God to force the demons to flee. To fly away.

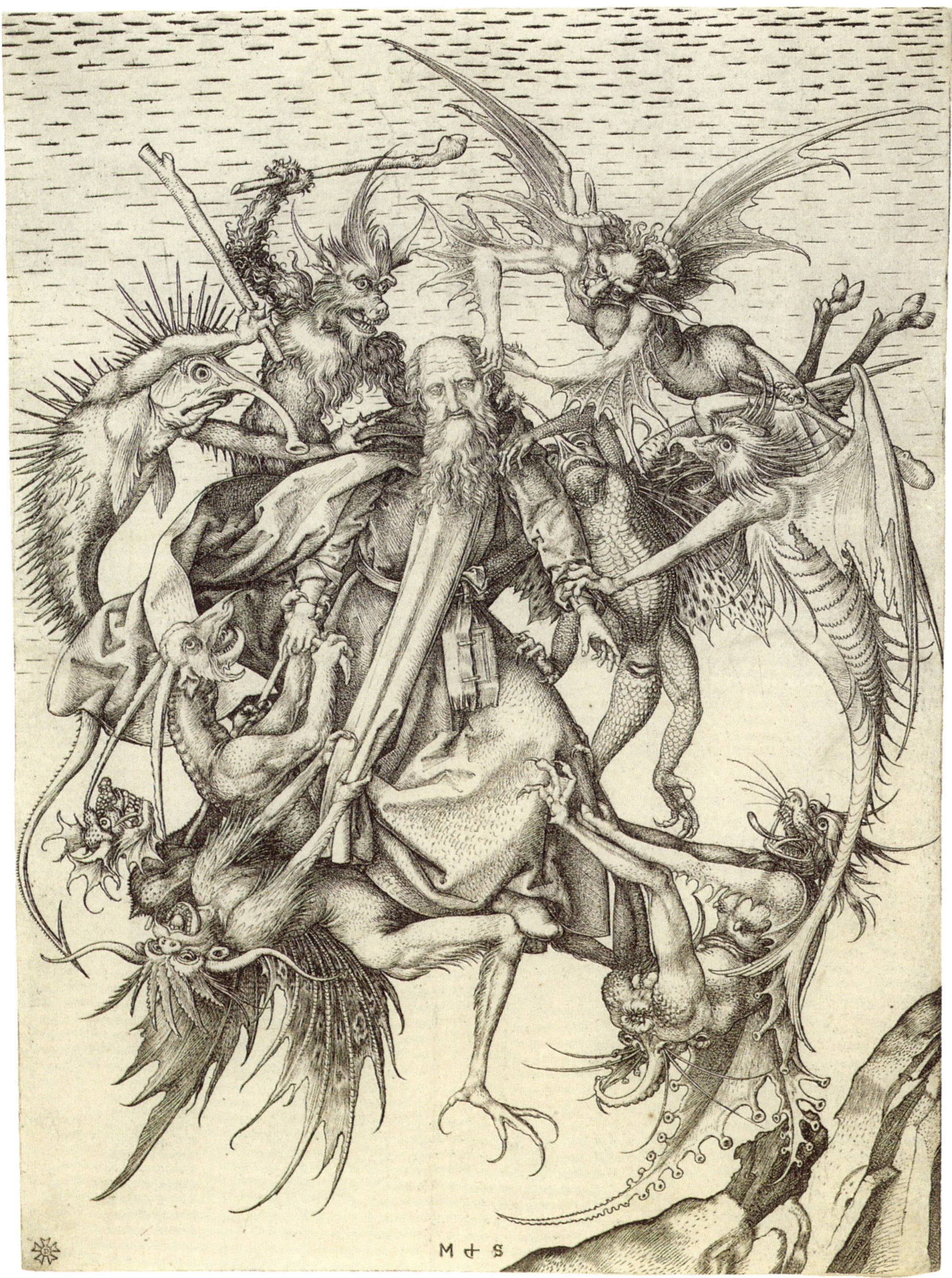

90

91
BECCAFUMI
Scene of torment

This is torture by gravity. Trussed high with ropes, gravity on the body itself creates the pain. A man arraigned before the tribunal of the Inquisition on unspecified religious crimes is tortured. And his torture is suspension. The pull of his weighted body is apparent in the fierce and strong diagonal of the rope and the strain of the rope pullers, whilst all the time the Virgin and her Child shine down in this dark place. He is being tortured to reveal the secrets of flying, for flying is prohibited.

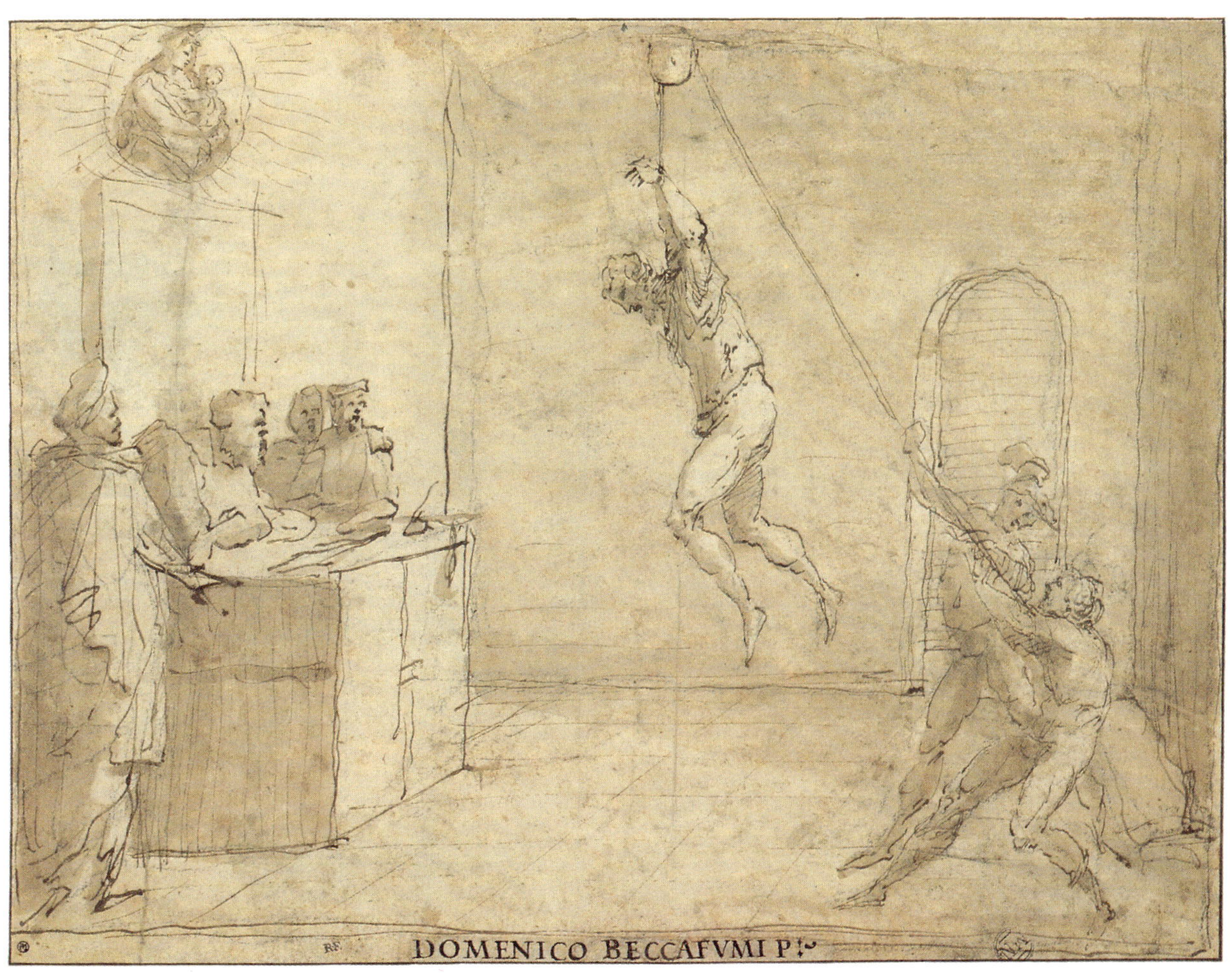

91

92
Victor HUGO
The Hanged Man

With a hanged man, the body can be its own cause of death. How else can the body kill itself? How convenient the anatomy of a man is, that he should be able to hang himself by his own weight, and either break his neck, or squeeze his own windpipe so tight it will not function. A heavy man will kill himself quickly, though it has been known that the dramatic fall of a heavy man might just break the rope.

This man hangs high in the dark air from a journeyman gibbet: three bulks of timber and ten meters of rope. What was he standing on before the rope tightened around his neck?

This drawing is a protest against judicial murder on the eye-for-an-eye, tooth-for-a-tooth pattern. Now we have other means of execution that involve electricity, gas, and drugs, but these are not so ingeniously neat and cheap, and not so self-reflexive. Any movement now from this man is caused by the wind swinging his dead weight. He is high above the ground, with powerless feet, and no wings. Gravity has strung this creature up at the same time as it has laid this creature low.

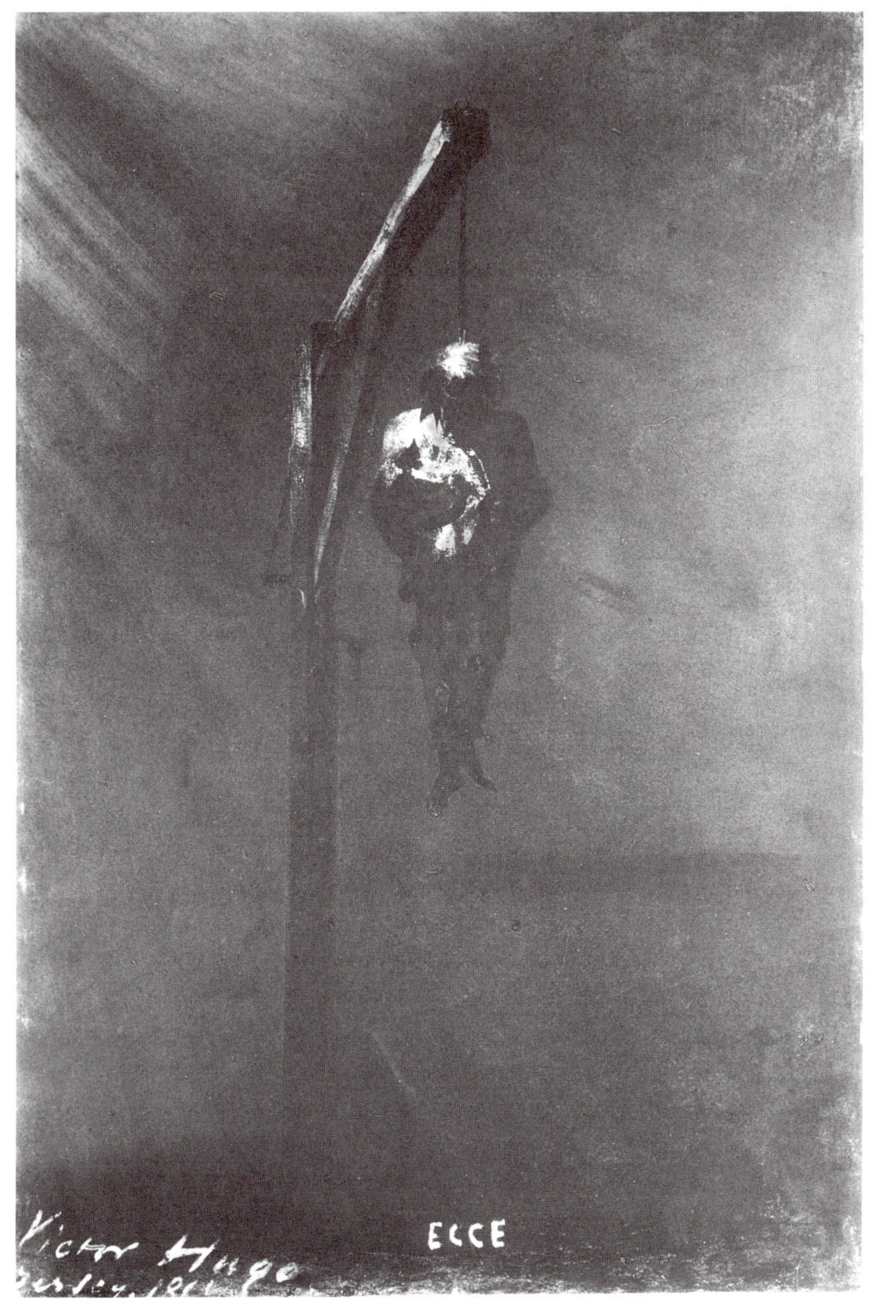

92

93
REDON
The Ball

And finally the dead-weight, the full stop, the gravity-sphere again. Like some fifth-columnist, it has drawn attention to its presence in not a few of the drawings of this exhibition. It is back in an inevitable return in this round of flight; Redon's philosophical sphere, but bereft of its philosopher. Just a ball with a shadow, of unknown size, because there is no reference for size. A heaviness and a next-to-nothingness, the earth and an atom all in one. The reflected light of its smooth surface is contained and acknowledged within its own shadow. And a mocking highlight reflects what? The light of the sun?

Flight has been prohibited. We must start again.

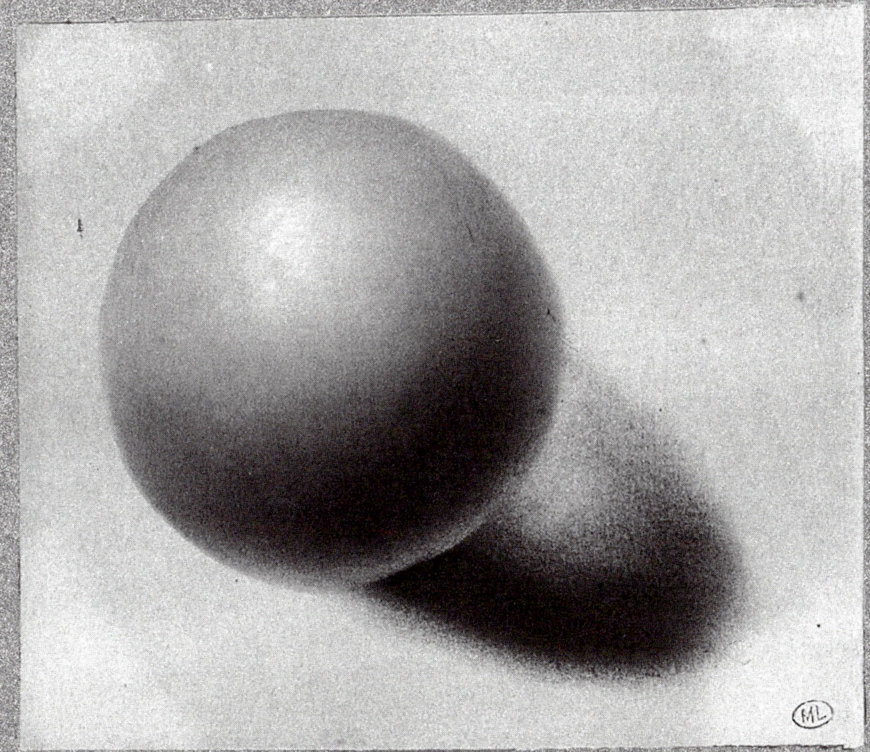

Illustrations

9   *Virtus Deserta* (Allegory of Humanity Saved), Louvre Museum, Edmond de Rothschild Collection   21
        Engraving (29.9 × 43.6). Inscription engraved lower left: *VIRTUS COM-BUSTA*, and on the stone: */VIRTU/TI/S. A. I.*

10 Francisco José de Goya y Lucientes (Goya), *It Is Her Name Day (Es dia de su Santo)*   24
        C'est le jour de sa fête. Brush and gray wash (23.5 × 14.6). Inscribed with brush, lower left: *es dia de su Santo,* and upper right: *Caricat.* Numbered with brush, on right: *61,* and at top with pen and brown ink, in another hand: *4.*

11 School of Mantegna, *Hercules and Antaeus,* Louvre Museum, Edmond de Rothschild Collection   26
        Hercule et Antée. Burin (33.7 × 25.0). Inscription engraved on left: *"DIVO HERCVLI INVICTO."*

12 Luca Cambiaso (1527–85), *The Flight of Aeneas*   29
        La Fuite d'Enée. Pen and brown ink (40.4 × 29.0). Sheet damaged with several losses. Inscribed at bottom in black crayon: *Luca C.*

13 Anne-Louis de Girodet-Trioson (Girodet) (1767–1824), *The Flood*   30
        Le Déluge. Black chalk, heightened with white, on yellow ochre paper (52.8 × 38.6).

14 Flemish School of the Fifteenth Century, after Jan van Eyck, *Saint Christopher*   32
        Saint Christophe. Pen and india ink (19.1 × 14.1). Inscribed upper right: *Johannes.*

15 Italian School of the Sixteenth Century, after Michelangelo, *Leda*   38
        Léda et le Cygne (Leda and the Swan). Red chalk (19.2 × 29.5). Inscribed lower right: *Michaelangelo.*

16 Anton van Dyck (?) (1599–1641), *The Stigmata of Saint Francis*   40
        Les Stigmates de saint François. Black chalk with brown wash, heightened with white, on paper slightly tinted with reddish brown, retouched with a brush (51.8 × 35.2). Retraced for engraving.

17 Serafino da Verona (ca. 1533–ca. 1605), *The Expulsion from Paradise*   43
        Adam et Eve chassés du paradis (Adam and Eve Expelled from Paradise). Pen and brown ink, brown wash, heightened with white, sketch in black chalk on ochre paper. Retouched by Michel Corneille (27.9 × 41.8).

18 Annibale Carracci, *Ulysses before Circe*   45
        Ulysse devant Circé. Black chalk, heightened with white, on cream paper (38.5 × 56.5). Inscribed lower right with pen: *23,* and another number that has been trimmed.

43 Auguste Rodin, *Iris, Messenger of the Gods,* Rodin Museum, Paris 87

> *Iris, messagère des dieux.* Bronze (95.0 × 87.0 × 40.0). Signed: *A. Rodin* on the left foot (Lebossé for mixing of the plaster and G. Rudier for the casting). Inventory S. 1068.

44 Odilon Redon, *Winged Old Man,* Orsay Museum 92

> *Vieillard ailé.* Pastels on gray-beige paper (56.9 × 39.7). Signed lower right, in graphite: *ODILON REDON.*

45 Odilon Redon, *Winged Demon,* Louvre Museum, Orsay Museum Collection 93

> *Démon ailé portant un masque* (Winged Demon Carrying a Mask). Charcoal on yellow ochre paper (46.0 × 34.0).

46 Odilon Redon, *Winged Woman,* Louvre Museum, Orsay Museum Collection 95

> *Femme ailée sur deux nuages* (Winged Woman on Two Clouds). Black crayon (20.0 × 13.0). Signed lower right with the initials: *Od.R.*

47 Guido Reni (1575–1642), *The Separation of Day from Night* 97

> *Le Séparation du Jour et de la Nuit.* Pen and brown ink, brown wash (32.0 × 26.3). Inscribed at bottom right in pen: *Lelio de novelare.*

48 Francesco Montelatici (Cecco Bravo) (1601–61), *Flying Figures* 99

> *Deux Figures volantes dans une architecture* (Two Flying Figures in Architecture). Black and red chalks (22.0 × 32.5). Inscribed on mounting in pen and black ink: *Cecco Bravo,* and brown ink: *on his dream.* Cropped at top and bottom.

49 Giulio Pippi (Giulio Romano). *Three Angels Bearing the Virgin's Crown* 101

> *Trois anges portant la couronne de la Vierge.* Black chalk, pen and brown ink, brown wash, heightened with white, on two sheets of beige paper joined vertically (27.7 × 27.5); outlines incised. On the pilaster at lower right, with brush and white gouache: *IVL. RO;* number bottom right, in pen and black ink: *142.*

50 Carlo Bianconi (1732–1802), *The Abduction of Ganymede* 103

> *L'Enlèvement de Ganymède.* Pen and brown ink, brown wash (17.9 × 24.5). Signed and dated lower left, in pen and brown ink: *CB. 1778.* Dedication on mounting in pen and brown ink: *Comiti d'Orsay bonarum artium cultori, et amatori eximio momentaneum Ganimedis raptum momentaneo labore a se exaratum Carolus Bianconi Patrono suo, et Amico incomparibile D.D.D. Romae 5e Kal. Feb. 1778* (To the Count d'Orsay, patron of the fine arts and eminent art lover, Carlo Bianconi dedicates and gives to Rome on 28 January 1778, to his protector and incomparable friend, this Ganymede being abducted, at the very moment of completing the drawing).

Source Notes

Notes on exhibited works are arranged in the order they appear in the text and in the exhibition, since numbers in the two cases are identical. Artists' names are arranged alphabetically in the index.

Unless otherwise noted, all exhibited works belong to Louvre collections (department of Graphic Arts).

Notes were compiled by Véronique Barjot-Faux (nos. 1–2, 4, 8–10, 13, 19, 24–30, 42–46, 49, 53–54, 56, 58, 60, 65, 73, 77–78, 80–82, 87–88, 92–93) and Régine Bonnefoit (nos. 3, 5–7, 11–12, 14–18, 20–23, 31–41, 47–48, 50–52, 55, 57, 59, 61–64, 66–72, 74–76, 79, 83–86, 89–91) (for the exhibition catalog. Dimensions [height × width × depth] are given in centimeters).

The authors of the catalog would like to express their profound gratitude to Régis Michel for his consistently insightful advice.

Index of Artists

These references refer to figure numbers.